This book belongs to:

Name

School

The Life of Benjamin Franklin

To this day, many Americans consider Benjamin Franklin to be one of the country's most influential and vital Founding Fathers. "First American," as some call him, would be an accurate description. Franklin was a "Renaissance Man" who was good at many things, like science, politics, writing, music, invention, diplomacy, and writing.

Benjamin Franklin was born in Boston, Massachusetts, on January 17th, 1706. He was the son of a chandler (someone who makes candles and soap). Ben was the youngest son in a family of sixteen brothers and sisters. In Ben's case, he had only a few years of formal education. He had to drop out of school when he was ten years old to work with his father. The following year, he was hired by his brother James as an apprentice to work as a printer's apprentice. Though he had no formal education, Ben was an avid reader and gained a great deal of wisdom from his habit of devouring books.

When Ben was 17 years old, he rushed away from Boston, abandoning his brother's apprenticeship. He moved to Philadelphia, Pennsylvania, and got a job as a printer after graduation.

Franklin worked in London and Philadelphia for several years after that, doing a variety of professions. As of 1729, Benjamin Franklin was the publisher of the Pennsylvania Gazette, a newspaper. Franklin rose to prominence in Pennsylvania politics as a newspaper publisher, and his name spread across the American colonies as a result. Franklin spent much of the 1750s and 1760s in London, England. At first, people in Pennsylvania used him to speak for them in Parliament, mostly to say that they didn't like how much power William Penn's relatives had over their new colony. William Penn was the founder of Philadelphia and the State of Pennsylvania. When he spoke out against the Stamp Act of 1765, he spoke for all American colonies. In the end, it was because of his arguments that Parliament was able to get the law repealed.

Franklin first published Poor Richard's Almanack in 1732. Franklin used the alias "Richard Saunders," often known as "Poor Richard, " in Poor Richard's Almanac," to pen a yearly publication. Poems, a calendar, fascinating sayings, weather forecasts, and scientific data were all included in the booklet. Selling the booklet was a profitable venture for Franklin. For the next 25 years, he produced up to 10,000 copies per year.

Benjamin Franklin was still living in London when the Revolutionary War neared. Franklin came up with the idea of the First Continental Congress in 1774, and he was the one to put it into action. Franklin then took their petition to King George III of England. On his return to Philadelphia in 1775, Franklin was re-elected as a delegate to the Second Continental Congress for Pennsylvania. The American Revolution had already begun by this point. Franklin was a key player in the Revolutionary War's early stages. This man helped put pen to paper on what would become America's first constitution and was its first postmaster general.

Ben Franklin made a trip to France in the year 1776. He worked tirelessly to rally French support for the American cause for the following few years. When France and the colonies formed an alliance in 1778, they could take on the British. When it came to winning the war, the United States relied heavily on its partnership with France. In France, Franklin stayed throughout the war. The Treaty of Paris, signed in 1783, put an end to the Revolutionary War.

To top it all off, Ben Franklin was an accomplished inventor and scientist and an important figure in the creation of the United States.

Perhaps the most notable accomplishment of Ben Franklin is his electrical experiments. He conducted numerous experiments to verify that lightning is, in fact, electricity. To prevent structures from being damaged by a lightning strike, he came up with a solution: a lightning rod. Ben Franklin also invented bifocals (a form of glasses), the Franklin stove, a carriage odometer, and the glass harp. Electricity, cooling, meteorology, printing, and the wave theory of light were among his many scientific interests.

The year was 1785, and Franklin had just returned from a trip to France. At the Constitutional Convention, he was the only founding father to sign the Declaration of Independence and the Alliance Treaty, Paris Treaty, and United States Constitution all at the same time. Then, he was also the President of the state of Pennsylvania (like the governor). Franklin passed away on April 17th, 1790, in Philadelphia.

Benjamin Franklin

1. Franklin first published Poor Richard's Almanack in 1742.
   a. True in 1742 and 1745
   b. False in 1732

2. Benjamin Franklin was the publisher of the Pennsylvania _____.
   a. Gazette
   b. Philadelphian

3. Benjamin Franklin was born in Boston, Massachusetts.
   a. True
   b. False

4. Ben dropped out of school when he was 12 years old to work with his father.
   a. True
   b. False

5. _____ was the founder of Philadelphia and the State of Pennsylvania.
   a. Richard Saunders
   b. William Penn

6. Franklin came up with the idea of the First _____ Congress in _____.
   a. Founding, 1772
   b. Continental, 1774

7. The _____, signed in 1783, put an end to the Revolutionary War.
   a. Treaty of Paris
   b. Treaty of America

8. When it came to winning the war, the United States relied heavily on its partnership with _____.
   a. France
   b. Spain

9. Franklin helped put pen to paper on what would become America's first _____ and was its first _____ general.
   a. congressional, founder
   b. constitution, postmaster

10. Ben Franklin also invented bifocals, the Franklin stove, a carriage ___, and the ___ harp
    a. the dollar bill, metal
    b. odometer, glass

11. Ben was the President of the state of Pennsylvania.
    a. True
    b. False

12. Ben was the only founding father to sign the Declaration of Independence and the _____Treaty, Paris Treaty, and United States Constitution all at the same time.
    a. Law, Congress
    b. Alliance, Constitution

Alice & The Rabbit-Hole

First, read the entire story. After that, go back and fill in the blanks. You can skip the blanks you're unsure about and finish them later.

sister	courageous	tunnel	pictures	hurry
dark	jar	feet	Rabbit	remarkable

ALICE was growing tired of sitting beside her _____ on the bank and having nothing to do: she had peeped into the book her sister was reading once or twice, but it was lacking _____ or words; "and what use is a book," Alice argued, "without pictures or conversations?" Thus, she was wondering in her mind (as best she could, given how sleepy and foolish she felt due to the heat) whether the pleasure of creating a cute daisy chain was worth the difficulty of getting up and gathering the daisies when a white _____ with pink eyes darted nearby her.

There was nothing _____ about that; nor did Alice consider it strange to hear the Rabbit exclaim to itself, "Oh no! Oh no! I will arrive too late!" (On reflection, she should have been surprised, but at the time, it seemed perfectly natural). Still, when the Rabbit actually removed a watch from its waistcoat-pocket, examined it, and then hurried on, Alice jumped to her _____, for it flashed across her mind that she had never seen a rabbit with either a waistcoat-pocket or a watch to remove from it, and burning with curiosity, she ran across the field after it. Alice saw the Rabbit go down a hole under the hedge. Alice followed it down in a _____, never once thinking how she would get out again.

The rabbit-hole continued straight ahead like a _____ for some distance and then suddenly dipped down, so quickly that Alice had no time to think about stopping herself before falling into what appeared to be a very deep well.

Either the well was really deep, or she dropped very slowly, as she had plenty of time to look around her and ponder on what might happen next. She first attempted to glance down and see what she was approaching, but it was too _____ to see anything; then, she discovered the sides of the well were lined with cupboards and bookcases; here and there, she observed maps and images hung on hooks. She removed a _____ from one of the shelves as she passed; it was labeled "ORANGE MARMALADE," but it was empty; she did not want to drop the jar for fear of killing someone beneath, so she managed to stuff it into one of the cupboards as she passed it.

"Perfect!" Alice exclaimed to herself. "After such a tumble, I shall have no worries about falling downstairs! How _____ they will all believe I am at home!

History: United States Armed Forces

The President of the United States is the Commander in Chief of the United States Armed Forces.

The United States, like many other countries, maintains a military to safeguard its borders and interests. The military has played an essential role in the formation and history of the United States since the Revolutionary War.

The **United States Department of Defense** (DoD) is in charge of controlling each branch of the military, except the United States Coast Guard, which is under the control of the Department of Homeland Security.

The Department of Defense is the world's largest 'company,' employing over 2 million civilians and military personnel.

The United States military is divided into six branches: the Air Force, Army, Coast Guard, Marine Corps, Navy, and Space Force.

The mission of the **United States Air Force** is to defend the country from outside forces. They also provide air support to other branches of the military, such as the Army and Navy.

The **United States Army** is responsible for defending against aggression that threatens the peace and security of the United States.

There are **Army National Guard** units in all 50 states, which their respective governments govern. The Constitution requires only one branch of the military. Members of the National Guard volunteer some of their time to keep the peace. They are not full-time soldiers, but they respond when called upon, for example, to quell violence when the police need assistance.

The primary concern of **the United States Coast Guard** is to protect domestic waterways (lakes, rivers, ports, etc.). The Coast Guard is managed by the United States Department of Homeland Security.

The **Marines** are a quick-response force. They are prepared to fight on both land and sea. The Marine Corps is a branch of the United States Navy. The Marine Corps conducts operations onboard warfare ships all over the world.

The **United States Navy** conducts its missions at sea to secure and protect the world's oceans. Their mission is to ensure safe sea travel and trade.

The **United States Space Force** is the newest branch of the military, established in December 2019. The world's first and currently only independent space force. It is in charge of operating and defending military satellites and ground stations that provide communications, navigation, and Earth observation, such as missile launch detection.

1. **The United States military is divided into ___ branches.**
   a. six
   b. five

2. **_____ is managed by the United States Department of Homeland Security.**
   a. The National Guard
   b. The Coast Guard

3. **The _____ of the United States is the Commander in Chief of the United States Armed Forces.**
   a. Governor
   b. President

4. **The United States maintains a military to safeguard its _____ and interests.**
   a. borders
   b. cities

5. **DoD is in charge of controlling each _____ of the military.**
   a. branch
   b. army

6. **The Marines are prepared to fight on both land and ____.**
   a. battlefield
   b. sea

7. **The United States Space Force is in charge of operating and defending military ____ and ground stations.**
   a. soldiers
   b. satellites

8. **The mission of the _____ is to defend the country from outside forces.**
   a. United States DoD Forces
   b. United States Air Force

9. There are _____ units in all 50 states.
    a. Army National Guard
    b. Armed Nations Guard

10. The United States Navy conducts its missions at sea to secure and protect the world's _____.
    a. oceans
    b. borders

11. The primary concern of the United States Coast Guard is to protect_____.
    a. domestic waterways
    b. domesticated cities

12. The United States military is: the Amy Force, Army, Coast Guard, Mario Corps, Old Navy, and Space Force.
    a. True
    b. False

Extra Credit: Has America ever been invaded?

Geography: Time Zones

First, go over the entire message. Then go back and fill in the blanks. You can skip the blanks you're unsure about and come back to them later.

different	outside	message	shines	classmate
exist	clocks	time	ball	day

Have you ever tried to call or send a _____ to someone who was on the other side of the country or the world? It can be tough to reach a faraway location from you because the time of _____ may be different from your own. The purpose of time zones and why we have them will be discussed in this session.

Kim, Mike's _____ who recently relocated across the country, is texting him. After a short time, Kim sends Mike a text message saying that it is time for her to go to sleep for the night. The sun is beaming brightly _____, and Mike is confused about why Kim would choose this time of day to go to sleep. 'Can you tell me what _____ it is, please?' Mike asked. 'It's 9:00 p.m. now!' Kim replies.

What exactly is going on here? Was Mike able to travel back in time in some way?

What is happening to Mike and Kim is nothing more than a natural occurrence that occurs on our planet daily. Since Kim relocated across the country, she is now in a _____ time zone than she was previously.

A time zone is a geographical location on the planet with a fixed time that all citizens can observe by setting their _____ to that time. As you go from east to west (or west to east) on the globe's surface, you will encounter different time zones. The greater the distance traveled, the greater the number of time zones crossed.

Time zones are not something that arises in nature by chance. Humans created the concept of time zones and determined which regions of the world are located in which time zones.

Because of time zones, everyone experiences the same pattern of dawn in the early morning and sunset in the late afternoon. We require time zones because the earth is shaped like a _____ and therefore requires them. As the sun beams down on the planet, not every location receives the same amount of sunshine. The sun _____ on one side of the earth and brightens it during the day, while the other side is dark during the night (nighttime). If time zones didn't _____, many people worldwide would experience quite strange sunshine patterns during the day if there were no time zones.

One key skill that everyone should be able to perform is determining whether a location on earth is in a later or earlier time zone than they are. The general guideline is as follows:

If your friend lives in a location that is west of you, they are in a different time zone than you. If they live in a time zone later than yours, they are located east of you.

West is considered to be earlier, whereas the east is considered later.

The following are the primary time zones in the United States:
Eastern (New York, Georgia, Ohio, and other east coast states)
Central (Alabama, Iowa, Minnesota, and more)
Mountain (Arizona, Montana, Utah, and more)
Pacific (California, Nevada, and other west coast states)

History: Darius the Great

First, go over the entire message. Then go back and fill in the blanks. You can skip the blanks you're unsure about and come back to them later.

ruler	storm	Battle	carved	army
famous	happy	experience	Middle	led

Many stories have appeared on the news about conflicts in the _____ East from Egypt to Iran. Do you think you have what it takes to lead this area of the country? It's a difficult challenge, but 2500 years ago, a single person ruled over this entire region and dealt with its issues. The Middle East was once a part of a vast region known as the Persian Empire. Darius the Great, the Persian Empire's most _____ ruler, ruled during the empire's height of power and size.

The Behistun Inscription, which means writing, has revealed much about Darius' life. Darius had his biography and accomplishments _____ into the face of a mountain for them to be remembered and respected. According to the Inscription, Darius was the son of a Persian nobleman, but not the son of the previous emperor. Darius overthrew the emperor's son and became the new _____ of Persia with the assistance of six other nobles.

In order to maintain control, Darius had to devote time to fighting rebellions. After destroying his last known enemies, he considered expanding his kingdom. Darius began by joining parts of northern India. Following that, he _____ his army into Scythia, the northern part of the Black Sea and a vital trading region.

Afterward, the Persian Empire stretched from Europe to the Indian Ocean, making it one of the largest empires. Darius may have ruled over up to half of humanity. He is renowned for decorating his palace hall with images of _____ people throughout the empire rather than conflict and war. However, he went one step further by choosing to fight the Greeks.

The Greeks and Persians had never gotten along, but both had left the other alone for much of their history. On the other hand, Darius desired to combine Greece into his empire. A protest or retaliation against the Persians took place among the Greeks who lived in modern-day Turkey. Darius attempted to make peace with the Greeks at first but ultimately decided it would be easier to conquer them with his gigantic _____. There were two main goals for Darius: punish the Greek leaders of the rebels and seize as many Greek cities as possible.

At first, Darius and the Persians won a series of minor victories over the Greeks, conquering cities and many of Greece's islands, and believed they could beat the rest of the region. However, he began to _____ significant difficulties. The first was a massive _____ that destroyed 200 of his ships and possibly 30,000 of his soldiers.

Following that, Darius' army fought and lost against the Greeks at the _____ of Marathon. The 26-mile race is named after this battle because a messenger ran the distance to Athens to announce the Persian defeat. The Battle of Marathon did not end the Greek-Persian wars, but Darius died shortly afterward, and his son Xerxes took over the war.

Science: Dolphins Life Cycle

Score: _____

Date: _____

First, read the entire story. After that, go back and fill in the blanks. You can skip the blanks you're unsure about and finish them later.

family	blowhole	old	milk	infants
small	protect	television	friendly	lifespan

You may have seen dolphins on _____ or in person, but did you know they are among the most intelligent animals on the planet or that baby dolphins are referred to as calves?

Dolphins occasionally mate through swimming and interacting with one another. While the idea of a dolphin socializing may seem silly, dolphins are incredibly sociable and _____ creatures. Dolphins are pretty similar to humans in this regard. They live in pod communities and act as friends and neighbors, protecting and caring for one another.

Between the ages of 5 and 10, a female dolphin becomes reproductive and capable of reproducing. Fertility refers to your body's readiness to give birth. Every one to three years, dolphins give birth to a new generation of calves. Following mating, the male dolphin occasionally swims in pretty patterns and produces noises with his _____ to alert other male dolphins in the area that he has mated with a female dolphin.

Calves are the term used to refer to dolphin _____. They are born tail-first and are subsequently transported to the water's surface to breathe. The calf can breathe and swim on its own quite early after birth. As with all mammals, the calf remains close to the mother until it has mastered critical survival abilities.

Dolphins, like humans and all mammals, generate milk for their young. Their milk is highly nutritious, and the dolphin calf feeds exclusively on its mother's _____ for six months to two years, depending on the species. Another way dolphin calves are comparable to human infants is that they begin eating food other than milk at the age of six months. This includes fish and crustaceans for dolphins. Crustaceans, such as lobsters and shrimp, are _____ sea animals with several legs, a sectioned body, and a hard shell.

Calves remain with their mothers until they reach adolescence. The dolphin is fertile and able to mate at that age. As previously said, dolphins typically dwell in pods. Sometimes pods are composed of multiple species of dolphins, or they may consist of a single male, a female, and a group of baby dolphins, much like a _____. Dolphins can live to be 50 years old; however, their average _____ is about 30 years; however, if they are captured and not allowed to dwell in their natural habitats, their lifespans are typically shorter.

Dolphins possess a unique ability called echolocation. Dolphins use echolocation to identify other creatures' size, shape, movement, and distance by making clicking noises through their blowholes. This is advantageous for dolphin survival since it enables them to _____ and hunt.

Dolphins die for various reasons, but some of the more prevalent ones include _____ age, heart illness, parasites, and viruses. Dolphins can also succumb to diseases that are recognizable to people, such as stomach ulcers, tumors, and skin ailments.

Science: Mars

Mars is the planet for you if your favorite color is red. It is coated in red dust and rocks composed of iron and oxygen, referred to as iron oxide. When anything rusts on Earth, this is what you get.

For centuries, humans have been fascinated by our neighboring planet. The prospect of another planet on which we could possibly live is mind-boggling. It's been debated whether or not Mars is our best hope. However, as technology advances, we have discovered that Mars is not a habitable planet for humans.

While our red neighbor is not as teeming with life as Earth, it has several characteristics with our world. As on Earth, the Martian day is approximately 24 hours long. And while they are longer than ours, Mars likewise has four seasons.

Mars' landscape shares specific characteristics with ours. It is heavily forested and covered in canyons, gorges, plateaus, flatlands, and mountains. They simply lack water, vegetation, and animals.

There are ice caps on our planet's north and south poles filled with life. Mars likewise possesses ice caps at its north and south poles, but they are not made of water and are non-existent: they are made of carbon dioxide, also known as dry ice.

Assume you did indeed land on Mars and began exploring. The first step is to wear your specialist suit in preparation to depart the space shuttle. Your suit includes an oxygen tank, as Mars lacks oxygen, and its thin atmosphere is dense with toxic carbon dioxide. Additionally, it has weighted feet since Mars has considerably lower gravity than Earth, which also explains why it has essentially no atmosphere; there isn't enough gravity to keep it in orbit around the planet. Your outfit shields you from sunburn. Mars' atmosphere does not protect you from dangerous rays the way ours does.

The first thing you notice is the planet's red loveliness all around you - but then you realize it's freezing! If memory serves, you arrived during the summer season, correct? Mars is a frigid planet due to its thin atmosphere, which cannot retain the sun's heat. You begin by collecting pebbles and soil to take home.

Suddenly, you notice the largest, thickest cloud of dust speeding toward you. You've read about Mars' tremendous dust storms. To escape being covered in red dust and bombarded, you hurriedly hop into the spacecraft you'll be driving and wait for the storm to pass.

You spend the day driving around the planet, avoiding asteroids. They can reach the surface of Mars because of its thin atmosphere. They are destroyed before they get to the Earth's surface due to the heat generated by the atmosphere. And even though Mars is only half the size of Earth, you have seen so much and are awestruck by your journey on this planet!

1. **Mars is the color_____.**
   a. red
   b. orange

2. **Mars is coated in red dust and rocks composed of ____ and oxygen.**
   a. iron
   b. metal

3. **Mars is not a habitable planet for humans.**
   a. True
   b. False

4. **Mars has _____ seasons.**
   a. four
   b. three

5. **Mar is covered in _____, gorges, plateaus, flatlands, and mountains.**
   a. sand
   b. canyons

6. **Mars lacks ____.**
   a. energy
   b. oxygen

7. **Mars' thin atmosphere is dense with toxic ____.**
   a. carbon dioxide
   b. minerals carbon

8. **Mars has tremendous ____ storms.**
   a. dust
   b. rain

Geography: Rivers

A river is a moving, flowing body of water. Typically, a river discharges its water into an ocean, lake, pond, or even another river. Rivers vary in size, and there is no hard and fast rule about how large a flow of water must be to be classified as a river. Rain, melting snow, lakes, ponds, and even glaciers can all contribute to river water. Rivers flow downhill from their headwaters. They are classified as freshwater biomes.

A river is a body of primarily freshwater that flows across the land's surface, usually traversing its way to the sea.

A river channel is a type of channel found in rivers.

All rivers flow in channels, and the bottom of the channel is known as the bed, while the sides are known as the banks.

When one stream meets another, they merge. The smaller stream is referred to as a tributary. A large number of tributaries form a river.

A river expands as it collects more and more water from its tributaries.

When a river comes to an end, it's known as the mouth.

Rivers provide us with food, energy, recreation, boating routes, and, of course, water for drinking and watering crops.

3 Longest Rivers:

The Nile River runs for 4,135 miles. It is found on the African continent, primarily in the countries of Egypt and Sudan. It flows into the Mediterranean Sea from the north.

The Amazon River stretches for 3,980 miles. It flows through several countries on the South American continent, including Brazil, Venezuela, Bolivia, and Ecuador. It comes to an end at the Atlantic Ocean.

The Mississippi River and Missouri River systems form the longest river system in North America.The Missouri River is a tributary of the Mississippi River. It is 6,279 kilometers long. It is a river that flows into the Gulf of Mexico.

Do you understand there is a difference between upstream and downstream? Upstream refers to the direction from which the water source originates, such as a mountain. Downstream refers to the direction in which the water flows to reach its final destination.

Fast Facts:

There are 76 rivers in the world that are more than 1000 miles long.

Many people believe that rivers always flow south, but four of the world's ten longest rivers flow north.

There are approximately 3.5 million miles of rivers in the United States alone.

1. **Rivers vary in _____.**
   a. height
   b. size

2. **A river is a moving, flowing _____ of water.**
   a. body
   b. streams

3. A river is a body of primarily _____ that flows across the land's surface.
   a. freshwater
   b. biome

4. When one stream meets another, they_____.
   a. cross over
   b. merge

5. When a river comes to an end, it's known as the _____.
   a. mouth
   b. lake

6. A large number of _____ form a river.
   a. tributaries
   b. oceans

7. A river expands as it _____ more and more water from its tributaries.
   a. collects
   b. decreases

8. The _____ runs for 4,135 miles.
   a. Nile River
   b. Mississippi River

9. _____ flows through several countries on the South American continent, including Brazil.
   a. Amazon River
   b. Antarctica River

10. _____ and _____ systems form the longest river system in North America.
   a. Mississippi River and Missouri River
   b. Mississippi River and Michigan River

Extra Credit: Answer The Following 3 Questions:

(1.) Where is majority of all water located on Earth?

(2.) What is all the water on earth called?

(3.) Why the Earth is called Blue planet?

_____

_____

_____

_____

_____

_____

_____

_____

Grammar: Homophones vs Homographs vs. Homonyms

How do you know which 'there,' 'their,' or 'they're' to use when you're writing? Isn't it a difficult one? These words sound similar but have completely different meanings.

Words with the same sound but different meanings are referred to as **homophones**. Homophones can be spelled differently or the same way. Rose (the flower), rose (the past tense of 'rise,' and rows (a line of items or people) are all homophones.

Homographs are two or more words that have the same spelling but different meanings and it **doesn't have to sound the same**. Because homographs are words with multiple meanings, how can you tell which one is being used? Readers can determine which form of a homograph is being used by looking for context clues, or words surrounding it that provide information about the definition. Take a look at these homograph examples.

A **bat** is either a piece of sporting equipment or an animal.
Bass is either a type of fish or a musical genre.
A **pen** is a writing instrument or a small enclosure in which animals are kept.
Lean is a word that means to be thin or to rest against something.
A **skip** is a fictitious jump or missing out on something.

Homonyms are words that have the same spelling or pronunciation but different meanings. These words can be perplexing at times, especially for students learning to spell them. For example, right means moral, the opposite of left, and a personal freedom. Homonyms can refer to both homophones and homographs. Both a homograph and a homophone are included in the definition of a homonym. For example, the words 'bear,' 'tear,' and 'lead' are all homographs, but they also meet the criteria for homonyms. They simply have to have the same look or sound. Similarly, while the words 'sell,' 'cell,' 'by,' and 'buy' are all homophones, they are also homonyms.

1. 'there,' 'their,' or 'they're' are examples of _____.
   a. Homophones
   b. Homographs

2. _____ are words that have the same spelling or pronunciation but different meanings.
   a. Homonyms
   b. Hemograms

3. Choose the correct homophone for this sentence: Please don't drop and _____that bottle of hand sanitizer!
   a. brake
   b. break

4. Homographs are two or more words that have the same spelling but different _____.
   a. ending sounds
   b. meanings

5. Current (A flow of water / Up to date) is both homograph and homophone.
   a. True
   b. False

6. To, two, and too are _____.
   a. Homonyms
   b. Homagraphs

7. The candle filled the _____ with a delicious scent.
   a. air
   b. heir

8. Kim drove _____ the tunnel.
   a. threw
   b. through

9. John wants to go to _____ house for dinner, but they don't like her, so _____ going to say no.
   a. there, they're
   b. their, they're

10. We won a $95,000 _____!
    a. check
    b. cheque

11. For example, a pencil is not really made with _____.
    a. led
    b. lead

12. Choose the correct homophone for this sentence: Timmy was standing _____ in line.
    a. fourth
    b. forth

13. Homophones are two words that sound the same but have a different meanings.
    a. True
    b. False

14. The word ring in the following two sentences is considered what? She wore a ruby ring. | We heard the doorbell ring.
    a. hologram
    b. homograph

15. A Homograph is a word that has more than one meaning and doesn't have to sound the same.
    a. True
    b. False

16. Homophones occur when there are multiple ways to spell the same sound.
    a. True
    b. False

17. Select the correct homophone: I have very little (patience/patients) when students do not follow directions.
    a. patience
    b. patients

18. The correct homophone (s) are used in the sentence: Personally, I hate the smell of read meet.
    a. True
    b. False

19. The correct homophone(s) is used in the sentence: We saw a herd of cattle in the farmer's field.
    a. True
    b. False

20. What is NOT an example of a homograph?
    a. or, oar
    b. live, live

21. I love my _____ class.
    a. dear
    b. deer

22. We will go _____ after we finish our lesson.
    a. there
    b. their

23. Please grab _____ jacket for recess.
    a. you're
    b. your

24. There is _____ more water at the concession stand.
    a. no
    b. know

Life Skills: Internet Safety

First, read the entire passage. After that, go back and fill in the blanks. You can skip the blanks you're unsure about and finish them later.

inappropriate	videos	unsupervised	downloading	violation
safety	skills	passwords	personal	permission
hurtful	protect	uncomfortable	agree	

Internet _____ is the act of making one's self safer while surfing the web. This includes being aware of the risks associated with your online activity and implementing a few solutions to minimize or eliminate these risks.

You may enjoy going online to watch _____, play games, and communicate with friends and family. You may be using the internet for schoolwork and homework as well. Computers, mobile phones, tablets, and other internet-enabled devices, including toys, can be used for this purpose.

Because you are becoming more independent online and may go online _____, you face more internet safety risks than younger children. There are additional dangers if you use the internet to communicate with others, such as on social media or in games.

You _____ yourself from potentially harmful or inappropriate content and activities when you take practical internet safety precautions. And you get to make the most of your online experience, which allows you to learn, explore, be creative, and connect with others.

10 Rules To Follow:

1. Unless my parents have given me permission, I will not give out _____ information such as my home address, phone number, or my parents' work address/phone number.

2. If I come across something that makes me _____, I will immediately notify my parents.

3. I will never _____ to meet someone I "met" online without first discussing with my parents. If my parents agree to the meeting, I will make sure that it is held in a public location and bring a parent with me.

4. If my parents think a picture of me or someone else online is _____, I will

discuss the issue with them and refrain from posting it.

5. I will not respond to any _____ messages or make me feel uncomfortable in any way. I don't believe that it is my fault if I receive such a message. If I do, I will immediately notify my parents.

6) I will talk to my parents about setting up rules for using the internet and mobile phones. We will work together to determine when I can be online, how long I can be online, and where I can go. Without their _____, I will not be able to access other areas or break these rules.

7. Other than my parents, I will not share my _____ with anyone else (even if they are my best friends).

8. I will consult with my parents before _____ or installing software or doing anything else that could potentially harm our computer or mobile device or that could compromise my family's privacy.

9. I will responsibly conduct myself on the internet, refraining from doing anything that is harmful to others or in _____ of the law.

10. I will educate my parents on how I have fun and learn new _____ online and teach them about the internet, computers, and other technology.

Extra Credit: Answer These 2 questions:

1. What is meant by Internet safety?

2. How can you stay safe on the Internet?

_____

_____

_____

_____

_____

_____

_____

_____

_____

Life Skills: Making Friends

Score: _____

Date: _____

First, read the entire passage. After that, go back and fill in the blanks. You can skip the blanks you're unsure about and finish them later.

entire	brag	persuade	grin	dream
bike	friendships	walk	opening	important

Hello, my name is Timmy! I've always found it challenging to make friends, to the point of anxiety. People find it difficult to

believe, but I used to _____ around school by myself. I wanted to meet people, make friends, and have others show interest

in me, but it just didn't happen. I was a good kid. I was intriguing. I was prepared to make new friends, but I couldn't make the

other kids notice me. I was approaching everything incorrectly. I spent all of my energy attempting to _____ other

students that I was interesting. But, when I realized that trying to pique the interest of others in me was pointless, I changed my

behavior. Being interested in others was the key to _____ the door to making friends for me. As a result of this, I was

able to connect with children much more quickly. I made more good friends in a few weeks than I had in all of my previous

school years combined.

SIMLE

A smile may appear to be such a simple thing to do, but it can open the path to a lot of good_____. It is

difficult to walk around with a smile on your face if you are in a situation where you are not making friends, no matter how hard

you try. However, not smiling can make you feel even more out of place.

Now, I'm not suggesting that you walk around with a _____ on your face all day because people will think you're weird. But

I'm talking about lightening up and sending out positive energy. Laugh at your classmates' jokes (even if they aren't funny) and

smile at people as you pass by. You have a much better chance of making friends if you let people in a little.

LISTEN

Everyone wishes to be heard. It's easy to believe that the best way to make friends is to _____ about how cool you are.

Doesn't this involve talking about yourself to others? Actually, no, it doesn't. It consists of being a part of a group, and listening

to others is a big part. All of this is a natural part of maturing. When you were three, you could walk into a room and start talking,

and everyone would stop and listen. But you no longer have that power. If you walk into a room full of your peers and begin

bragging about how great you are, they will almost certainly tune you out.

FEEL IMPORTANT

Everyone wants to feel like they are the most _____ person in the room. It is a natural process that occurs to all of us. There's nothing wrong with feeling that way. When someone pays attention to you, you feel ten feet tall and walk around all day with a smile on your face and a spring in your step (remember that). You must be able to convey this feeling to others. If this makes you happy, know that it will make others happy as well.

I used to _____ about being so well-known that I didn't have time to do anything other than saying "hi" to people as I walked by. Just consider that for a moment. What's the point of that? Making friends involves not only "knowing a lot of people," but also "spending quality time with people."

You will have a much happier school life if you have a few good friends rather than a tight connection to the _____ school. What you are interested in is reflected in your friends. You grow together and share beautiful experiences that you will remember for months or years to come. Having close friends has a real impact on your life. The power of a few good friends is a thousand times greater than the power of 500 social media connections.

Knowing who you allow you to be yourself. Perhaps you enjoy watching silly stuff on YouTube, riding your _____, or cooking Tacos every Tuesday. My point is, don't pretend to be someone you're not just to fit in. You might miss out on a friendship with someone who shares your interests.

Extra Credit: Answer These 2 questions:

1. What are 3 ways to make friends?

2. What is the difference between acquaintance and friend?

....

....

....

....

....

....

Science: All About Beavers

First, read the entire passage. After that, go back and fill in the blanks. You can skip the blanks you're unsure about and finish them later.

hammer	growing	slow	building	wild
plants	fur	slap	underwater	rodents

Beavers are mammals well-known for their _____ abilities. Dams are built out of branches, stones, and mud. A dam stretches across a stream and blocks the flow of water. This results in a large pond. Beavers build their homes in these ponds' still waters rather than in rushing streams.

Beavers are _____, which are a type of animal. They have a kinship with mice, squirrels, and muskrats. Beavers are classified into two species or types. North America is home to the American beaver. The Eurasian beaver can be found in Europe and Asia. Beavers can be found in rivers, streams, and lakes. They spend some time on land as well.

Beavers have a total length of about 4 feet (1.3 meters), including the tail. Beavertails are scaly, flat, and paddle-shaped. Their stocky bodies and short legs are covered in thick brown fur. Beavers carry objects with their tiny front feet. Beavers are _____ on land, but their webbed back feet help them swim. Beavers can submerge for up to 15 minutes underwater.

Beavers are herbivores, which means they eat _____. They primarily consume tree buds, leaves, twigs, and the layer beneath the bark.

Beavers cut down young trees with their powerful jaws and teeth. The beaver's large front teeth never stop _____. The constant gnawing on wood by beavers helps to keep their teeth from growing too long.

They work in groups to construct dams. Beaver couples create lodges out of sticks and mud. A lodge can be up to 5 feet (1.5 meters) tall. It has a dome-shaped roof. Beavers are strong swimmers who can stay submerged for up to 15 minutes. Beavers have a translucent third eyelid (called a nictitating membrane) that covers and protects their eyes while still allowing some sight _____. Their ears and noses are valvular, which means they can close while diving underwater.

Even in the wee hours of the morning, Beavers have a hard time keeping their hands off the _____.___ They are prolific builders during the night.   As a result, they are "as busy as a beaver."

Beavers will _____ the water with their broad, scaly tail to warn other beavers in the area that a predator is approaching.

There were once more than 60 million beavers in North America. However, due to hunting for its _____ and glands for medicine, as well as the beavers' tree-felling and damming affecting other land uses, the population has declined to around 12 million.

Beavers can live in the _____ for up to 24 years.

Extra Credit: Answer These 3 questions:

1. Are beavers friendly?

2. Why are beavers' teeth orange?

3. How many beavers live in a dam?

Occupation **Lawyer, university administrator, writer,**

BORN DATE: **January 27, 1954**   Nationality **American**

DEATH DATE: **still alive and well**   Education **Princeton & Harvard University**   Children **2 girls**

Childhood and Family Background Facts

Born as Mary Robinson in Chicago, Illinois.

Dad's name John Robinson III & mom's name Rose Robinson.

One brother named Malcolm Robinson, he's a college basketball coach.

Her great-great-great-grandmother, Cindy Shields, was born into slavery in South Carolina.

Her childhood home was in New York.

Her great-aunt who was a piano teacher, taught her how to play the piano.

Work and Career Facts

- First job was babysitting.
- Mary majored in sociology at Princeton, where she graduated with honors, and went to Harvard Law School.
- She once worked in public service as an assistant to the mayor.
- She was the Vice President of Community and External Affairs at the University of Chicago Medical Center.

Friends, Social Life and Other Interesting Facts

- When she was a teen, she became friends with Kim Jackson.
- Her college bestie Suzanne Alele died from cancer at a young age in 1990.
- Her two favorite children's books: "Goodnight Moon" and "Where the Wild Things Are."
- Celebrity Crush: Denzel & Will Smith

Children, Marriage or Significant Relationships

- She suffered a heartbreaking miscarriage.
- Gave birth to two beautiful daughters Monica and Jennifer.
- She met her husband Tom when she was assigned to be his mentor when he was a summer associate at the law firm she worked at.

Did you enjoy researching this person?
Rating: ☆ ☆ ☆ ☆ ☆

TODAY IS RESEARCH DAY!   GRADE_____

DATE_____   RESEARCH: Galileo Galilei

Occupation _____

BORN DATE:_____ Nationality_____

DEATH DATE:_____ Education _____ #Children _____

Childhood and Family Background Facts

Work and Career Facts

Children, Marriage and or Significant Relationships

Friends, Social Life and Other Interesting Facts

Did you enjoy researching this person?

Give a Rating: ☆ ☆ ☆ ☆ ☆

DATE_____   **RESEARCH: Mark Twain**

Occupation _____

BORN DATE:_____   Nationality_____

DEATH DATE:_____   Education _____   #Children _____

Childhood and Family Background Facts

Work and Career Facts

Children, Marriage and or Significant Relationships

Friends, Social Life and Other Interesting Facts

Did you enjoy researching this person?

Give a Rating: ☆ ☆ ☆ ☆ ☆

GRADE_____

DATE_____   **RESEARCH: Marie Curie**

Occupation _____

BORN DATE:_____   Nationality_____

DEATH DATE:_____   Education _____   #Children _____

Childhood and Family Background Facts

Work and Career Facts

Children, Marriage and or Significant Relationships

Friends, Social Life and Other Interesting Facts

Did you enjoy researching this person?

Give a Rating: ☆ ☆ ☆ ☆ ☆

GRADE_____

DATE_____

RESEARCH: Princess Diana

Occupation _____

BORN DATE: _____ Nationality _____

DEATH DATE: _____ Education _____ #Children _____

Childhood and Family Background Facts

Work and Career Facts

Children, Marriage and or Significant Relationships

Friends, Social Life and Other Interesting Facts

Did you enjoy researching this person?

Give a Rating: ☆ ☆ ☆ ☆ ☆

Science: Helium

One of the lightest elements in the universe, helium is also one of its most common. In the periodic table, it is at the top of the noble gas group.

Helium is an odorless, tasteless, and colorless gas at room temperature. It has very low boiling and melting points, so it is usually found in the gas phase except in the most extreme conditions. Helium is the only element that does not solidify at normal pressures and remains a liquid even when temperatures reach absolute zero.

Helium is classified as an inert or noble gas. This means that the electrons in its outer electron shell are filled. As a result, it is highly inert and non-flammable.

Helium is a relatively rare element on Earth. It eventually escapes into space because it is so light; it is very little in the Earth's atmosphere.

Scientists believe that the majority of the helium in the universe was created during the universe's formation. However, new helium is produced in the cores of stars and through radioactive decay on Earth. Helium can be found trapped underground in natural gas reservoirs as a result of radioactive decay. The majority of the world's helium comes from gas deposits in the United States. Smaller quantities are available in Qatar, Algeria, Russia, Canada, China, and Poland.

The internal cores of stars are constantly producing helium. Intense pressures deep within a star cause hydrogen atoms to convert to helium atoms. This generates the energy, heat, and light required to power the stars and the sun. This process is known as nuclear fusion.

Helium is used to make balloons and airships float. Although it is not as light as hydrogen, it is a safer gas because hydrogen is highly flammable. Underwater, deep-sea divers breathe a mixture of helium and oxygen. Helium protects divers from being poisoned by too much oxygen. However, inhaling too much helium is also dangerous. The body may not receive enough oxygen, causing the person to suffocate.

MRI scanners, which use the gas to keep superconducting magnets cool, are the largest industrial users of helium gas. Other applications include silicon wafers for electronics and arc welding protection gas.

Astronomer Pierre Janssen discovered helium for the first time in 1868. When he was studying a solar eclipse, he found a new element. The element was discovered on Earth for the first time in 1895.

Helium derives its name from the Greek word "helios," which means "sun." Helios is also the name of the Greek Sun God.

Helium has eight different isotopes. Helium-4 is the most abundant of the helium isotopes, and it was largely created at the beginning of the universe.

1. Helium is an ___, ___, and colorless gas at room temperature.
   a. orderly, tasteful
   b. odorless, tasteless

2. Helium is one of the ____ elements in the universe.
   a. heaviest
   b. lightest

3. Helium is classified as an inert or ____ gas.
   a. noble
   b. odor

4. ____Pierre Janssen discovered helium for the first time in 1868.
   a. Scientist
   b. Astronomer

5. Helium is used to make _____ and airships float.
   a. kites
   b. balloons

6. The internal cores of _____ are constantly producing helium.
   a. stars
   b. the sun

7. Helium protects divers from being poisoned by too much _____.
   a. oxygen
   b. gas

8. Helium can be found trapped underground in _____ gas reservoirs as a result of radioactive decay.
   a. natural
   b. minerals

Extra Credit: Answer The Following 3 Questions:

1. What is helium made from?

2. Can you make a balloon float without helium?

3. Why did my helium balloons sink overnight?

Science: The First Moon Walk Part II

Looking out the windows, Armstrong and Aldrin saw a lifeless and barren lunar landscape from inside the spacecraft. In other words, the moon surface appeared dry, bare with no sign of life

The pair inside the Eagle prepared to exit the module after six and a half hours. Armstrong took the lead as mission commander and became the first person to set foot on the moon.

Aldrin descended the ladder and joined his partner twenty minutes later. Following a plaque reading that stated they "came in peace for all mankind," the two planted the American flag on the surface. President Richard Nixon called to express his congratulations to the astronauts.

Armstrong and Aldrin returned to their jobs, collecting moon rocks and dust samples for future research and development. After more than two hours, the astronauts re-boarded the lunar module and prepared to rejoin Collins. It was time to return home.

On July 24, 1969, the Apollo 11 crew returned to Earth. Ten astronauts would follow in Armstrong and Aldrin's footsteps over the next several years. The last moon mission took place in 1972.

Despite the fact that humans have not returned to the moon since then, they have continued to explore the cosmos. They even built the International Space Station (ISS), a space research station where they can conduct experiments and study space from a close distance.

NASA is currently working on sending humans to another planet: Mars. NASA is optimistic about its chances as a result of the Apollo 11 moon landing. The act of landing three people on the moon and safely returning them proved that successful human space exploration is possible.

1. **NASA is currently working on sending humans to another planet: _____.**
   a. Saturn
   b. Mars

2. **On _____, the Apollo 11 crew returned to Earth.**
   a. July 24, 1969
   b. July 25, 1967

3. **The _____ is a space research station.**
   a. US International Center Moon
   b. International Space Station

4. **Armstrong took the lead as mission _____ and became the first person to set foot on the moon.**
   a. commander
   b. scientist

5. **The astronauts saw a _____ reading that stated they "came in peace for all mankind,".**
   a. written letter
   b. plaque

6. **The last moon mission took place in _____.**
   a. 1972
   b. 1975

The Moon Walk Extra Credit: Answer The Following 3 Questions:

1. How old was Neil Armstrong when he landed on the moon?

2. Is the flag still on the moon?

3. What was the first animal in space?

Science: The Moon Walk

On July 20, 1969, a record-breaking event occurred when millions of people gathered around their television sets to witness two American astronauts accomplish something no one had ever done before. Neil Armstrong and Edwin "Buzz" Aldrin became the first humans to walk on the moon, wearing bulky spacesuits and oxygen backpacks.

Armstrong famously said after the two stepped onto the lunar surface, "That's one small step for a man, one giant leap for mankind."

Russia launched the first artificial satellite, Sputnik 1, into space in 1957. Following that, the United States launched several satellites of its own. Both countries wanted to be the first to send a person into space.

It wasn't until 1961 that a person went into space: Russian Yuri Gagarin became the first on April 12, 1961. Alan Shepard of the United States became the first American in space less than a month later. Following these achievements, President John F. Kennedy challenged the National Aeronautics and Space Administration (NASA) to land a man on the moon in ten years or less.

NASA got right to work. On July 16, 1969, the Apollo 11 spacecraft was preparing to launch three astronauts into space.

As part of the selection process for the Apollo 11 astronauts, officials from NASA chose Neil Armstrong, Buzz Aldrin, and Michael Collins. The spacecraft approached the moon's surface just four days after taking off from Florida's Kennedy Space Center.

The three men separated before landing. Collins boarded Apollo 11's command module, the Columbia, from which he would remain in lunar orbit. Armstrong and Aldrin boarded the Eagle, Apollo 11's lunar module, and began their descent to the moon's surface.

The Eagle made a daring landing in a shallow moon crater known as the Sea of Tranquility, which was a risky move. Most people who watched the landing on television were unaware that the Eagle had only 20 seconds of landing fuel remaining at this point in the flight.

1. Neil _____ and Edwin "Buzz" _____ became the first humans to walk on the moon.
   a. Armstrong and Aldrin
   b. Armadale and Aladdin

2. Russia launched the first artificial satellite called ____.
   a. Spank 1.0
   b. Sputnik 1

3. The Eagle made a daring landing in a shallow moon crater known as the ____.
   a. Sea of Tranquility
   b. U.S.A Sea of Trinity

4. On _____, the Apollo 11 spacecraft was preparing to launch three astronauts into space.
   a. July 16, 1989
   b. July 16, 1969

5. Russian _____ became the first person in space on April 12, 1961
   a. Yuri Gagarin
   b. Yari Kim Jun

6. Armstrong and Aldrin boarded the _____, Apollo 11's lunar module, and began their descent to the moon's surface.
   a. Eagle
   b. Black Bird

Score: _____

Date: _____

Geography
Vocabulary Crossword

Complete the crossword by filling in a word that fits each clue. Fill in the correct answers, one letter per square, both across and down, from the given clues. There will be a gray space between multi-word answers.

Tip: Solve the easy clues first, and then go back and answer the more difficult ones.

Across

1. a bowl-shaped vessel used for holding food or liquids
9. water that has condensed on a cool surface overnight
10. droplets of water vapor suspended in the air near the ground
11. ice crystals forming a white deposit
12. a slowly moving mass of ice
16. a shelter serving as a place of safety or sanctuary
17. a relatively flat highland
18. an extensive plain without trees
20. topographic study of a given place
21. a long steep-sided depression in the ocean floor
23. A circular, spiral, or helical motion in a fluid
24. a low area where the land is saturated with water

Down

2. an indentation of a shoreline smaller than a gulf
3. a large cave or a large chamber in a cave
4. a steep rock face
5. the shore of a sea or ocean
6. the territory occupied by a nation
7. an open valley in a hilly area
8. arid land with little or no vegetation
13. precipitation of ice pellets
14. a large frozen mass floating at sea
15. a thin fog with condensation near the ground
18. air pollution by a mixture of smoke and fog
23. a valley
25. a slight wind

GLACIER ZEPHYR ICEBERG
DESERT FROST DALE HAIL
SMOG BASIN VALE BAY
OASIS COUNTRY COAST
TOPOLOGY WETLAND MIST
STEPPE VORTEX PLATEAU
FOG DEW CLIFF TRENCH
CAVERN

Geography: Castles in Germany

Score: _____

Date:_____

Castles are now iconic symbols of magnificence and mythical tales. Aside from their dazzling appearance and antiquity, they reveal an old vivid, and true fable.

German castles date from the 9th to 10th centuries, when the Great Age of Castles began. Castles embody the need for nations to be protected from invasions by other countries and serve as residences for old royal families. These incredible structures are examples of tactical and solid rocky constructions built by kings and emperors to guard the nation's territories during warfare and impose rule among populaces during peacetime.

German castles evolved during the "Medieval Ages," following the fall of Ancient Rome and the beginning of the Renaissance Period in the 14th century, and are considered an area of art and architecture. The architecture of German castles consists of a combination of towers and fortified walls, with amazingly decorated interior and exterior, located in high peaks of mountains and valleys, near waterways, and allowing total surveillance of the surrounding territory.

Modern Germany has a magnificent castle heritage, with over 2100 castles spread throughout the country. A very bright and amusing history awaits behind the doors of these impressive castles. Around 100 years ago, not so long ago, kings, emperors, and their families visited, lived, and operated there. Historical resolutions were reached there, and many soldiers died there defending their country from invaders.

Let us take some time to explore some of Germany's magnificent castles.

Neuschwanstein Castle: Located in the Bavarian Alps near the town of Füssen in southeast Bavaria, Germany, this is one of Europe's and the world's most impressive castles.

Hohenzollern Castle is situated on the crest of Mount Hohenzollern in the German state of Swabia. It was first built in the 11th century.

Eltz Castle: The beautiful and ancient castle of Eltz is located in the Moselle valley, between Koblenz and Trier, Germany, and is surrounded on three sides by the Eltzbach River. The castle was built as a residence rather than a fortress and served as a residence for the Rodendorf, Kempenich, and Rübenach families.

Heidelberg Castle: Heidelberg Castle (German: *Heidelberger Schloss*) is unquestionably Germany's most famous castle ruin. The magnificent palace commands a commanding position on a hill overlooking historic Heidelberg. Schloss Heidelberg has inspired poets for centuries, so it's no surprise that it's a popular tourist destination and well-known worldwide.

Schwerin Castle: Schwerin Castle is located in the city of Schwerin, Germany. Schwerin Castle is now the seat of the local government and an art museum displaying works from antiquity to the twentieth century. The museum's seventeenth-century Dutch and Flemish paintings are among its most important exhibits.

1. _____ is now the seat of the local government and an art museum.
   a. Schwerin Castle
   b. Swaziland Castle

2. Hohenzollern Castle is situated on the _____ of Mount Hohenzollern.
   a. crest
   b. end

3. The architecture of German castles consists of a combination of towers and _____.
   a. beautiful curtains
   b. fortified walls

4. German castles evolved during the "_____ Ages".
   a. Century
   b. Medieval

5. This castle was built as a residence rather than a fortress.
   a. Eltz Castle
   b. Schwerin Castle

6. Castles are now iconic symbols of magnificence and _____ tales.
   a. real life
   b. mythical

7. _____has inspired poets for centuries.
   a. Schloss Heidelberg
   b. Steven Spielberg

8. _____Castle is located in the Bavarian Alps near the town of Füssen.
   a. Norwegian
   b. Neuschwanstein

Life Skills: Peer Pressure

First, read the entire passage. After that, go back and fill in the blanks. You can skip the blanks you're unsure about and finish them later.

impact	drink	trust	struggling	influence
positive	negative	classmates	avoid	victim

Almost all of us will come into contact with the apparent problem of peer pressure or the feeling that we have to do something because our friends or _____ think it is cool. Peer pressure can be a serious issue, whether we're talking about fourth-graders being pressured to play games, they don't want to play, or college students being pressured to smoke or _____ alcohol. As you get older, you'll realize you're responsible for the peer pressure you're subjected to and inadvertently exert on others. Though you can never completely eliminate peer pressure, you can mitigate some of its negative effects.

Peers have an _____ on your life, even if you are unaware of it, simply by spending time with you. You learn from them, and they do the same for you. It's only natural to listen to and learn from people your own age.

Peers can have a _____ impact on one another. Perhaps another student in your science class taught you an easy way to remember the planets in the solar system, or someone on your soccer team taught you a cool ball trick. You might look up to a friend who is always a good sport and try to emulate him or her. Perhaps you piqued the interest of others in your new favorite book, and now everyone is reading it. These are examples of how peers positively _____ one another daily.

Peers can have a _____ influence on one another. For example, a few kids at school may try to persuade you to skip class with them, a soccer friend may try to convince you to be mean to another player and never pass the ball to her, or a kid in the neighborhood may try to persuade you to shoplift with him.

It is common for kids to fall _____ to the pressure of their peers because they want to be liked, to fit in, or because they are afraid that other kids will make fun of them if they don't follow suit. Others join in because they want to try something new that others are doing. The notion that "everyone is doing it" can lead some children to disregard their better judgment or common sense.

You've probably heard your parents or teachers tell you to "pick your friends wisely." Peer pressure is a major reason for this. If you choose friends who don't do drugs, skip class, smoke cigarettes, or lie to their parents, you're less likely to do the same, even if other kids do. Try to assist a friend who is _____ to resist peer pressure. It can be powerful for one child to simply say, "I'm with you - let's go."

Even if you're alone and subjected to peer pressure, there are things you can do. You can _____ peers who put you under pressure to do things you know are wrong. You can say "no" and walk away. Even better, find other friends and classmates to hang out with.

If you continue to experience peer pressure and find it challenging to deal with, talk to someone you _____. If you've made a mistake or two, don't feel bad about it. Talking to a parent, teacher, or school counselor can make you feel much better and prepare you for peer pressure the next time you are subjected to it.

Science: The Seasons

First, read the entire passage. After that, go back and fill in the blanks. You can skip the blanks you're unsure about and finish them later.

planet	leaves	North	chicks	green
summer	shines	June	heats	frost

Our _____ has four seasons each year: autumn, winter, spring, and _____.

The Earth spins in a slightly tilted position as it orbits the sun (on an axis tilted 23.5 degrees from a straight-up, vertical position). Because different parts of the planet are angled towards or away from the sun's light throughout the year, this tilt causes our seasons. More or less sunlight and heat influence the length of each day, the average daily temperature, and the amount of rainfall in different seasons.

The tilt has two major effects: the sun's angle to the Earth and the length of the days. The Earth is tilted so that the _____ Pole is more pointed towards the sun for half of the year. The South Pole is pointing at the sun for the other half. When the North Pole is angled toward the sun, the days in the northern hemisphere (north of the equator) receive more sunlight, resulting in longer days and shorter nights. The northern hemisphere _____ up and experiences summer as the days lengthen. As the year progresses, the Earth's tilt shifts to the North Pole points away from the sun, resulting in winter.

As a result, seasons north of the equator are opposed to seasons south of the equator. When Europe and the United States are experiencing winter, Brazil and Australia will be experiencing summer.

We discussed how the length of the day changes, but the angle of the sun also changes. In the summer, the sun _____ more directly on the Earth, providing more energy to the surface and heating it. In the winter, sunlight strikes the Earth at an angle. This produces less energy and heats the Earthless.

The longest day in the Northern Hemisphere is _____ 21st, while the longest night is December 21st. The opposite is true in the Southern Hemisphere, where December 21st is the longest day, and June 21st is the longest night. There are only two days a year when the day and night are the same. These are September 22nd and March 21st.

The amount of time it is light for decreases in autumn, and the _____ begin to change color and fall off the trees. In the United States of America, autumn is referred to as Fall.

Winter brings colder weather, sometimes snow and _____, no leaves on the trees, and the amount of daylight during the day are at its shortest.

The weather usually warms up in the spring, trees begin to sprout leaves, plants begin to bloom, and young animals such as _____ and lambs are born.

The weather is usually warm in the summer, the trees have entire _____ leaves, and the amount of daylight during the day is extended.

Storytime Reading: The Wolf & 7 Kids

Hello Friend! You're going to read a story that's **not** real; it is fiction. Fiction is any story made up by an author. It is a creation of the author's imagination.

First, read the entire passage. After that, go back and fill in the blanks. You can skip the blanks you're unsure about and finish them last.

poor	terrified	table	good	snoring
rose	scissors	swallowed	dashed	returned
hunger	knocked	inserted	rattled	paws
forest	wide	mother	stomach	water

The story goes that once upon a time, an old Goat had seven little Kids and adored them with all the affection a _____ would have for her children.

She wanted to go into the _____ and get some food one day. So she called up all seven children to her and said, "Dear Children, I must go into the forest." Keep an eye out for the Wolf. If he gets in, he'll eat your whole skin, hair, and all. The wretch frequently disguises himself, but you'll recognize him right away by his rough voice and black feet."

"Dear Mother, we will take _____ care of ourselves," the children said. You may leave without wariness."

The old one bleated and went on her way, her mind at ease.

It wasn't long before someone _____ on the door and yelled, "Open the door, dear Children! Your mother has arrived, and she has brought something for each of you."

The little Kids, however, recognized the Wolf by his rough voice. "We will not open the door," they cried, "because you are not our mother." Your voice is rough, whereas hers is soft and pleasant. "You are Wolf!"

The Wolf then went to a shopkeeper and bought a large lump of chalk, which he ate and used to soften his voice. Then he returned, knocked on the door, and cried, "Open the door, dear Children! Your mother has arrived and has brought something for each of you."

However, the Wolf had placed his black _____ against the window, and when the children saw them, they cried out, "We will not open the door; our mother does not have black feet like you." "You are Wolf!"

The Wolf then _____ over to a baker and said, "I've hurt my feet; rub some dough over them for me."

After rubbing his feet, the baker ran to the miller and said, "Strew some white meal over my feet for me." "The Wolf wants to deceive someone," the miller reasoned, and he refused. "If you don't do it," the Wolf said, "I will devour you." The miller became _____ and whitened his paws for him. Yes, and so are men!

Now, for the third time, the wretch went to the house-door, knocked, and said, "Open the door for me, Children!" Your dear little mother has _____ home, and she has brought something from the forest for each of you."

"First show us your paws so we can tell if you are our dear little mother," the children cried.

Then he _____ his paws through the window. When the kids saw they were white, they believed everything he said and opened the door. But who else but the Wolf should enter?

They were terrified and wished to remain hidden. One jumped under the _____, another into the bed, a third into the stove, a fourth into the kitchen, a fifth into the cupboard, a sixth into the washing bowl, and a seventh into the clock case. But the Wolf found them all and _____ them down his throat one after the other. The only one he didn't find was the youngest in the clock case.

When the Wolf had satisfied his _____, he exited the building, sat down under a tree in the green meadow outside, and fell asleep.

Soon after, the old Goat returned from the forest. What a sight she saw over there! The front door was _____ open. The table, chairs, and benches were thrown to the ground, the washing bowl was shattered, and the quilts and pillows were yanked from the bed.

She went looking for her children, but they were nowhere to be found. She called out their names one by one, but no one answered. When she finally summoned the youngest, a soft voice cried out, "Dear Mother, I am in the clock-case."

She took the Kid out, and it informed her that the Wolf had arrived and devoured all the others. You can only imagine how she cried over her _____ children!

In her grief, she eventually went out, and the youngest Kid followed her. When they arrived at the meadow, the Wolf by the tree was _____ so loudly that the branches shook. She examined him from every angle and noticed that something was moving and struggling in his stomach. "Ah!" she exclaimed, "is it possible that my poor children, whom he has devoured for his supper, are still alive?"

The Kid then had to dash home to get _____, a needle and thread, and the Goat to cut open the monster's stomach. She had barely made one cut when a little Kid thrust its head out, and when she had cut further, all six sprang out one after the other, all still alive and unharmed, because the monster had swallowed them whole in his greed.

There was a lot of joy! They ran up to their mother and jumped like a tailor at his wedding. "Now go and look for some big stones," the mother said. We'll stuff them into the wicked beast's _____ while he's sleeping."

The seven Kids then dragged the stones with all haste, stuffing as many as they could into his stomach. And the mother sewed him up again in haste so that he was unaware of anything and never moved.

When the Wolf awoke from his slumber, he _____ to his feet, and because the stones in his stomach were making him thirsty, he desired to go to a well to drink. When he started walking and moving around, the stones in his stomach knocked against each other and _____. Then he cried out:

"What is it that rumbles and tumbles Against my poor bones?"
I thought it was six children, but it's just big stones!"

And as he approached the well, stooped over the _____, and was about to drink, the heavy stones caused him to fall in. There was no way to save him, so he had to drown!

When the seven Kids saw this, they dashed to the spot and exclaimed, "The Wolf is dead! "The Wolf has died!" and joyfully danced around the well with their mother.

Art: Abstract Art

In the United States, there was an Abstract Art movement. Abstract art has no subject in its purest form. It consists solely of lines, shapes, and colors. Abstract Expressionism is the name given to the Abstract Art movement because, despite the lack of a subject, the art attempts to convey some emotion.

Following World War II, the Abstract Expressionism movement began in the 1940s in New York City. However, some Expressionists, particularly Wassily Kandinsky, painted the first true Abstract Art in the early 1900s.

The main feature of abstract art is that it lacks a recognizable subject. Some Abstract Artists had theories about the emotions elicited by different colors and shapes. They meticulously planned their seemingly random paintings. Other Abstract Artists painted with emotion and randomness in the hope of capturing their feelings and subconscious thoughts on canvas.

Mondrian's paintings are filled with precision and geometric shapes. In this painting, he uses straight black lines, white spaces, and primary colors to create a sense of balance. He painted several other pictures in the same style.

Mark Rothko created many large color blocks in his paintings. There was usually a border, and the edges of the blocks were blurred together, as in this painting. Rothko never explained what the painting was supposed to mean. He left it up to the viewer to make their interpretations. As simple as it appears here, this painting sold for more than $72 million in 2007.

Jackson Pollock developed his distinct painting style. He would splatter and dribble paint directly from the can onto the canvas. This art form was later dubbed "Action Painting." Yellow and brown paint is drizzled in this painting to create an exciting nest of colors and textures. The painting was sold for a whopping $140 million in 2006.

1. Who splatters and dribbles paint directly from the can onto the canvas?
   a. Mark Rothko
   b. Jackson Pollock

2. Abstract Art consists solely of lines, ___, and colors.
   a. pictures
   b. shapes

3. Abstract Expressionism movement began in the 1940s in _____.
   a. Washington
   b. New York City

4. _____ created many large color blocks in his paintings.
   a. Mark Rothko
   b. John Mondrian

5. The main feature of abstract art is that it lacks a _____ subject.
   a. recognizable
   b. colorful

6. _____ paintings are filled with precision and geometric shapes.
   a. Mondrian's
   b. Rothko

7. The Abstract Expressionism movement began in the ____.
   a. The 1940s
   b. The 1840s

8. Based on what you read, what do you think is the main idea of abstract art?
   a. Not to tell a story, but to encourage involvement and imagination.
   b. Tell a true story and show emotions.

9. Who painted the first true Abstract Art in the early 1900s?
   a. Walter Kondiskny
   b. Wassily Kandinsky

10. Some abstract artists painted with emotion and ____.
    a. randomness
    b. black lines and dots

Science: Food Chain and Food Web

In the wild, the food chain describes who eats whom. Every living thing, from single-celled algae to massive blue whales, requires food to survive. Each food chain represents a potential path for energy and nutrients to travel through the ecosystem.

Grass, for example, generates its food from sunlight. A rabbit is eating the grass. A fox devours the rabbit. When a fox dies, bacteria decompose its body and return it to the soil, providing nutrients to plants such as grass. To survive, every living plant and animal requires energy. Plants get their energy from the soil, water, and the sun. Plants and other animals provide energy to animals.

Plants and animals in an ecosystem rely on one another to survive. Scientists may use a food chain or a food web to describe this dependence.

Of course, many different animals consume grass, and rabbits can consume plants other than grass. Foxes, in turn, can consume a wide range of animals and plants. Each of these living things has the potential to be a part of multiple food chains. A food web is made up of all of the interconnected and overlapping food chains in an ecosystem.

Each link in the food chain has a name to help describe it. The names are determined mainly by what the organism eats and how it contributes to its energy.

Producers - Plants are creators. This is because they generate energy for the ecosystem. They do this because photosynthesis absorbs energy from the sun. They require water and nutrients from the soil as well, but plants are the only source of new energy.

Consumers - Consumers include animals. This is since they do not generate energy; instead, they consume it. Primary consumers, also known as herbivores, are animals that eat plants. Secondary consumers or carnivores are animals that eat other animals. A carnivore is referred to as a tertiary consumer when it consumes another carnivore. Some animals perform both functions, eating both plants and animals. They are known as omnivores.

All of the energy produced in the food chain is produced by producers or plants, who convert sunlight into energy through photosynthesis. The rest of the food chain merely consumes energy. As a result, as you move up the food chain, less and less energy is available. As a result, as you move up the food chain, there are fewer and fewer organisms.

Many different food chains that make up a food web can be found in various habitats and ecosystems.

Single-celled organisms known as phytoplankton provide food for tiny shrimp known as krill in one marine food chain. Krill are the primary food source for blue whales, which are classified as being on the third trophic level.

A grasshopper may consume grass, a producer, in a grassland ecosystem. The grasshopper may be eaten by a rat, which a snake then eats. Finally, an apex predator, a hawk, swoops down and snatches up the snake.

The autotroph in a pond could be algae. A mosquito larva consumes the algae, and then a dragonfly larva consumes the young mosquito. The dragonfly larva is eaten by a fish, which then becomes a tasty meal for a raccoon.

Remember that there may be some question-answer relationship (QAR) questions, so please keep that in mind when answering the questions below.

1. **In ecology, it is the sequence of transfers of matter and energy in the form of food from organism to organism.**
   a. Food Sequencing
   b. Food Transport
   c. Food Chain

2. **_____ can increase the total food supply by cutting out one step in the food chain.**
   a. Birds
   b. Animals
   c. People

3. **Plants, which convert solar energy to food by photosynthesis, are the _____.**
   a. secondary food source
   b. tertiary food source
   c. primary food source

4. **_____ help us understand how changes to ecosystems affect many different species, both directly and indirectly.**
   a. Food Transport
   b. Food Chain
   c. Food Web

5. _____ eat decaying matter and are the ones who help put nutrients back into the soil for plants to eat.
   a. Decomposers
   b. Consumers
   c. Producers

6. _____ are producers because they produce energy for the ecosystem.
   a. Animals
   b. Decomposers
   c. Plants

7. Each organism in an ecosystem occupies a specific _____ in the food chain or web.
   a. trophic level
   b. space
   c. place

8. What do you call an organism that eats both plants and animals?
   a. Omnivores
   b. Herbivores
   c. Carnivores

9. Carnivore is from the Latin word that means _____.
   a. "flesh devourers"
   b. "eats both plants and animals"
   c. "plant eaters"

10. A food web is all of the interactions between the species within a community that involve the transfer of energy through _____.
    a. consumption
    b. reservation
    c. adaptation

11. Why are animals considered consumers?
    a. because they produce energy for the ecosystem
    b. because they don't produce energy, they just use it up
    c. because they only produce energy for themselves

12. How do plants turn sunlight energy into chemical energy?
    a. through the process of photosynthesis
    b. through the process of adaptation
    c. through the process of cancelation

13. Grass produces its own food from_____,
    a. animals
    b. sunlight
    c. soil

14. Each of these living things can be a part of _____ food chains.
    a. zero
    b. multiple
    c. only one

15. When an animal dies, _____ breaks down its body.
    a. bacteria
    b. grass
    c. sunlight

Geography: The North Pole

First, read the entire passage. After that, go back and fill in the blanks. You can skip the blanks you're unsure about and finish them later.

historians	cold	frozen	solar	survive
Frederick	Arctic	bears	axis	fish

What is the world's most northern location? You may be familiar with it as the location of Santa's workshop, but let's take a look at the North Pole's history, environment, and wildlife. It is situated in the middle of the _____ Ocean, which is almost entirely _____ all year. The only direction you could travel if you stood precisely on the North Pole is south!

For hundreds of years, explorers have attempted to reach the North Pole. Many exploration trips ended in disaster or with the explorers turning around and returning home due to inclement weather. _____ Cook was an American explorer who claimed to have discovered the North Pole for the first time in 1908. A year later, another American explorer, Robert Peary, made the same claim. Scientists and _____ have not been able to back up these claims. There are currently numerous expeditions to the North Pole, many traveling by airplane, boat, or submarine.

We all know the North Pole is _____, but compared to the South Pole, the weather is like summer. That is if you consider average winter temperatures of -22 degrees Fahrenheit to be comparable to summer temperatures! Summer temperatures hover around 32 degrees Fahrenheit on average. Pack your shorts and flip-flops for a trip to the North Pole!

There aren't many animals that can _____ in this environment because it's so cold all year. Many people believe that polar _____ live in the North Pole, but they do not travel that far north. Several bird species, including the Arctic snow bunting and the Arctic tern, travel to the North Pole. Every year, the tern travels to and from the South and North Poles!

Sealife is also scarce. Scientists discovered shrimp and _____, including Arctic cod, in the Arctic Ocean near the North Pole. Many sea animals, however, do not travel far enough north to reach the North Pole.

At the North Pole, day and night are very different. Because the Earth's _____ is tilted and the North Pole is at the top of the world, there is only one sunrise and one sunset each year. In the winter, there is constant darkness, whereas, in the summer, there is daylight all day and night!

An aurora is a unique event that occurs in polar areas, both north and south. These are brilliant colorful flashes of light in the night sky that are commonly referred to as polar lights. Auroras are caused by _____ winds and electromagnetic activity in the atmosphere.

Multiple Choice Quiz: Fiji

Score: _____

Date:_____

Select the best answer for each question.

1. Fiji, officially the Republic of Fiji, is an island country in the _____.
   a. Arctic Ocean
   b. North Pacific Ocean
   c. South Pacific Ocean

2. Bula, which means _____ in Fijian, is the first word you'll need to learn because you'll hear it everywhere.
   a. Hello
   b. Welcome
   c. Good day

3. What is the capital and largest city of Fiji?
   a. Suva
   b. Lautoka
   c. Nadi

4. What is the climate in Fiji?
   a. Dry
   b. Temperate continental
   c. Tropical marine

5. ____, ____, and _____ are the official languages of Fiji.
   a. English, Fijian, and Samoan
   b. Fijian, Māori, and Rotuman
   c. English, Fijian, and Hindustan

6. The native Fijians are mostly _____ and the Indo-Fijians are mostly Hindu.
   a. Christians
   b. Buddhist
   c. Catholics

7. The traditional cooking method in Fiji is called _____.
   a. lovo
   b. ahima'a
   c. uma

8. After 96 years of British rule, Fiji became independent in _____ but remained part of the British Commonwealth.
   a. May 10, 1977
   b. October 10, 1970
   c. June 11, 1970

9. The original settlers of Fiji were _____ and _____ peoples who have lived on the islands for thousands of years.
   a. Austronesian, Micronesian
   b. Polynesian and Micronesian
   c. Polynesian, Melanesian

10. _____ is a Fijian military leader who led a 2006 coup that resulted in his becoming acting president (2006–07) and later acting prime minister (2007–14) of Fiji.
    a. Ratu Epeli Nailatikau
    b. Frank Bainimarama
    c. Laisenia Qarase

11. Fiji was ruled by one military coup after another until a democratic election was held in _____.
    a. November of 2014
    b. October of 2014
    c. September of 2014

12. What are Fiji's two largest islands?
    a. Viti Levu & Vanua Levu
    b. Kadavu & Mamanuca
    c. Rotuma & Lomaiviti

Reading Comprehension: Marco Polo

Marco Polo was a merchant and explorer who spent much of his life traveling throughout the Far East and China. For many years, his stories were the foundation of what much of Europe knew about Ancient China. He lived between 1254 and 1324.

Marco was born in 1254 in Venice, Italy. Marco's father was a merchant in Venice, a prosperous trading city.

The Silk Road was a network of trade routes that connected major cities and trading posts from Eastern Europe to Northern China. The Silk Road was named because silk cloth was China's main export. Few people completed the entire route. Trading was mostly done between cities or small sections of the route, and goods would slowly make their way from one end to the other, changing hands several times along the way. Marco Polo's father and uncle desired to try something new. They intended to travel all the way to China and return the goods to Venice. They believed that by doing so, they would be able to make a fortune. It took them nine years, but they eventually returned home.

Marco left for China for the first time when he was 17 years old. He accompanied his father and uncle on the trip. During their first trip to China, his father and uncle met the Mongol Emperor Kublai Khan and promised him they would return. At the time, Kublai was the ruler of all of China.

Marco Polo traveled to China for three years. Along the way, he visited many great cities and sites, including the holy city of Jerusalem, the Hindu Kush mountains, Persia, and the Gobi Desert. He met a wide range of people and had numerous adventures.

Marco spent many years in China, where he learned the language. As a messenger and spy for Kublai Khan, he traveled throughout China. He even went as far south as Myanmar and Vietnam are today. He learned about different cultures, foods, cities, and people during these visits. He saw places and things that no European had ever seen before.

Marco was captivated by the wealth and luxury of Chinese cities and the court of Kublai Khan. It was nothing like what he had seen in Europe. Kinsay's capital city was large but well-organized and clean. Wide roads and massive civil engineering projects like the Grand Canal were far beyond what he had seen back home. Everything was new and exciting, from the food to the people to the animals, such as orangutans and rhinos.

1. The _____ Road was a network of trade routes that connected major cities and trading posts.
   a. Reddit
   b. Silk
   c. Forest

2. Who intended to travel all the way to China and return the goods to Venice?
   a. Marco Polo's father and uncle
   b. Marco Polo
   c. Marco Polo mother and aunt

3. Marco Polo was a merchant and _____.
   a. artist
   b. explorer
   c. painter

4. Marco was born in 1254 in _____, Italy
   a. Vincent
   b. Vance
   c. Venice

5. Marco left for China for the first time when he was _____.
   a. seventeen years old
   b. eighteen years old.
   c. 21 years old

6. The Silk Road was named because silk _____ was China's main export.
   a. cloth
   b. curtains
   c. shoes

7. _____ was the ruler of all of China.
   a. Kubilla
   b. Kublai
   c. Kyle

8. How many year Marco Polo traveled to China?
   a. for four years.
   b. for 3 years.
   c. for 5 years.

Science Multiple Choice Quiz: Coral Reef Biome

Select the best answer for each question.

1. _____ is a ring of land surrounding a pool of water called a lagoon.
   a. A Fringe reef
   b. An Atoll
   c. A Coral reef

2. Most of the reef of an atoll is _____.
   a. on the shore
   b. underwater
   c. above the water

3. The _____ in the Indian Ocean and the _____ in the Pacific are countries made up of atolls and other islands.
   a. Maldives, Marshall Islands
   b. Marshall Islands, Boracay
   c. Valley Indonesia, Maldives

4. How many percent of the known marine species live in coral reefs?
   a. Greater than 50%
   b. Around 25 %
   c. Less than 10%

5. How many different types of coral reefs are there?
   a. 3
   b. 7
   c. 4

6. _____ are the primary makers of reefs and come in a variety of shapes and sizes.
   a. Seaweeds
   b. Coral polyps
   c. Sea grass

7. The majority of the plants living on the coral reef are various species of _____, _____, and _____.
   a. seaweeds, crabs, fishes
   b. crabs, shrimps, sea horse
   c. sea grass, seaweed, algae

8. Large reefs grow at a rate of _____ per year.
   a. 5 to 6 cm
   b. 1 to 2 cm
   c. 3 to 4 cm

9. It is a ridge or hummock formed in shallow ocean areas by algae and the calcareous skeletons of certain coelenterates.
   a. Shore
   b. River
   c. Coral reef

10. The coral reef can be divided by?
    a. Barriers
    b. Water
    c. Zones

11. Coral reefs have been called _____.
    a. "the rain forests of the seas"
    b. "the underwater garden of the seas"
    c. "the Amazon rainforest of the seas"

12. Corals live with algae in a type of relationship called _____.
    a. apodosis
    b. symbiosis
    c. amaurosis

Science: Tyrannosaurus

First, read the entire passage. After that, go back and fill in the blanks. You can skip the blanks you're unsure about and finish them later.

fossils	Mexico	teeth	walk	Jurassic
meat	skull	largest	scientists	museums

Tyrannosaurus Rex, one of the most famous and notable dinosaurs, is a theropod dinosaur. Many Tyrannosaurus _____ have been discovered, allowing scientists to learn more about how big it was, how it hunted, and how it lived.

Tyrannosaurus rex was a land predator dinosaur that was one of the _____. The T-rex could grow to be 43 feet long and weigh up to 7.5 tons. Because of its size and overall fearsome image, the dinosaur is frequently used in movies and films such as _____ Park.

Tyrannosaurus rex was a two-legged dinosaur. This means it could _____ and run on two legs. These two legs were large and strong enough to support the dinosaur's massive weight. The T-arms, rex's on the other hand, were relatively small. However, it is believed that the small arms were powerful to hold onto prey.

The Tyrannosaurus' massive _____ and large _____ are among its most terrifying features. T-rex skulls as long as 5 feet have been discovered! Other evidence suggests that the Tyrannosaurus had a powerful bite that allowed it to crush other dinosaurs' bones easily when combined with sharp teeth.

The Tyrannosaurus Rex ate _____ from other animals and dinosaurs. Still, it is unclear whether it was a predator (hunted and killed its own food) or a scavenger (meaning it stole food from other predators). Many _____ believe the dinosaur did both. Much is dependent on how fast the dinosaur was. Some claim that the T-Rex was fast and capable of catching its own prey. Others argue that the dinosaur was slow and used its fearsome jaws to frighten off other predators and steal their prey.

There are numerous significant Tyrannosaurus specimens in _____ around the world. "Sue" at the Field Museum of Natural History in Chicago is one of the largest and most comprehensive. "Stan," another significant T-Rex specimen, can be found at the Black Hills Museum of Natural History Exhibit in Hill City, South Dakota. Also on display at the American Museum of Natural History in New York, paleontologist Barnum Brown's largest Tyrannosaurus find (he discovered five in total).

The only known Tyrannosaurus Rex track can be found at Philmont Scout Ranch in New _____.

Spelling: Unscramble

Unscramble the spelling words below.

Tip: Unscramble the words you are sure about first.

sailor	misunderstand	heroes	decision	remarkable	ambulance
intermission	sentence	shampoo	creative	discussion	forgiveness
roam	recently	performance	remind	minus	comfortable

1. ytcleenr   r _ c _ _ _ _ _

2. psomhao   _ h _ _ _ _ o

3. eiacrvte   _ r _ a _ _ _ _

4. nriuadmsetsnd   _ _ _ _ n _ e _ _ t _ _ _

5. deinmr   _ _ m _ _ d

6. aomr   _ _ _ m

7. nceulbama   a _ _ _ l _ _ _ _

8. rmbaeekral   r e _ _ r _ _ _ _ _

9. vegofsnries   _ _ r _ i _ _ _ _ s _

10. boreoftcmla   _ _ m _ _ _ t a _ _ _

11. lsioar   s _ _ _ _ r

12. misnu   _ i _ _ _

13. enetcsen   s _ _ _ e _ _ _

14. incsoied   _ _ _ i _ _ o _

15. sdoicisuns   _ i _ c _ _ _ i _ _

16. esoerh   h _ _ _ e _

17. ferpenmroac   _ _ _ _ o _ _ a _ _ e

18. tireiinosmsn   _ n _ _ _ m _ _ _ i _ _

Sentence Vocabulary

Score: _____

Date: _____

Fill in the blanks with the correct spelling word.

colorful	massive	likable	reasonable	cheerful
thoughtful	wonderful	around	memorable	predictable
careless	creative	impressive	breakable	breathless
honorable	destroy	remarkable	adaptable	hopeless
thousands	spotless	peaceful		

1. Amy painted a _____ picture of a rainbow.

2. We have a _____ amount of time to study for our test.

3. Doesn't the night sky look _____ with all the stars shining so brightly?

4. The dishes that Mrs. Price bought were not _____ .

5. Our bus driver is one of the most _____ people I know.

6. The situation isn't _____ ; we can find a solution.

7. Cynthia enjoys writing _____ stories and reading them to her family.

8. Wow! Every room in your house looks _____ !

9. The young figure skater performed an _____ routine at her first state competition.

10. Krishna ran _____ the backyard with his dog.

11. One _____ camper could be responsible for an enormous forest fire.

12. The school bus comes to Lizzie's house at a _____ time each morning.

13. Rhett did an _____ thing by turning in the wallet he found to his teacher.

14. This is the most _____ cake I've ever tasted!

15. Steven wrote _____ thank-you notes to everyone who came to his birthday party.

16. There were _____ of people at the art festival last weekend.

17. Jamie's family moves around a lot, so she has learned to become _____ .

18. Running outside in the freezing temperature made Nora feel _____ .

19. Tia's most _____ holiday was the year her baby sister was born on Christmas Day.

20. Have you ever seen a cat _____ a roll of toilet paper?

21. A _____ boulder fell from the side of the mountain and blocked the hiking trail.

22. Mrs. Dobmire, the lunch lady, is one of the most _____ people you'll ever meet.

23. The fact that the local newspaper is one of the oldest in the country is _____

AREA 51 WORDSEARCH

Score: _____

Date: _____

Area 51, a classified United States Air Force military installation near Groom Lake in southern Nevada. Edwards Air Force Base in southern California is in charge of it. The facility has been the subject of numerous conspiracies involving **extraterrestrial life**, despite the fact that its only confirmed use is as a flight testing facility.

```
B  Q  V  X  N  Y  X  W  M  L  P  R  G  L  Y  O  E  P  I  N
U  Y  J  D  M  Y  C  G  K  Q  D  I  P  I  M  M  N  T  R  I
J  R  E  K  E  P  K  R  S  O  Z  D  H  I  J  N  N  G  E  L
X  J  E  T  Z  N  A  D  D  L  U  S  Q  S  A  H  O  H  T  B
V  G  O  T  W  M  N  E  J  U  K  H  X  B  E  U  X  M  S  O
N  Y  Q  K  E  M  I  I  F  D  S  H  S  Z  Y  C  H  T  N  G
K  K  Q  I  J  F  I  J  K  I  K  R  G  K  U  H  A  B  O  E
U  N  P  H  N  G  B  L  N  S  X  D  P  U  A  U  G  P  M  L
T  Q  H  R  D  M  U  E  G  S  Y  S  L  F  U  M  J  A  S  L
J  T  S  P  A  D  E  S  H  A  P  E  D  H  E  A  D  Y  D  I
W  J  O  L  T  R  N  E  M  N  E  E  R  G  D  N  G  I  O  V
S  D  P  I  G  A  O  Z  X  B  Y  M  S  G  R  O  M  Y  O  S
S  D  V  M  Z  V  I  D  X  L  T  R  S  E  L  I  F  X  W  N
P  S  H  W  A  G  T  J  W  E  A  H  U  X  N  D  Z  J  T  I
X  J  R  U  O  L  C  C  S  E  Y  E  E  U  L  B  T  O  A  K
H  F  B  O  W  D  U  R  O  Q  E  Z  T  W  J  J  J  C  L  P
X  K  V  V  X  F  D  N  Q  Q  E  I  J  M  U  S  F  C  F  O
V  O  P  O  J  L  B  Q  O  B  V  C  M  L  F  K  U  E  S  H
B  Z  Q  X  X  F  A  J  D  E  E  H  K  C  O  L  I  J  W  K
N  J  T  P  P  S  F  G  W  Q  W  K  Y  C  S  A  U  D  K  B
```

Humanoid	Spade Shaped Head	Flatwoods Monster	No Ears	Grey Skinned
Xfiles	Ufos	Greenish	Hopkinsville Goblin	Green Men
Spaceship	Diminutive	Abduction	Blue Eyes	Lockheed

Fictional vs. Fictitious vs. Fictive

Fictional is invented as part of a work of fiction

SYNONYMS:
Fabricated
Imaginary

Fictitious is created, taken, or assumed for the sake of concealment; not genuine; false

SYNONYMS:
Bogus
Counterfeit

Fictive - fictitious; imaginary. pertaining to the creation of fiction
- is capable of imaginative creation.

SYNONYMS:

Make-believe
Fabricated

1. He dismissed recent rumors about his private life as _____.
   a. fictitious
   b. fictional
   c. fictive

2. I have the impression that this _____ marriage of ours is like a ghost in a play.
   a. fictional
   b. fictitious
   c. fictive

3. The setting is a _____ island in the Chesapeake River.
   a. fictitious
   b. fictional
   c. fictive

4. The writer has _____ talent.
   a. fictitious
   b. fictional
   c. fictive

5. Almost all _____ detectives are unreal.
   a. fictitious
   b. fictional
   c. fictive

6. The names of the shops are entirely _____.
   a. fictive
   b. fictional
   c. fictitious

How It's Made: Money

It's not very often that people think about how the money in their wallets was made or who made it. The federal agency in charge of money creation in the United States is the Department of Treasury. It looks after two branches that make money. The United States Mint produces coins, whereas the United States Bureau of Engraving and Printing produces dollar notes. Let's look at the entire money-making process, from conception to distribution.

Paper money and coin designs are sketched and modeled by designers employed by the United States Department of Treasury. The Secretary of the Treasury selects one of the designs submitted by the designers for production into currency, albeit the final design may be subject to further revisions at this point.

However, why are fresh designs necessary? Technology has made it easier for anyone to create their own counterfeit money. Counterfeiting, the act of creating phony money, is a crime. The government has redesigned our currency to reduce counterfeiting.

Dollar bills and computer paper don't have the same weight and feel. Since paper money is created from a particular cotton and linen blend, it is more difficult to forge. The Bureau of Engraving and Printing also manufactures the ink. Some recent bills (in values of $10 and higher) contain metallic or color-shifting ink to help prevent counterfeiting, which is used on all paper money.

Coins in the United States are created from a combination of metals and alloys. In addition to reducing coin counterfeiting, this usage of bi-metallic elements significantly lowers the cost of minting coins. Coins that are made of pure metal can be worth more than their face value. As a result, instead of utilizing the coins as money, others may opt to melt them and sell the metals they contain.

The Bureau of Engraving and Printing engraves the design onto a plate once it has been created for paper money. The same plate is then replicated numerous times onto a much larger plate that can print multiple bills simultaneously on numerous printers. Ink is applied to the plate, which is then pushed onto the paper. Each side of a sheet of banknotes must dry for 72 hours.

Following the design of the coins, the designs are replicated on stamps that press the design onto the bi-metallic substance. Coins are made from enormous metal sheets, but that's just the beginning. The metal sheets are fed into a machine that punches out coins. Before being stamped with the design, the blank coins are heated and cleaned.

The bills are examined once they've been printed and dried. They remove and discard any bills that have errors. Money that fits the criteria is cut and packaged for distribution. Additionally, the coins are examined, and any that are found to be flawed are disposed of. However, a few of these coins manage to slip through the cracks. When that occurs, the value of these extremely rare coins might skyrocket!

Following an inspection, banks are given the money they require, if needed. After that, the funds are dispersed among the banks' clients. The currency is now in circulation!

Remember, the federal agency in charge of money creation in the United States is the Department of Treasury. The Bureau of Engraving and Printing produces paper currency, whereas the United States Mint produces coins. Numerous safeguards are used during the design, material selection, and production of money to avoid counterfeiting or the production of counterfeit money.

MONEY

1. The _____ agency is in charge of money creation.
   a. federal
   b. government

2. The United States Mint produces coins and dollar bills.
   a. True - coins and dollar bills
   b. False - only coins

3. Each side of a sheet of banknotes must dry for ___ hours.
   a. 72
   b. 24

4. Dollar bills and computer paper don't have the same _____ and feel.
   a. design
   b. weight

5. The metal sheets are fed into a machine that punches out _____.
   a. coins
   b. silver dollars

6. United States Bureau of _____ produces dollar notes.
   a. Engraving and Printing
   b. Engravers and Commission

7. The Secretary of the _____ selects one of the designs submitted by the designers for production.
   a. Treasury
   b. Bank

8. Coins in the United States are created from a combination of _____.
   a. metals and alloys
   b. silver and nickels

9. Before being stamped with the design, the blank coins are _____.
   a. heated and cleaned
   b. shined and reserved

10. Paper money is created from a particular _____ blend, it is more difficult to forge.
   a. parcel and green dye
   b. cotton and linen

Introvert vs. Extrovert

Introvert is a person who prefers calm environments, limits social engagement, or embraces a greater than average preference for solitude.

SYNONYMS:
brooder
loner
solitary

Extrovert is an outgoing, gregarious person who thrives in dynamic environments and seeks to maximize social engagement.

SYNONYMS:
character
exhibitionist
show-off
showboat

Fill in the blank with the correct word. [introvert, introverts, extrovert, extroverts]

1. Sue is the _____ in the family; opinionated, talkative and passionate about politics.

2. He was described as an _____, a reserved man who spoke little.

3. _____ are often described as the life of the party.

4. An _____ is often thought of as a quiet, reserved, and thoughtful individual.

5. _____ enjoy being around other people and tend to focus on the outside world.

6. Typically _____ tend to enjoy more time to themselves.

7. Jane is an _____ whose only hobby is reading.

8. I am still not as "outgoing" as an _____ is.

9. I had been a very _____ person, living life to the full.

10. I am an _____, I am a loner.

11. Because Pat is an _____ who enjoys chatting with others, she is the ideal talk show host.

12. She is basically an _____, uncomfortable with loud women and confrontations.

Quiz: Famous Entrepreneurs

Match the well-known entrepreneurs below to the correct company or industry.

Need help? Try Google.

1. Arianna Huffington
   a. CNN reporter
   b. Huffington Post

2. Sergey Brin and Larry Page
   a. Yahoo
   b. Google

3. Elon Musk
   a. Mercedes
   b. Tesla

4. Mark Zuckerberg
   a. Facebook
   b. Twitter

5. Estee Lauder
   a. cosmetics
   b. fashion

6. Richard Branson
   a. media, aviation, banking
   b.

7. Weili Dai
   a. Walmart Chief Executive
   b. Marvell Technologies (semi-conductors)

8. Coco Chanel
   a. fashion
   b. chocolate

9. Steve Jobs
   a. Samsung
   b. Apple Inc.

10. Bill Gates
   a. Microsoft
   b. Snap Chat

11. Kiran Mazumdar-Shaw
   a. Biocon (biotech)
   b. Instagram

12. JK Rowling
   a. Hello Kitty empire
   b. Harry Potter empire

13. Jack Ma Yun
   a. eBay
   b. Alibaba

14. Jeff Bezos
   a. Amazon
   b. Esty

15. Ken Kutaragi
   a. Xbox
   b. PlayStation

16. Vivian Horner
   a. Nickelodeon
   b. Disney

Dealing With Acne

Acne is a skin disorder that results in bumps. Whiteheads, blackheads, pimples, and pus-filled bumps are all sorts of blemishes. What's the source of these annoying bumps? Pores and hair follicles make up most of your skin's top layer. Sebum (pronounced "see-bum"), the natural oil that moisturizes hair and skin, is produced in the pores by oil glands.

Generally, the glands produce adequate sebum, and the pores are good. However, oil, dead skin cells, and bacteria can block a pore if they accumulate in it to an unhealthy level. Acne may result as a result of this.

Puberty-induced hormonal changes are to blame for acne in children. If your parent suffered from acne as a teen, you will likely as well because your pores may produce more sebum when under stress; stress may worsen acne. Acne is usually gone by the time a person reaches their twenties.

Here are a few tips for preventing breakouts if you suffer from acne:

- It would help if you washed your face with warm water and a light soap or cleanser in the morning before school and before bed.
- Avoid scrubbing your face. Acne can be exacerbated by irritating the skin, so scrubbing is not recommended.
- Makeup should be washed off at the end of the day if you wear it.
- Ensure to wash your face after a workout if you've been sweating heavily.
- Acne-fighting lotions and creams are readily available over-the-counter. Talk to your parents or doctor about the options available to you.

Make sure you follow the guidelines on any acne medication you use. If you're unsure whether you're allergic to the cream or lotion, use a small amount at first. If you don't notice results the next day, don't give up. Acne medication can take weeks or months to take effect. If you use more than recommended, your skin may become extremely dry and red.

Acne-suffering children can seek treatment from their doctor. Doctors can prescribe stronger medications than what you can get over the counter.

The following are some other factors to consider:

- Avoid touching your face if you can.
- Pimples should not be picked, squeezed, or popped.
- Long hair should be kept away from the face, and it should be washed regularly to reduce oil production.

It is possible to get pimples on the hairline by wearing headgear like baseball caps. Stay away from them if you suspect they're contributing to your acne problems.

Despite their best efforts, many children will get acne at some point in their lives. The situation isn't out of the ordinary.

If you suffer from acne, you now have several options for treating it. Remind yourself of this: You are not alone. Take a look around at your buddies and you'll notice that the majority of children and adolescents are dealing with acne, too!

1. Puberty _____ changes are to blame for acne in children.
- a. harmonic
- b. hormonal

2. Pores and hair _____ make up most of your skin's top layer.
- a. follicles
- b. folate

3. Avoid _____ your face.
- a. using cleanser
- b. scrubbing

4. _____ is the oil that moisturizes hair and skin, is produced in the pores by oil glands.
- a. Acne
- b. Sebum

Smart Ways to Deal With a Bully

First, read over the entire passage(s). Then go back and fill in the blanks. You can skip the blanks you're unsure about and come back to them later.

control	popular	confident	ground	society
threats	negative	skip	Fighting	mocking

One of the most serious issues in our _____ today is bullying. It's not uncommon for young people to experience a range of _____ emotions due to this. Bullies may use physical force (such as punches, kicks, or shoves) or verbal abuse (such as calling someone a name, making fun of them, or scaring them) to harm others.

Some examples of bullying include calling someone names, stealing from them and _____ them, or ostracizing them from a group.

Some bullies want to be the center of attention. As a strategy to be _____ or get what they want, they may believe bullying is acceptable. Bullies are usually motivated by a desire to elevate their own status. As a result of picking on someone else, they can feel more power and authority.

Bullies frequently target someone they believe they can _____. Kids who are easily agitated or have difficulty standing up for themselves are likely targets. Getting a strong reaction from someone can give bullies the illusion that they have the power they desire. There are times when bullies pick on someone who is more intelligent than them or who looks different from them somehow.

Preventing a Bully's Attack
Do not give in to the bully. Avoid the bully as much as possible. Of course, you aren't allowed to disappear or _____ class. However, if you can escape the bully by taking a different path, do so.

Bravely stand your _____. Scared people aren't usually the most courageous people. Bullies can be stopped by just showing courage in the face of them. Just how do you present yourself as a fearless person? To send a message that says, "Don't mess with me," stand tall. It is much easier to be brave when you are confident in yourself.

Don't Pay Attention to What the Bully Says or Does. If you can, do your best not to listen to the bully's _____. Act as though you aren't aware of their presence and immediately go away to a safe place. It's what bullies want: a big reaction to their teasing and being mean. If you don't respond to a bully's actions by pretending you don't notice or care, you may be able to stop them.

Defend your rights. Pretend you're _____ and brave. In a loud voice, tell the bully, "No! Stop it!" Then take a step back or even take off running if necessary. No matter what a bully says, say "no" and walk away if it doesn't feel right. If you do what a bully tells you to do, the bully is more likely to keep bullying you; kids who don't stand up for themselves are more likely to be targeted by bullies.

Don't retaliate by being a bully yourself. Don't fight back against someone who's bullying you or your pals by punching, kicking, or shoving them. _____ back only makes the bully happier, and it's also risky since someone can be injured. You're also going to be in a lot of trouble. It's essential to stick with your friends, keep safe, and seek adult assistance.

Inform a responsible adult of the situation. Telling an adult if you're being bullied is crucial. Find someone you can confide in and tell them what's going on with you. It is up to everyone in the school, from teachers to principals to parents to lunchroom assistants, to stop the bullies. As soon as a teacher discovers the bullying, the bully usually stops because they are worried that their parents will punish them for their behavior. Bullying is terrible, and everyone who is bullied or witnesses bullying should speak up.

The Human Bones

At birth, a baby's body has about 300 bones. These bones will one day grow together and become the 206 bones that adults have. Some of a baby's bones are made entirely of cartilage, a special material that helps them grow. Other bones in a baby are partially cartilage-covered. This cartilage is soft and easy to move. During childhood, the cartilage grows and is slowly replaced by bone, with the help of calcium, as you get bigger and stronger.

At about 25, this process will be done. Once this occurs, there is no more room for bone growth; the bones have reached their maximum size. There are a lot of bones that make up a skeleton that is both strong and light.

Spine: It's easy to look at your spine: When you touch your back, you'll feel bumps on it. The spine lets you twist and bend, and it also keeps your body in place. That's not all: It also helps protect the spinal cord, a long group of nerves that sends information from the brain to the rest of your body. You can't just have one or two bones in your spine. It's made of 33! Vertebrae are the bones that make up the spine, and each one is shaped like a ring.

Ribs: Heart, lung, and liver are all essential, and ribs will keep them safe. This makes your chest look like a cage of bones. A few inches below your heart, you can run your fingers along the sides and front of your body to get a sense of the bottom of this cage. It's easy to feel your ribs when you breathe deeply. Some very thin kids can even see some of their ribs through their skin.

Skull: The brain is the most important thing in your body, so your skull protects it the best. There are places where you can feel your skull when you push on your head, like in the back a few inches above your neck. Different bones make up the skull. They protect your brain, while other bones make up the shape of your face. If you touch below your eyes, you can feel the bone that makes the hole where your eye goes.

Arm: When an arm moves, it connects to a large triangular bone on the upper back corner of each side of the ribcage called a "shoulder blade." You have three bones in your arm: the humerus, which is above your elbow, the radius and ulna, which are below your elbow.

Pelvis: The pelvis, a ring of bones at the base of your spine, is where your legs attach. The pelvis, which is like a bowl, holds the spine in place. Large hip bones are in front of the sacrum and coccyx, which are behind. It is made up of the two large hip bones. The pelvis is a hard ring that protects parts of the digestive, urinary, and reproductive systems.

Joint: A joint is where two bones meet. This is how some joints work, and some don't: Fixed joints don't move at all. Young people have a lot of these joints in their skulls, called sutures. These joints close up the bones of the skull in their head. One of these joints is called the parieto-temporal suture, which is the one that runs along the side of the skull. It's called this because it connects the two sides of the skull together.

You need to keep your bones healthy. Drinking milk or eating oranges is good for you. They are calcium-rich. Calcium aids in the development of strong bones.

Have you ever suffered from bone fractures? Ouch! A doctor places the bone in its proper position. During the healing process, it is covered in a cast.

The bones of your body are located below the surface of your skin. They can only be seen with an X-ray machine. An X-ray is a type of picture. It allows medical professionals to see if a bone has been broken.

1. A baby's body has about _____ bones.
   a. 320
   b. 300

2. The _____, which is like a bowl, holds the spine in place.
   a. pelvis
   b. spinal cord

3. A _____ is where two bones meet.
   a. legs
   b. joint

4. At what age is there no more room for growth?
   a. 25
   b. 18

5. Adults have how many bones?
   a. 206
   b. 200

6. The _____ lets you twist and bend.
   a. hip bones
   b. spine

7. Your skull protects your what?
   a. brain
   b. joints

8. Your ribs protect your what?
   a. Heart, spine, and arms
   b. heart, lung, and liver

9. The _____ connects to a large triangular bone on the upper back corner of each side of the ribcage.
   a. shoulder blade
   b. joints blade

10. You have _____ bones in your arm.
    a. two
    b. three

US Government: Running for Office

First, read over the entire passage(s). Then go back and fill in the blanks. You can skip the blanks you're unsure about and come back to them later.

political	strategy	presidential	government	outlining
council	rapport	worries	financial	healthcare
requirements	priority	victory	coordinate	memorable

When running for public office, candidates must persuade voters that they are the best candidate for the position. Running for office is a term for this type of endeavor. Running for office can be a full-time job in some cases, such as the _____ race. When running for office, there are a lot of things to do.

To run for office, the first step is to ensure that you meet all of the _____. For example, one must be at least 18 years of age and a US citizen in order to apply.

Almost everyone joins a political party to run for public office these days. The primary election, in which they run to represent that party, is frequently the first election they must win. The Democratic Party and the Republican Party are the two most influential _____ organizations in the United States today.

Without money, it's challenging to run for office. Candidates frequently use billboards, television commercials, and travel to give speeches to promote their campaigns. All of this comes at a price. The people who want to help a candidate win the election provide them with money. As a result, the budget is established. This is critical, as the person with the most significant _____ resources may be able to sway the greatest number of voters, ultimately leading to their victory.

A candidate's campaign staff should be assembled as well. These are people who will assist the candidate in their bid for the presidency. They _____ volunteers, manage funds, plan events, and generally assist the candidate in winning the election. It is the campaign manager's responsibility to lead the campaign team.

Many candidates attempt to stand out from the crowd by creating a memorable campaign slogan. This is a catchy phrase that will stick in voters' minds as they cast their ballots. Calvin Coolidge and Dwight Eisenhower both had _____ campaign slogans, "I Like Ike" for Eisenhower and "Keep Cool with Coolidge" for Coolidge.

At some point, the candidate will begin a public campaign. A lot of "shaking hands and hugging babies" is involved in the process of running for office. There are a lot of speeches they give _____ what they plan to do when they get into the White House. It's their job to explain why they're better than their rivals.

When a candidate runs for office, they usually take a position on several issues relevant to the position for which they are running. A wide range of topics, such as education, clean water, taxation, war, and _____, are examples.

The debate is yet another aspect of running for office. At a debate, all of the candidates for a particular office sit down together to discuss their positions on a specific issue. Candidates take turns speaking and responding to each other's arguments during the debate. The outcome of a debate between two candidates can mean the difference between

_____ and defeat.

After months of campaigning, the election is finally upon us. They'll cast their ballots and then get right back to work. Attending rallies or shaking hands with strangers on the street may be part of their campaign _____. All the candidates can do is wait until the polls close. Family, friends, and campaign members usually gather to see how things turn out. If they are successful, they are likely to deliver a victory speech and then go to a party to celebrate.

Becoming Your Class President

Start working toward your goal of becoming class or high school president as soon as possible if you want to one day hold that position.

If you want to get involved in student _____ your freshman year, go ahead and join, but don't hold your breath waiting to be elected president. Elections for the freshman class council are frequently a complete disaster. Since freshman elections are held within a month of the start of school, no one has had a chance to get to know one another. The person elected president is usually the one whose name has been mentioned the most by other students. A lot of the time, it's not based on competence or trust.

Building trust and _____ with your classmates is essential from the beginning of the school year. This is the most crucial step in the process of becoming a Class Officer President.

Electing someone they like and trust is a top _____ for today's college students. Be a role model for your students. In order to demonstrate your competence, participate in class discussions and get good grades. Avoid being the class clown or the laziest or most absent-minded member of the group.

Become a part of the students' lives. Attend lunch with a variety of people from various backgrounds. Ask them about their _____ and their hopes for the school's future.

Make an effort to attend student _____ meetings even if you aren't currently a member. If you're interested in joining the student council, you may be able to sit in on their meetings, or you may be able to attend an occasional meeting where non-council members can express their concerns and ideas.

Reading Comprehension
Alphabetical Order

1. Which word follows "engage" in the dictionary?
   a. encounter
   b. erase
   c. energy
   d. emigrant

2. Which word would follow "honor" in the dictionary?
   a. hiccup
   b. hesitate
   c. humble
   d. hideout

3. Which word would follow "linoleum" in the dictionary?
   a. literature
   b. lightning
   c. lilac
   d. liberty

4. Which word would follow "minute" in the dictionary?
   a. method
   b. mimic
   c. misery
   d. minister

5. Which word would follow "pleasure" in the dicitonary?
   a. pliers
   b. photo
   c. platinum
   d. place

6. What word follows "proceed" in the dictionary?
   a. product
   b. program
   c. probable
   d. priority

7. What word follow "respiration" in the dictionary?
   a. resound
   b. resign
   c. resort
   d. respond

8. What word follows "sneeze" in the dictionary?
   a. slumber
   b. snarl
   c. snatch
   d. snorkel

9. What word follows "territory" in the dictionary?
   a. textile
   b. terrific
   c. telescope
   d. tarnish

10. What word follows "curtain" in the dictionary?
    a. crumble
    b. curse
    c. cube
    d. customer

Understanding Questions-
Answer Relationship

The question-answer relationship (QAR) strategy helps students understand the different types of questions. By learning that the answers to some questions are "Right There" in the text, that some answers require a reader to "Think and Search," and that some answers can only be answered "On My Own," students recognize that they must first consider the question before developing an answer.

Throughout your education, you may be asked four different types of questions on a quiz:

Right There Questions: Literal questions with answers in the text. The words used in the question are frequently the same as those found in the text.

Think and Search Questions: Answers are obtained from various parts of the text and combined to form meaning.

The Author and You: These questions are based on information from the text, but you must apply it to your own experience. Although the answer is not directly in the text, you must have read it in order to respond to the question.

On My Own: These questions may require you to do some research outside of reading the passage. You can use primary sources to help such as online research articles, books, historical documents, and autobiographies.

Why is the question-answer relationship used?

It has the potential to improve your reading comprehension.
It teaches you how to ask questions about what you're reading and where to look for answers.
It encourages you to think about the text you're reading as well as beyond it.
It motivates you to think creatively and collaboratively, while also challenging you to use higher-level thinking skills.

1. Literal questions with answers in the text are_____.
    a. Right There Questions
    b. Right Here Questions

2. These questions are based on information from the text, but you must apply it to your own
    a. The Teacher and You
    b. The Author and You

3. Answers are obtained from various parts of the text.
    a. Think and Search Questions
    b. Check Your Knowledge Questions

4. These questions may require you to do some research outside of reading the passage.
    a. On My Own
    b. Find The Author

Weather Vocabulary Words Match Up

The weather is simply the state of the atmosphere at any given time, which includes temperature, precipitation, air pressure, and cloud cover. Winds and storms cause daily changes in the weather. Seasonal changes are caused by the Earth's rotation around the sun.

The sun's rays do not fall evenly on the land and oceans because the Earth is round rather than flat. The sun shines more directly near the equator, bringing more warmth to these areas. On the other hand, the polar regions are at such an angle to the sun that they receive little or no sunlight during the winter, resulting in colder temperatures. These temperature differences cause a frantic movement of air and water in great swirling currents, distributing heat energy from the sun across the planet. When the air in one region is warmer than air in another, it becomes less dense and begins to rise, drawing more air in beneath it. Cooler, denser air sinks elsewhere, pushing air outward to flow along the surface and complete the cycle.

Match to the correct answer.

1	☐	Anemometer		something that happens quickly usually due to heavy rain	A
2	☐	Barometer		tiny water droplets floating in the atmosphere that you can see	B
3	☐	Blizzard		A region with low air pressure and warm, moist air	C
4	☐	Cloud		A region with high air pressure and cool, dry air	D
5	☐	Coriolis effect		line on a weather map that represents a given barometric pressure	E
6	☐	Flash flood		meteorological instrument used to measure the atmospheric pressure	F
7	☐	High-pressure system		It affects weather patterns - affects an object that's moving over something that's rotating	G
8	☐	Hurricane		meteorological instrument used to measure wind speed	H
9	☐	Isobar		snow storm that has winds of 35 miles per hour or more	I
10	☐	Low-pressure system		tropical cyclone that formed in the North Atlantic Ocean	J

Each word problem should be read and solved. Make sure you comprehend all of the words and concepts. It is possible that you will need to read the problem twice or more. If you don't understand a word, look it up in a dictionary or on the internet.

Score : _____

Date : _____

Word Problems

1) There are sixteen pencils in the drawer. Sandy placed forty - one more pencils in the drawer. How many pencils are now there in total ?

_____

2) Tom had 77 pennies in his bank. He spent 37 of his pennies. How many pennies does he have now ?

_____

3) There are 33 oak trees currently in the park. Park workers will plant 44 more oak trees today. How many oak trees will the park have when the workers are finished ?

_____

4) Dan picked thirty - three lemons and Jessica picked sixty - one lemons from the lemon tree. How many lemons were picked in all ?

_____

5) Tom has 63 books. Nancy has 22 books. How many books do they have together ?

_____

6) Mary has 89 black marbles, she gave Sally 73 of the marbles. How many black marbles does she now have ?

_____

7) Nancy found 67 seashells on the beach, she gave Sandy 37 of the seashells. How many seashells does she now have ?

_____

8) Keith has ninety - eight Pokemon cards. Sally bought fifty - two of Keith's Pokemon cards. How many Pokemon cards does Keith have now ?

_____

9) Sally grew thirteen carrots. Tom grew seventy - six carrots. How many carrots did they grow in all ?

_____

10) Joan's high school played eighty - four hockey games this year. She attended thirteen games. How many hockey games did Joan miss ?

_____

Word Problems

1) Dan was at the beach for five days and found eight seashells every day.
How many seashells did Dan find during the beach trip ?   _____

2) Sam goes out to lunch with Fred and Keith. Each person orders the
$9 lunch special. Sam agrees to pay the bill. How much will he have to pay ?

_____

3) Melanie worked 2 hours for 6 days.
How many hours did she work in total ?   _____

4) A restaurant sold 5 sandwiches every day for a week.
How many sandwiches were sold during the week ?   _____

5) Melanie goes fishing with Sally. Melanie catches nine trout. Sally
catches twice as many trout as Melanie. How many trout did Sally catch ? _____

6) Nancy has 9 black balloons. Melanie has 3 times more
black balloons than Nancy. How many black balloons does Melanie have now ?

_____

7) Sally has nine five dollars bills. How much money does she have ?

_____

8) Jessica, Mike, and Sally each have 6 rulers.
How many rulers do they have have in all ?   _____

9) Sam has six quarters in his bank.
How much money does Sam have in quarters ?   _____

10) There were a total of 5 soccer games a month.
The season is played for 4 months. How many soccer games are in the seasons ?

_____

GRADE_____

DATE_____

RESEARCH: Elizabeth Fries Lummis Ellet

Occupation _____

BORN DATE:_____ Nationality_____

DEATH DATE:_____ Education _____ #Children _____

Childhood and Family Background Facts

Work and Career Facts

Children, Marriage and or Significant Relationships

Friends, Social Life and Other Interesting Facts

Did you enjoy researching this person?

Give a Rating: ☆ ☆ ☆ ☆ ☆

GRADE_____

DATE_____

RESEARCH: Susan B. Anthony

Occupation _____

BORN DATE:_____ Nationality _____

DEATH DATE:_____ Education _____ #Children _____

Childhood and Family Background Facts

Work and Career Facts

Children, Marriage and or Significant Relationships

Friends, Social Life and Other Interesting Facts

Did you enjoy researching this person?

Give a Rating: ☆ ☆ ☆ ☆ ☆

GRADE_____

DATE_____   **RESEARCH:** Juliette Gordon Low

Occupation _____

BORN DATE:_____   Nationality_____

DEATH DATE:_____   Education _____   #Children _____

Childhood and Family Background Facts

Work and Career Facts

Children, Marriage and or Significant Relationships

Friends, Social Life and Other Interesting Facts

Did you enjoy researching this person?

Give a Rating: ☆ ☆ ☆ ☆ ☆

TODAY IS RESEARCH DAY!   GRADE_____

DATE_____   **RESEARCH: Buddha**

      Occupation _____

BORN DATE:_____   Nationality _____

DEATH DATE:_____   Education _____   #Children _____

Childhood and Family Background Facts

Work and Career Facts

Children, Marriage and or Significant Relationships

Friends, Social Life and Other Interesting Facts

Did you enjoy researching this person?

Give a Rating: ☆ ☆ ☆ ☆ ☆

GRADE_____

DATE_____   **RESEARCH:** Martin Cooper

Occupation _____

BORN DATE:_____ Nationality_____

DEATH DATE:_____ Education _____ #Children _____

Childhood and Family Background Facts

Work and Career Facts

Children, Marriage and or Significant Relationships

Friends, Social Life and Other Interesting Facts

Did you enjoy researching this person?

Give a Rating: ☆ ☆ ☆ ☆ ☆

GRADE_____

DATE_____   **RESEARCH: Aristotle**

Occupation _____

BORN DATE: _____   Nationality _____

DEATH DATE: _____   Education _____   #Children _____

Childhood and Family Background Facts

Work and Career Facts

Children, Marriage and or Significant Relationships

Friends, Social Life and Other Interesting Facts

Did you enjoy researching this person?

Give a Rating: ☆

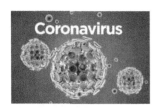

Corona Virus - COVID 19 Pandemic

Score: _____

Date:_____

Student Task: Use the clues and the words in the box to complete this crossword.

Across

1. A virus is considered zoonotic when its origins can be traced to animals.
2. People should stay away from public spaces with large gatherings of people.
3. When an epidemic has spread to multiple continents or countries.
5. The amount of time it takes for an infected person to start showing symptoms,
10. An individual is asymptomatic when they don't show any symptoms

Down

4. A large outbreak of a disease in a short period of time.
6. A restriction of movement and isolation for those exposed to COVID 19.
7. To stay at home in isolation from the general public.
8. The infectious disease caused by the most recently discovered coronavirus
9. A large family of viruses that cause a range of illnesses ranging from the common cold to more severe diseases,

PANDEMIC   COVID19
ZOONOTIC   EPIDEMIC
SOCIAL DISTANCING
ASYMPTOMATIC
QUARANTINE
INCUBATION
CORONAVIRUS   SELF
ISOLATION

Getting Your Temporary Driver's License

First, read the entire passage. After that, go back and fill in the blanks. You can skip the blanks you're unsure about and finish them later.

Department	paperwork	comfortable	guardian	standard
trial	certified	legal	transport	handbook

1. Meet the requirements

No matter what state you live in, there are _____ requirements you must meet before you can take the driving test and get your license. Most of the time, these requirements are:

FINISHING A DRIVER EDU COURSE
A LEARNER'S PERMIT IS APPLIED FOR AND RECEIVED
GETTING A CERTAIN NUMBER OF HOURS OF MONITORED PRACTICE

Even though the exact requirements vary from state to state, there will be a _____ to meet before taking the driving test. At least six months before you turn 16, find out your state's rules and get everything in order. Do not be without a license on your 18th birthday.

2. Take and pass the exam

Now comes the hard part, which is passing the test. Even though each state has its own rules, most require that you get a specific score on both a written and a driving test. After about six hours of driver's education, you can usually take the written test. During the written part of the DMV test, you will be asked questions about road signs, traffic laws, and safe driving rules. Find the test _____ for your state to get practice questions and information about the traffic laws in your state.

After you've finished driver's ed, you can take the part of the test where you drive. Depending on where you live, you may have to do this part with a _____ driving instructor or a state trooper at the Department of Motor Vehicles (DMV). The examiner will give you a set of driving instructions to see how well you can follow them.

3. Be prepared

On the day of the exam, you will need to bring proper identification, proof of your social security number, proof of legal residency and school enrollment (when required), a legal _____, and payment for any fees that may be incurred. Believe me when I say nothing could be more frustrating than showing up at the Department of Motor Vehicles, waiting in line for an hour, and finally reaching the attendant, only to find out that you forgot a vital form on the kitchen counter. Before leaving for the test, check and double-check that you have everything you need.

4. Visit the DMV.

You've done it! You're done with school, you've passed all your tests, and it's finally your 16th birthday. It's time to get your license! Depending on the state, it may be known as the _____ of Motor Vehicles (DMV), the Motor Vehicle Division (MVD), the Department of Public Safety (DPS), the Motor Vehicle Agency (MVA), the Department of Revenue (DOR), or the Secretary of State (SOS). Do your research ahead of time, so you know exactly where to go on the day of.

A driving test on-site is required if you haven't already passed either the written or driving portions of the exam. Bring the necessary _____ and payment, and ensure you look your best. Don't forget that this picture will be on your driver's license for at least a year.

5. Stick to the rules.

Most states won't give you a full license immediately if you are under 18. Instead, they give you a license that is only good for about 6 months. This is a _____ period to see if you are ready to drive without a parent or guardian with you. Be sure to follow all rules and guidelines.

It would be horrible to finally get a license and then have it taken away because you didn't follow all the rules. For example, some states restrict how many hours you can drive per day and how many passengers you can _____, while others limit the distance you can travel outside your home county.

6. Limit your passengers

Limiting the number of passengers you take on your first few trips, regardless of whether your license is temporary in nature or not, is wise advice irrespective of your license status. Every extra person in the car adds another thing to think about while driving. Driving with friends can be great fun, but if you're not entirely _____ behind the wheel, this fun can quickly turn into danger.

Of course, it's critical to abide by all state and federal laws and regulations. If you follow the rules of safe driving and use common sense, your first drive after getting your license can be a great time.

Littering

First, read the entire passage. After that, go back and fill in the blanks. You can skip the blanks you're unsure about and finish them later.

butts	jail	negative	neighborhood	amount
suspension	recreational	streets	fine	community

The annual cost of cleaning up litter in the nation's _____, parks, and coastal areas is estimated to be in the millions of dollars. The cleanup of trash has a direct expense, but it also has a _____ impact on the surrounding environment, the value of property, and other economic activity. Food packaging, bottles, cans, plastic bags, and paper are the most common sources of litter. Did you know cigarette _____ remain the most littered item in the U.S. and across the globe? One of the many strategies that states can use to reduce the amount of litter in their communities is to enact and strictly adhere to laws that carry criminal penalties for the behavior. The penalties for littering vary significantly from state to state, depending on the _____, nature, and location of the litter. The seriousness of the offense is determined by the weight or volume of litter in 10 states, for example. For instance, several states penalize people for disposing of large goods like furniture or major appliances in public places. Legislation addressing trash on public roadways, along the beaches, and in _____ areas has been passed in several states due to these concerns.

In situations that are considered to be relatively small, the courts will typically impose a fine. They may also compel the defendant to perform _____ service, such as picking up garbage. In Massachusetts, for instance, the minimum _____ is $25, whereas, in the state of Maryland, the maximum penalty is $30,000. When a crime is more serious, the offender may be sentenced to up to six years in _____, depending on the state. In addition, the laws in the states of Maryland, Massachusetts, and Louisiana all include provisions that allow the _____ of a driver's license for those who violate the laws. In almost every state, a person's sentence worsens with each subsequent conviction.

It doesn't matter if someone throws trash out on purpose or accidentally; either way, they're contributing to pollution by doing so. Our city's parks, sidewalks, roads, and private property and parks are all impacted by litter. Research has shown that litter leads to the accumulation of even more garbage. A clean _____, on the other hand, lowers the incidence of littering and enhances both the local living standards and the quality of life.

STATE BIKE LAWS

There are two levels of enforcement for bicycle laws: state and local. However, while bikers are generally required to adhere to the same traffic laws as cars, most jurisdictions also have legislation specifically for people operating bicycles on public roads. Other bicycle-specific rules and regulations can be found in state and local legislation, such as those prohibiting riding a bike on the sidewalk or while intoxicated.

Biker (and pedestrian) safety has been called into question due to some local bicycle regulations, such as those requiring bicyclists to ride on the sidewalk or walk their bikes across intersections. Bicyclists should familiarize themselves with the laws along frequently traveled routes because they can vary from municipality to municipality and are not always straightforward. Continue reading to find out more about the operation of bicycle legislation.

Violations of the law when operating a bicycle are treated the same as any other type of moving offense. There is no effect on your motor insurance when you receive a traffic ticket that specifies whether the infraction occurred while riding a bicycle.

Rules for Bicyclists on the Road

Bicyclists are expected to use hand signals when turning, changing lanes, or stopping, even if their bicycles have turn signals. A traffic penalty can be issued if a cyclist fails to indicate while riding in traffic:

Right Turn/Lane Change: The right hand extended straight out
Left Turn/Lane Change: The right hand at the elbow bent 90 degrees.
Stop: Right hand bent down 90 degrees at the elbow
Mandatory wear of a helmet

Children under the age of 16 or 18 are generally required to wear bicycle helmets in most states and the District of Columbia. Even though there are no state laws that require cyclists of any age to wear helmets, many local laws do. For example, Washington state has no law about helmets, but many cities, like Seattle, require cyclists of all ages to wear helmets.

Reflectors and Lights

Red lights on back and white lights on the front are required in nearly every state, as well as white and red reflectors on the front and back. Depending on the legislation in each state and locality, the specifics can be somewhat different.

Bike Riding on the Sidewalk

Most state and local laws say that people over a certain age (13 in San Francisco, for example) can't ride their bikes on sidewalks, but bikers always have to give way to pedestrians. On the other hand, some municipal rules make it legal to bicycle on sidewalks, while others make it illegal to ride bicycles on particular streets.

Not Stopping at a Red Light or Stop Sign

Bicyclists, like motorists, are not permitted to ride through a stop sign or stoplight without first stopping entirely. It may not seem practical to come to a complete stop when riding a bicycle, especially if you are stopping while going uphill. Yet, failure to do so could result in a citation being issued to the rider.

1. State laws and local ordinances often include measures requiring cyclists to wear _____.
   a. headlights
   b. helmets

2. A bicycle violation will not affect your automobile insurance.
   a. True
   b. False

3. Bicyclists are expected to use the appropriate _____ while turning, changing lanes, or stopping, even though some bicycles come equipped with turn signals.
   a. motion sensors
   b. hand signals

4. Rules pertaining to the use of bicycles are enforced at the _____ levels, just like other traffic laws.
   a. state and local
   b. state and countrywide

5. Bicyclists are prohibited from proceeding through a _____ or _____ without first coming to a complete stop, just like vehicles are.
   a. stop sign, stoplight
   b. yield sign, yellow light

6. _____ on back and _____ lights on the front are required in nearly every state, as well as white and red reflectors on the front and back.
   a. Red lights, white
   b. White lights, flashing

UNDERSTANDING RIDESHARE

Score: _____

Date: _____

First, read the entire passage. After that, go back and fill in the blanks. You can skip the blanks you're unsure about and finish them later.

ratings	destination	luxury	alternative	fares
carpooling	declining	flagging	smartphone	legislation

The way in which people travel is undergoing significant change. Ride-sharing and ride-hailing services, such as Uber, provide an _____ to the taxi business. When ridesharing startup Uber first debuted its services, the world of private transportation shifted radically. They offered a _____ black car service as an alternative to the usual taxi ride.

In the past, ridesharing was a lot like _____, where the person riding along often paid for half of the trip. Both the driver and passenger were traveling in the same direction, and the rider would contribute to the trip's cost. Ridesharing today is for-profit, and the driver has no _____ in mind rather than providing transportation services like a taxi. A third-party app or website charges a fee to connect riders and drivers.

It's common to see the term "rideshare" replaced with "ride-hail." However, this can be deceptive, as "hailing" usually refers to the act of _____ down a cab from a distance. Hail requests can't be accepted by drivers for ridesharing services like Lyft, Uber, and TappCar because the companies don't support the feature. The _____ also prohibits drivers from receiving hails. Otherwise, the service would be categorized as a taxi service. Instead, users must use their smartphone to "haul" a driver through their preferred ridesharing app.

Rideshare companies use a _____ app to connect drivers with passengers in the local region. The driver opens the app and changes their status to "online" to show they are ready to take a ride.

Customer pick-up and drop-off requests are sent to the driver, who responds by accepting or _____ the ride.

After accepting the trip and picking up the passenger, the driver proceeds to the passenger's destination.

The passenger will exit the vehicle once the driver reaches the final location.

Because payments for _____ are processed within the app, no money exchange occurs between the driver and the passenger.

Additionally, the app enables passengers and drivers to provide _____ for one another. Both the driver and rider benefit from this grading system, which ensures a high level of service and respect for both parties.

Organ Donations

A common question on driver's license applications and renewals is whether or not you'd like to be an organ donor. To make it easier to communicate your desires in the event of an untimely death, many states have joined with donor programs.

Being an organ donor is a big deal. It's possible that when you're asked this question while getting your driver's license, you won't know whether to select "yes" or "no" on the checkbox. Before you make a decision, consider the following information.

Who is eligible to become a donor?

People of all ages and medical backgrounds are welcome to sign up, regardless of prior medical history or current well-being. Through your state DMV, you can easily register to donate organs. However, you must be at least 18 years old to join on your own. Those under the age of 18 may be able to donate their organs if they have the approval of their parents. There are no restrictions on who can donate outside their age; persons of any color, ethnicity, or religion can do so if they are comfortable doing so.

What can you donate in terms of organs and tissues, and what can you do with them?

The heart, lungs, liver, pancreas, kidneys, and small intestines are all organs that can be donated. Organ donation can save lives by transplanting healthy organs into patients with sick organs.   Skin, bone, corneas, heart valves, and veins are examples of tissues that can be donated. Corneas can be transplanted to restore vision, and heart valves are frequently used in the valve replacement operation that is routinely performed on children. Patients who have suffered burns often require skin grafts. Using bone, tendons, and ligaments can be beneficial in reconstructive procedures.

If it is found that a particular organ or tissue cannot be used in a transplant, then it may be utilized for medical research and teaching, unless you have made other arrangements. You can designate which organs and tissues you are willing to donate and whether or not they should be disposed of properly.

What if I decide to go back on my decision?

If you already have the DONOR label on your driver's license or ID card and want it taken off, you must go to any DMV office and make the request. You will be sent a replacement license or ID that does not contain the indication you are a donor.

The decision to become an organ donor is an amazing way to bestow the gift of life on another person.

If you have questions about your state's donor program or any other driving-related questions, you can look in the driver's handbook for your state.

1. **You can quickly register to donate organs through the _____ in your state.**
   a. Department of Organ Donations
   b. Department of Motor Vehicles

2. **Donated organs can be _____ into another _____.**
   a. transplanted, person
   b. translational, facility

3. **To remove the DONOR label from your driver's license or ID card, visit any ____ office.**

   a. DVM

   b. DMV

4. **There are many different types of ____ that can be donated, including skin, bone, corneas, heart valves, and ____.**

   a. organism, plasma

   b. tissues, veins

5. **Those under the age of ____ may be able to donate their organs if they have the ____ of their parents.**

   a. 18, approval

   b. 17, agreement

6. **If an organ or tissue ____ be transplanted, it may be used for medical research and ____, unless you make other arrangements.**

   a. can, placement

   b. cannot, teaching

Commonly misspelled words that sound alike but are spelled differently

Carefully circle the correct spelling combinations of words.

	A	B	C	D
1.	Sun/Sn	Son/Son	Sun/Son	Son/Sn
2.	Hare/Hiar	Harre/Hair	Hare/Hair	Harre/Hiar
3.	Cache/Cassh	Cache/Cash	Cache/Casch	Cacha/Cash
4.	Cytte/Sight	Cite/Sight	Cyte/Sight	Citte/Sight
5.	Worrn/Warn	Wurn/Warn	Wurrn/Warn	Worn/Warn
6.	Minerr/Minor	Miner/Minur	Miner/Minor	Minerr/Minur
7.	Wratch/Retch	Wretch/Retch	Wrretch/Retch	Wrratch/Retch
8.	Floor/Flower	Flloor/Flower	Flour/Flower	Fllour/Flower
9.	Whille/Wile	While/Wile	Whylle/Wile	Whyle/Wile
10.	Calous/Callus	Caloos/Callus	Callous/Callus	Calloos/Callus
11.	Build/Biled	Build/Billed	Boild/Billed	Boild/Biled
12.	Marrten/Martin	Marten/Martin	Marten/Martyn	Marrten/Martyn
13.	Humerrus/Humorous	Humerus/Humorous	Humerrus/Humoroos	Humerus/Humoroos
14.	Housse/Hoes	Hose/Hoes	House/Hoes	Hosse/Hoes
15.	Mei Be/Maybe	Mai Be/Maybe	May Be/Maybe	Mey Be/Maybe
16.	Matal/Metle/Meddle	Metal/Mettle/Meddle	Matal/Mettle/Meddle	Metal/Metle/Meddle
17.	Halve/Have	Hallva/Have	Hallve/Have	Halva/Have
18.	Wee/We	Wea/We	We/We	Wa/We
19.	Taper/Tapir	Taperr/Tapyr	Taperr/Tapir	Taper/Tapyr
20.	Timberr/Timbre	Tymber/Timbre	Tymberr/Timbre	Timber/Timbre
21.	Minse/Mintts	Mince/Mintts	Minse/Mints	Mince/Mints
22.	Eies/Ayes	Eyesc/Ayes	Eyes/Ayes	Eyess/Ayes
23.	Guesced/Guest	Guessed/Guest	Guesed/Guest	Gueced/Guest
24.	Yore/Your/You'Re	Yore/Yoor/You'Re	Yorre/Your/You'Re	Yorre/Yoor/You'Re
25.	Oarr/Or/Ora	Oarr/Or/Ore	Oar/Or/Ore	Oar/Or/Ora
26.	Bate/Biat	Bate/Bait	Batte/Biat	Batte/Bait
27.	Tax/Tacks	Tax/Taks	Tax/Tacksc	Tax/Tackss

28.	Bald/Ballad/Bawled	Bald/Baled/Bawled	Bald/Balled/Bawled	Bald/Balad/Bawled
29.	Ewe/Yuo/Yew	Ewe/Yoo/Yew	Ewe/You/Yew	Ewe/Yoo/Yw
30.	Eei/I/Aye	Eie/I/Ae	Eye/I/Aye	Eie/I/Aye
31.	Hoes/Hose	Hoess/Hose	Hoess/House	Hoes/House
32.	Tou/Two/To	Tu/Two/To	To/Two/To	Too/Two/To
33.	Ceres/Series	Cerres/Series	Ceres/Sereis	Cerres/Sereis
34.	Hansom/Handsome	Hansum/Handsome	Hanscom/Handsome	Hanssom/Handsome
35.	Residance/Residents	Residence/Residents	Ressidence/Residents	Ressidance/Residents
36.	Surrf/Serf	Surf/Serf	Surrph/Serf	Surph/Serf
37.	Siall/Sale	Saill/Sale	Sail/Sale	Sial/Sale
38.	Therre's/Thiers	There's/Thiers	There's/Theirs	Therre's/Theirs
39.	Roed/Rode	Roed/Rude	Rued/Rude	Roed/Rue
40.	Aid/Aie	Ayd/Aide	Ayd/Aie	Aid/Aide
41.	Taem/Teem	Taem/Tem	Team/Tem	Team/Teem
42.	Ilusion/Allusion	Ilution/Allusion	Illution/Allusion	Illusion/Allusion
43.	Hi/Hih	Hy/High	Hi/High	Hy/Hih
44.	Barred/Bard	Bared/Bard	Barad/Bard	Barrad/Bard
45.	Mewll/Mule	Mewl/Mule	Mewll/Mole	Mewl/Mole
46.	Rowss/Rose	Rows/Rose	Rowss/Rouse	Rows/Rouse
47.	Chep/Cheap	Cheep/Chaep	Cheep/Cheap	Chep/Chaep
48.	Bah/Ba	Beh/Ba	Bah/Baa	Beh/Baa
49.	Gofer/Gopher	Gopher/Gopher	Gophfer/Gopher	Goffer/Gopher
50.	Don/Doe	Dun/Doe	Dun/Done	Don/Done
51.	Ryte/Write/Right	Ritte/Write/Right	Rytte/Write/Right	Rite/Write/Right
52.	Mite/Might	Mitte/Might	Myte/Might	Mytte/Might
53.	Latter/Ladder	Later/Ladder	Latar/Ladder	Lattar/Ladder
54.	Gorred/Goord	Gored/Gourd	Gored/Goord	Gorred/Gourd
55.	Ball/Belle	Bell/Belle	Bal/Belle	Bel/Belle
56.	Ruscell/Rustle	Russell/Rustle	Rusell/Rustle	Rucell/Rustle
57.	Tuat/Taught	Tautt/Taught	Tuatt/Taught	Taut/Taught
58.	Cozen/Cousin	Cozen/Coosin	Cozen/Coossin	Cozen/Coussin
59.	Morn/Mourn	Morrn/Moorn	Morrn/Mourn	Morn/Moorn
60.	Stare/Stiar	Stare/Stair	Sttare/Stiar	Sttare/Stair
61.	Wrrap/Rap	Wrrep/Rap	Wrap/Rap	Wrep/Rap

62.	Centts/Ssents	Centts/Scents	Cents/Scents	Cents/Ssents
63.	Basste/Based	Baste/Baced	Baste/Based	Bascte/Based
64.	Foorr/Fore/For	Foor/Fore/For	Fourr/Fore/For	Four/Fore/For
65.	Knikers/Nickers	Knickerrs/Nickers	Knikerrs/Nickers	Knickers/Nickers
66.	Marre/Mayor	Mare/Mayor	Mare/Meyor	Marre/Meyor
67.	Surrje/Serge	Surje/Serge	Surrge/Serge	Surge/Serge
68.	Steal/Steel	Steal/Stel	Stael/Steel	Stael/Stel
69.	Haerrt/Hart	Heart/Hart	Hearrt/Hart	Haert/Hart
70.	Holed/Hold	Huled/Hold	Holled/Hold	Hulled/Hold
71.	Way/Wiegh/Whey	Wai/Wiegh/Whey	Wai/Weigh/Whey	Way/Weigh/Whey
72.	Diieng/Dying	Dyieng/Dying	Dieing/Dying	Dyeing/Dying
73.	Holay/Holy/Wholly	Holay/Holy/Wholy	Holey/Holy/Wholy	Holey/Holy/Wholly
74.	Sworrd/Soared	Swurrd/Soared	Swurd/Soared	Sword/Soared
75.	Cane/Cyan	Cane/Cian	Cane/Cayn	Cane/Cain
76.	Arreil/Aerial	Ariel/Aerial	Arriel/Aerial	Areil/Aerial
77.	Brut/Brute	Brrot/Brute	Brot/Brute	Brrut/Brute
78.	Frrays/Phrase	Frays/Phrase	Frreys/Phrase	Freys/Phrase
79.	Throne/Thrown	Thrrune/Thrown	Thrune/Thrown	Thrrone/Thrown
80.	Ha'd/Hed	He'd/Heed	He'd/Hed	He'd/Head
81.	Waerr/Where/Ware	Wear/Where/Ware	Wearr/Where/Ware	Waer/Where/Ware
82.	Brraed/Bred	Bread/Bred	Braed/Bred	Brread/Bred
83.	We've/Waeve	We've/Weave	Wa've/Weave	Wa've/Waeve
84.	Hew/Hoe/Huh	Hew/Hue/Hugh	Hew/Hoe/Hugh	Hew/Hoe/Hogh
85.	Nikerrs/Knickers	Nickerrs/Knickers	Nikers/Knickers	Nickers/Knickers
86.	Call/Sell	Cell/Sell	Cal/Sell	Cel/Sell
87.	Isle/I'll/Aisle	Isle/I'll/Aisle	Isle/I'll/Aysle	Isle/I'll/Aysle
88.	Brruice/Brews	Bruise/Brews	Brruise/Brews	Bruice/Brews
89.	Except/Accept	Exsept/Accept	Exsept/Acept	Except/Acept

Grammar: Singular and Plural

Nouns can take many different forms. Singular and plural are two of these forms. A singular noun refers to a single person, place, thing, or idea. A plural noun is one that refers to two or more people, places, things, or ideas. How do you pluralize a singular noun? Making a singular noun plural is usually as simple as adding a **s** to the end of the word.
Example: Singular toy | Plural toys

Some nouns, however, do not follow this rule and are referred to as irregular nouns. How do I pluralize a singular irregular noun?

We'll start with **singular nouns** that end in s, ss, ch, sh, x, or z. If a singular noun **ends in s, ss, ch, sh, x, or z**, add **es** at the end.
Example: beach--->beaches

If the singular noun **ends in a vowel**, the letters a, e, I o, and u are usually suffixed with an **s**.
Example: video--->videos

If a singular noun **ends with a consonant + o**, it is common to add an **es** at the end. Except for a, e, I o, and u, consonants are all the letters of the alphabet.
Example: potato--->potatoes

Simply add a **s** to the end of the word if the singular noun **ends in a vowel + y** pattern.
Example: day--->days

Now we'll look at singular nouns that **end in f or fe**. If the singular noun ends in a f or fe, **change it to a v and then add es**.
Example: life--->lives

Consonant + y is another unusual noun. If the singular noun **ends with a consonant + y** pattern, **change the y to I before adding es**.
Example: bunny---> bunnies

Some nouns are spelled the same way in both the singular and plural forms.

It's now time to make some spelling changes. When you switch from the singular to plural form of a noun, the spelling changes. The following are some examples of common words that change spelling when formed into plurals:
Example: child--->childrens

Select the best answer for each question.

1. **Which word is NOT a plural noun?**
   a. books
   b. hat
   c. toys

2. **Which word is a singular noun?**
   a. bikes
   b. cars
   c. pencil

3. **Which word can be both singular and plural?**
   a. deer
   b. bears
   c. mice

4. **Tommy _____ badminton at the court.**
   a. playing
   b. plays
   c. play's

5. **They _____ to eat at fast food restaurants once in a while.**
   a. likes
   b. like
   c. likies

6. **Everybody _____ Janet Jackson.**
   a. know
   b. known
   c. knows

7. He ___ very fast. You have to listen carefully.

    a. spoken

    b. speak

    c. speaks

8. Which one is the singular form of women?

    a. womans

    b. woman

    c. women

9. The plural form of tooth is

    a. tooths

    b. toothes

    c. teeth

10. The singular form of mice is _____.

    a. mouse

    b. mices

    c. mouses

11. The plural form of glass is _____.

    a. glassies

    b. glasses

    c. glassy

12. The plural form of dress is _____.

    a. dressing

    b. dresses

    c. dressy

13. Plural means many.

    a. True

    b. False

14. Singular means 1.

    a. True

    b. False

15. Is this word singular or plural? monsters

    a. plural

    b. singular

16. Find the plural noun in the sentence. They gave her a nice vase full of flowers.

    a. they

    b. flowers

    c. vase

17. Find the plural noun in the sentence. Her baby brother grabbed the crayons out of the box and drew on the wall.

    a. crayons

    b. box

    c. brothers

18. Find the plural noun in the sentence. My friend, Lois, picked enough red strawberries for the whole class.

    a. strawberries

    b. friends

    c. classes

19. What is the correct plural form of the noun wish?

    a. wishes

    b. wishs

    c. wishy

20. What is the correct plural form of the noun flurry?

    a. flurrys

    b. flurryies

    c. flurries

21. What is the correct plural form of the noun box?

    a. boxs

    b. boxses

    c. boxes

22. What is the correct plural form of the noun bee?

    a. beess

    b. beeses

    c. bees

23. What is the correct plural form of the noun candy?

    a. candys

    b. candyies

    c. candies

24. Find the singular noun in the sentence. The boys and girls drew pictures on the sidewalk.

    a. boys

    b. drew

    c. sidewalk

Grammar: Homophones vs Homographs vs. Homonyms

How do you know which 'there,' 'their,' or 'they're' to use when you're writing? Isn't it a difficult one? These words sound similar but have completely different meanings.

Words with the same sound but different meanings are referred to as **homophones**. Homophones can be spelled differently or the same way. Rose (the flower), rose (the past tense of 'rise,' and rows (a line of items or people) are all homophones.

Homographs are two or more words that have the same spelling but different meanings and it **doesn't have to sound the same**. Because homographs are words with multiple meanings, how can you tell which one is being used? Readers can determine which form of a homograph is being used by looking for context clues, or words surrounding it that provide information about the definition. Take a look at these homograph examples.

A **bat** is either a piece of sporting equipment or an animal.
Bass is either a type of fish or a musical genre.
A **pen** is a writing instrument or a small enclosure in which animals are kept.
Lean is a word that means to be thin or to rest against something.
A **skip** is a fictitious jump or missing out on something.

Homonyms are words that have the same spelling or pronunciation but different meanings. These words can be perplexing at times, especially for students learning to spell them. For example, right means moral, the opposite of left, and a personal freedom. Homonyms can refer to both homophones and homographs. Both a homograph and a homophone are included in the definition of a homonym. For example, the words 'bear,' 'tear,' and 'lead' are all homographs, but they also meet the criteria for homonyms. They simply have to have the same look or sound. Similarly, while the words 'sell,' 'cell,' 'by,' and 'buy' are all homophones, they are also homonyms.

1. 'there,' 'their,' or 'they're' are examples of
   _____.

   a. Homophones
   b. Homographs

2. _____ are words that have the same spelling or pronunciation but different meanings.

   a. Homonyms
   b. Hemograms

3. Choose the correct homophone for this sentence: Please don't drop and _____that bottle of hand sanitizer!

   a. brake
   b. break

4. Homographs are two or more words that have the same spelling but different _____.

   a. ending sounds
   b. meanings

5. Current (A flow of water / Up to date) is both homograph and homophone.

   a. True
   b. False

6. To, two and too are _____.

   a. Homagraphs
   b. Homonyms

7. **The candle filled the _____ with a delicious scent.**
   a. heir
   b. air

8. **Kim drove _____ the tunnel.**
   a. threw
   b. through

9. **John wants to go to _____ house for dinner, but they don't like her, so _____ going to say no.**
   a. their, they're
   b. there, they're

10. **We won a $95,000 _____!**
    a. cheque
    b. check

11. **For example, a pencil is not really made with _____.**
    a. led
    b. lead

12. **Choose the correct homophone for this sentence: Timmy was standing _____ in line.**
    a. fourth
    b. forth

13. **Homophones are two words that sound the same but have a different meanings.**
    a. True
    b. False

14. **The word ring in the following two sentences is considered what? She wore a ruby ring. | We heard the doorbell ring.**
    a. hologram
    b. homograph

15. **A Homograph is a word that has more than one meaning and doesn't have to sound the same.**
    a. True
    b. False

16. **Homophones occur when there are multiple ways to spell the same sound.**
    a. True
    b. False

17. **Select the correct homophone: I have very little (patience/patients) when students do not follow directions.**
    a. patients
    b. patience

18. **The correct homophone (s) are used in the sentence: Personally, I hate the smell of read meet.**
    a. True
    b. False

19. **The correct homophone(s) is used in the sentence: We saw a herd of cattle in the farmer's field.**
    a. True
    b. False

20. **What is NOT an example of a homograph?**
    a. or, oar
    b. live, live

Reading a Timeline   DATE: _____   SCORE: _____

Use the timeline to answer the questions.

Lewis and Clark's Expedition

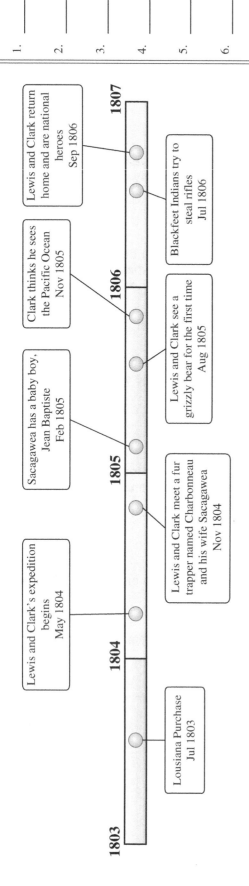

1803	**1804**	**1805**	**1806**	**1807**

Lousiana Purchase
Jul 1803

Lewis and Clark's expedition begins
May 1804

Lewis and Clark meet a fur trapper named Charbonneau and his wife Sacagawea
Nov 1804

Sacagawea has a baby boy, Jean Baptiste
Feb 1805

Lewis and Clark see a grizzly bear for the first time
Aug 1805

Clark thinks he sees the Pacific Ocean
Nov 1805

Blackfeet Indians try to steal rifles
Jul 1806

Lewis and Clark return home and are national heroes
Sep 1806

1) How many years did Lewis and Clark's expedition take? _____

2) Which happened earlier? A. Indians try to steal rifles or B. Lewis and Clark see a grizzly bear _____

3) What year was the Louisiana Purchase? _____

4) What year did Sacagawea have her child? _____

5) What is the span (number of years shown) of this timeline? _____

6) What year did Lewis and Clark meet Charbonneau? _____

7) What year did Lewis and Clark return home? _____

8) In September of 1804 Lewis and Clark saw a prairie dog. Could you put this event on the timeline above? (Yes / No) _____

9) What event happened in Nov 1805? _____

10) What is this timeline about? _____

Answers

1. _____
2. _____
3. _____
4. _____
5. _____
6. _____
7. _____
8. _____ Use Line
9. _____ Use Line
10. _____

GRADE_____

DATE_____   **RESEARCH:** Ken Kutaragi

Occupation _____

BORN DATE: _____   Nationality_____

DEATH DATE:_____   Education _____   #Children _____

Childhood and Family Background Facts

Work and Career Facts

Children, Marriage and or Significant Relationships

Friends, Social Life and Other Interesting Facts

Did you enjoy researching this person?

Give a Rating: ☆ ☆ ☆ ☆ ☆

TODAY IS RESEARCH DAY!

GRADE_____

DATE_____   **RESEARCH: Charles Macintosh**

Occupation _____

BORN DATE:_____   Nationality _____

DEATH DATE:_____   Education _____   #Children _____

Childhood and Family Background Facts

Work and Career Facts

Children, Marriage and or Significant Relationships

Friends, Social Life and Other Interesting Facts

Did you enjoy researching this person?

Give a Rating: ☆ ☆ ☆ ☆ ☆

GRADE_____

DATE_____

RESEARCH: Ilya Ilyich Mechnikov

Occupation _____

BORN DATE:_____ Nationality _____

DEATH DATE:_____ Education _____ #Children _____

Childhood and Family Background Facts

Work and Career Facts

Children, Marriage and or Significant Relationships

Friends, Social Life and Other Interesting Facts

Did you enjoy researching this person?

Give a Rating: ☆ ☆ ☆ ☆ ☆

TODAY IS RESEARCH DAY!   GRADE_____

DATE_____   **RESEARCH: Daniel David Palmer**

     Occupation _____

BORN DATE:_____   Nationality_____

DEATH DATE:_____   Education _____   #Children _____

Childhood and Family Background Facts

Work and Career Facts

Children, Marriage and or Significant Relationships

Friends, Social Life and Other Interesting Facts

Did you enjoy researching this person?

Give a Rating: ☆ ☆ ☆ ☆ ☆

GRADE_____

DATE_____   **RESEARCH: Adolphe Sax**

Occupation _____

BORN DATE:_____   Nationality _____

DEATH DATE:_____   Education _____   #Children _____

Childhood and Family Background Facts

Work and Career Facts

Children, Marriage and or Significant Relationships

Friends, Social Life and Other Interesting Facts

Did you enjoy researching this person?

Give a Rating: ☆ ☆ ☆ ☆ ☆

10th Grade Simple Math Refresher

Score: _____

Date: _____

1. Perform the following operation: 12 + 1 + 8 =
   a. 21
   b. 20
   c. 18

2. Solve 1,056 divided by 22.
   a. 92
   b. 48
   c. 36

3. Division is the math operation that tells you to _____ and is represented by the symbols _____.
   a. separate or combine two numbers together; - and /
   b. separate something into parts; ÷ and /
   c. combine three numbers together; - and /

4. Brad saved $605 for his yearly vacations. He has 11 days of vacation and wants to spend the same amount of money each day, how much will he spend each day?
   a. $95
   b. $55
   c. $104

5. Convert 3/7 to a percent.
   a. 38.1%
   b. 5.9%
   c. 42.9%

6. Change 0.142 to a fraction.
   a. 1/7
   b. 2/4
   c. 1/8

7. Change 2/5 to a decimal.
   a. 0.4
   b. 0.9
   c. 0.5

8. Write 4 8/9 as an improper fraction.
   a. 32/5
   b. 40/8
   c. 44/9

9. A(n) _____ is an improper fraction written with a whole number and a proper fraction.
   a. decimal
   b. proper fraction
   c. mixed number

10. Write 50% as a fraction.
    a. 1/2
    b. 0/5
    c. 5/0

11. Change 79.5% to a decimal.
    a. 0.795
    b. .79.5%
    c. 79.05%

12. Which of the following number has the highest numerical value?
    a. 2.8
    b. 0.28
    c. 4.5%

13. Order the following numbers from smallest to greatest: 0.25, 4.54, 0.015, 1.24

    a. 1.24, 4.54, 0.015, 0.25

    b. 0.015, 0.25, 1.24, 4.54

    c. 4.54, 0.015, 0.25, 1.24

14. What is the 28% of 80?

    a. 28.0

    b. 84%

    c. 22.4

15. Convert 6/7 to a percent.

    a. 7.6%

    b. 6.7%

    c. 86%

16. What is the denominator of 7/9?

    a. 7.9

    b. 7

    c. 9

17. Write 18.7% as a decimal.

    a. 0.187

    b. 1.87

    c. 18.7%

18. Convert 0.00047 to scientific notation.

    a. 4.0×10^{-7}

    b. 4.7×4^{-0}

    c. 4.7×10^{-4}

19. Multiply 4.25×10^{-5} by 4.

    a. 1.7×10^{-4}

    b. 2.7×10^{-4}

    c. 4.5×10^{1}

20. Janes Market sells a pack of 500 napkins for $2.50 and Taylor Grocery sells a pack that has 750 of the same napkins for $3.75. Which pack is the best deal?

    a. Janes Market

    b. Both packs have the same price per napkin

    c. Taylor Grocery

21. Maya earned $4,575 in 3 months. If earned the same amount each month, how much did she earn each month?

    a. $2,575

    b. $925

    c. $1,525

22. The independent variable of an exponential function is the _____.

    a. exponent

    b. logarithm

    c. fraction

23. Solve for X in the following equation $8 + 3^{X} = 35$

    a. X = 3

    b. X = 8

    c. X = 35

24. Grams. liters and centimeters are all examples of _____ units.

    a. pounds

    b. kilogram

    c. metric

25. One kilogram is equivalent to _____ grams.

    a. 100

    b. 10

    c. 1,000

10th Grade Geography Multiple Choice Quiz: Mountain Range

Select the best answer for each question.

1. The _____ run for 1,500 miles along the east coast of the US from northern Alabama to Maine.
   a. Sierra Nevada
   b. Rocky Mountains
   c. Appalachian Mountains

2. Which is of the following is famous for its tall peaks and stretches 1,491 miles through much of central Asia?
   a. Himalayas
   b. Andres
   c. Urals

3. The _____ are the world's longest mountain range, stretching approximately 4,300 miles.
   a. Alps
   b. Rockies
   c. Andes

4. Fault-block mountains were formed along a fault in the Earth's crust. Which of the following is a fault-block mountain?
   a. Appalachian
   b. Sierra Nevada
   c. Rockies

5. What is the process by which the world's tallest mountain ranges are formed?
   a. seafloor spreading
   b. continental drift
   c. plate tectonics

6. The theory of continental drift was proposed by which German meteorologist?
   a. Charles Thomson Rees Wilson
   b. Alfred Wegener
   c. John Dalton

7. Which of the following mountain ranges is the highest and most extensive in Europe?
   a. The Appalachian
   b. The Alps
   c. The Andes

8. What is the highest point of the Rockies that is 14,440 feet above sea level?
   a. Mount Elbert
   b. Mount Chamberlin
   c. Mount Whitney

9. The _____ is a mountain range in northeast New York.
   a. Alaska Range
   b. Adirondacks
   c. Brooks Range

10. Which famous city was built atop a mountain of the Andes Mountain range?
    a. Machu Picchu
    b. Tikal
    c. Tenochtitlan

11. What is the highest mountain range in North America?
    a. Brooks Range
    b. Cascade Range
    c. Alaska Range

12. The _____ is the largest mountain range between the Appalachians and the Rockies.
    a. Ozarks
    b. Urals
    c. Adirondacks

10th Grade Geography Multiple Choice Quiz: Islands

Select the best answer for each question.

1. An island is a body of land smaller than a continent that is surrounded _____ by water.
   a. entirely
   b. on three sides
   c. on two sides

2. A group of related islands, such as the Philippines, is called _____ .
   a. a continent
   b. an island
   c. an archipelago

3. _____ form when volcanoes erupt on the ocean floor.
   a. Artificial Island
   b. Continental islands
   c. Oceanic islands

4. Which of the following islands are classified as oceanic islands?
   a. Padre Island and Cape Hatteras
   b. Greenland and Madagascar
   c. Iceland and Hawaiian

5. Which of the following is the world's largest non-continental island?
   a. Madagascar
   b. Greenland
   c. Great Britain

6. Located off the southeast coast of Africa, _____ is the world's fourth largest island.
   a. Seychelles
   b. Madagascar
   c. Mauritius

7. _____are sections of the continental shelf that have become isolated due to sea-level rise.
   a. Oceanic islands
   b. Continental islands
   c. Barrier islands

8. Home to the famous volcano Mount Fuji, ____ is Japan's largest island.
   a. Hokkaido
   b. Honshu
   c. Kyushu

9. What is the largest island in the Mediterranean Sea?
   a. Sardinia
   b. Sicily
   c. Cyprus

10. Napoleon Bonaparte, Emperor of France was born on which island in France?
    a. Port-Cros
    b. Levant Island
    c. Corcica

11. _____ is the world's ninth largest island, the largest island in the British Isles, and the world's third most populous island.
    a. Great Britain
    b. Isle of Man
    c. Ireland

12. The largest and southernmost island in the Mariana Islands chain, located in the North Pacific Ocean is _____.
    a. Guam
    b. Saipan
    c. Tinian

10th Grade Geography Multiple Choice Quiz: Glaciers

Select the best answer for each question.

1. A glacier is a huge mass of _____ that moves slowly over _____.
    a. snow and clouds
    b. hail and water
    c. ice and land

2. Glaciers that cover more than 50,000 square kilometers are called?
    a. Alpine
    b. Ice caps
    c. Ice sheets

3. _____ form on mountainsides and move downward through valleys.
    a. Alpine glaciers
    b. Ice caps
    c. Ice sheets

4. A complex of _____ glaciers burying much of a mountain range is called an _____.
    a. valley and ice sheet
    b. hill and ice cap
    c. mountain and ice field

5. Glaciers also exist high in _____ such as the _____ and the _____.
    a. mountain ranges, Himalayas and Andes
    b. Plateaus, Arctic and Antarctica
    c. Hills, Australia and South Africa

6. Melting _____ contribute to rising sea levels.
    a. ice caps
    b. ice field
    c. ice sheets

7. Glaciers carry great amounts of _____, _____, and _____.
    a. snow, water and rock
    b. ice, rock and clay
    c. soil, rock and clay

8. A _____ is one that ends in a body of water like a lake or an ocean.
    a. hanging glaciers
    b. cirque glaciers
    c. calving glacier

9. A _____ glacier is one that is formed in an area where the temperature is always below the freezing point.
    a. temperate
    b. polar
    c. piedmont

10. Most glaciers are located near the _____ or _____.
    a. Greenland or Iceland
    b. Arctic or Antarctic
    c. North or South Poles

11. _____ refers to all processes that contribute mass to a glacier.
    a. Transformation
    b. Ablation
    c. Accumulation

12. _____ is a simple consequence of the weight and creep properties of ice.
    a. Glacier flow
    b. Ablation
    c. Accumulation

10th Grade Geography Multiple Choice Quiz: Deserts

Score: _____

Date: _____

Select the best answer for each question.

1. Which is the only continent with no large deserts?

    a. Europe

    b. North America

    c. Australia

2. Which desert in Asia stretches across parts of China and Mongolia?

    a. Great Victoria desert

    b. Sahara desert

    c. Gobi desert

3. What percentage of the world's land surface is a desert?

    a. 15

    b. 25

    c. 20

4. The _____ is the world's largest hot desert.

    a. Sahara

    b. Sonoran

    c. Kalahari

5. Which of the following is one of the most oil-rich places in the world?

    a. Mohave desert

    b. Arabian desert

    c. Kalahari desert

6. An oasis is a place in the desert with _____.

    a. a collection of desert edible plants

    b. a supply of fresh water

    c. a horde of desert animals

7. A subtropical desert is _____.

    a. a desert that exists near the leeward slopes of some mountain ranges

    b. sometimes called inland deserts

    c. caused by the circulation patterns of air masses

8. The _____ is a large desert located in Mexico and parts of the Southwestern United States.

    a. Great Victoria desert

    b. Sonoran desert

    c. Gobi desert

9. The amount of _____ in a desert often greatly exceeds the annual rainfall.

    a. condensation

    b. precipitation

    c. evaporation

10. _____ deserts exist near the leeward slopes of some mountain ranges.

    a. rain shadow

    b. costal

    c. interior

11. A home to Death Valley, the hottest and lowest spot in the US is the _____.

    a. Sonoran desert

    b. Mohave desert

    c. Kalahari desert

12. The Atacama Desert on the Pacific shores of Chile, is a _____, where some areas of it are often covered by fog.

    a. subtropical desert

    b. coastal desert

    c. interior desert

10th Grade The Metric System

Tip: After you've answered the easy ones, go back and work on the harder ones.

gram	metric	liter	Meter	Gram
centimeter	liter	weight	Celsius	Liter
meter	10	milliliters	kilogram	Celsius

Scientists all over the world use the _____ system. There's a very good reason for this-it's so everyone is doing the measuring the same way, all over the world. Most other countries already use the metric system for measuring everything.

Another good reason to use metric is that you don't have so much to remember-no 12 inches in a foot or 5,280 feet in a mile. It's all decimal! The larger or smaller units go up or down by _____, 100, or 1,000.

_____ is for length. A _____ is a little longer than a yard. For long distances, there is the kilometer (a thousand meters). For small things, there is the _____ (100 centimeters in a meter).

_____ is for volume. A _____ is a little larger than a quart. There are a thousand _____ in a _____.

_____ is for _____. A _____ is a little more than the weight of a paper clip. For heavier things, there is the _____ (a thousand grams).

Temperatures are in degrees Celsius (also called centigrade). Water freezes at 0 degrees _____ and boils at 100 degrees _____. That's easy!

Contractions Multiple Choice

A *contraction* is a way of making two words into one. Circle the correct answer.

1. aren't
   a. are not
   b. not are
   c. arenot

2. can't
   a. cants
   b. cannot
   c. cant

3. couldn't
   a. couldnt
   b. couldnts
   c. could not

4. didn't
   a. didn'ts
   b. did nots
   c. did not

5. don't
   a.
   b. do not

6. hadn't
   a. had not
   b. had nots
   c. hadn'ts

7. hasn't
   a. has nots
   b. has not
   c. hasnot

8. haven't
   a. have nots
   b. haven'ts
   c. have not

9. I'm
   a. I am
   b. I'ms
   c. I'am

10. I've
   a. I have
   b. I'ves
   c. I'have

11. isn't
   a. isn'ts
   b. is not
   c. is'not

12. let's
   a. lets
   b. let'us
   c. let us

13. mightn't
   a. mightnt
   b. might not
   c. might'not

14. mustn't
   a. mustnt
   b. must'not
   c. must not

10th Grade Art: Henri Matisse

Tip: After you've answered the easy ones, go back and work on the harder ones.

influenced	impressionism	bar	France	masterpiece
rules	appendicitis	modern	emotions	bright

Henri Matisse was born in the north of _____. Henri's father was a grain merchant who was strict

with him. He went to law school in Paris and graduated from there. In 1888, he passed the _____

and began working as a law clerk.

Henri was diagnosed with _____ in 1889. During his recovery, his mother bought him some art

supplies to keep him occupied. He became enamored with painting and art. He decided to pursue a career as an

artist, which made his father extremely dissatisfied. His mother encouraged him to break the _____

of art and experiment with new techniques and paint his _____. He studied art for a year at the

Academie Julian in Paris before leaving to train under the artist Gustave Moreau, where he could experiment with

more _____ painting styles. Matisse met painter John Peter Russell in 1897. Russell introduced him

to _____ and van Gogh's work.

In 1897, Matisse completed his first _____. It was known as The Dinner Table. He continued to

paint, _____ by artists such as Vincent van Gogh and Paul Cezanne. He also studied the works of

J.M.W. Turner and adopted some of Seurat's Pointillism style.

Matisse developed a new style in the early 1900s. He began to paint with _____ masses of freely

applied colors. He used colors to express emotion, often using colors that had nothing to do with the subject's

natural colors. Along with fellow artists Maurice de Vlaminck and Andre Derain, Matisse introduced their new style

to the world in 1905. One critic referred to them as "fauves," which translates as "wild beasts." The name stuck,

and their art style became known as Fauvism.

10th Grade Art: Recycled Art

Recycled art is an unusual but very creative art form in which existing materials are reused and recycled to create works of art. This is in contrast to more traditional art forms in which artists use paint, drawing materials, clay, or other mediums associated with artwork creation. Sometimes the materials used in recycled art are essentially garbage, while other materials are created for a purpose other than art and are being given a new lease on life. Recycled art can be made for several reasons. When people have limited materials to work with, it is often created out of necessity. In other cases, as discussed in this lesson, the materials used in the art are deliberately chosen to challenge viewers' perceptions of what is art, what is trash, and what is beautiful and meaningful. Many recycled art artists use their mediums to convey powerful environmental messages.

There are two types of recycled art: upcycled art and downcycled art. These are two complementary approaches that make use of recycled materials in opposing ways. Upcycled art transforms materials that are typically considered trash into beautiful and meaningful art. This practice is considered more common in the recycled art world because it allows artists to make powerful statements about waste. Upcycled art is created by an artist who creates a portrait out of discarded computer parts that would otherwise end up in a landfill.

Downcycled art is the inverse of upcycled art in that artists deconstruct or destroy objects before transforming them into art. Downcycled art is created by an artist who takes an old armchair and rips the stuffing out of it in an installation piece. While downcycled art exists, it is less common because the goal of recycled art is often to elevate materials that are considered worthless by incorporating them into art.

1. Sometimes the materials used in recycled art are essentially _____.
   a. wood
   b. garbage
   c. luxury items

2. _____ art transforms materials that are typically considered trash into beautiful and meaningful art.
   a. Abstract
   b. Acrylic paint
   c. Upcycled

3. _____ art is the inverse of upcycled art in that artists deconstruct or destroy objects before transforming them into art.
   a. Enamel
   b. Fine art
   c. Downcycled

4. There are two types of recycled art: _____ art and _____ art.
   a. decorative and airbrush
   b. upcycled and downcycled
   c. abstract and recycled

10th Grade Music Vocabulary Crossword

Music has most likely existed for as long as humans have, which could be over a hundred thousand years! The earliest music is thought to have involved singing and clapping, and then early humans began drumming with sticks or other natural objects. Flutes carved from bones, such as bear and woolly mammoth bones, were among the first known musical instruments. Some of these bone instruments date back to 45,000 years!

Scholars agree that there are no 100% reliable methods for determining the exact chronology of musical instruments across cultures. Comparing and organizing instruments based on their complexity is deceptive, because technological advances in musical instruments have sometimes reduced complexity. Early slit drums, for example, required felling and hollowing out large trees; later slit drums were made by opening bamboo stalks, a much simpler task.

Across

1. the distinctive property of a complex sound
2. the speed at which a composition is to be played
3. having or denoting a high range
5. the lowest part of the musical range
7. compatibility in opinion and action

Down

4. an interval during which a recurring sequence occurs
5. hit repeatedly
6. a succession of notes forming a distinctive sequence
8. a strong rod or stick with a specialized utilitarian purpose
10. a brief written record

BASS   BEAT   STAFF
TIMBRE   HARMONY
TREBLE   MELODY   NOTE
RHYTHM   TEMPO

10th Grade Music: Wolfgang Amadeus Mozart

Wolfgang Amadeus Mozart (January 27, 1756 – December 5, 1791; pronounced MOHT-sart) was an Austrian composer, instrumentalist, and music teacher. Johannes Chrysostomus Wolfgangus Theophillus Mozart was his full baptismal name. He was the youngest child of Leopold and Anna Maria Mozart and was born in Salzburg, Austria. The young Mozart displayed exceptional musical talent from an early age. He toured Europe with his parents and older sister "Nannerl," performing for royalty and the aristocratic elite for several years.

Mozart attempted but failed to establish himself as a composer in Paris as a young man. He returned to Salzburg and briefly worked in the Archbishop of Salzburg's court. He was restless, aware of his brilliance, and thought Salzburg was too small for him. He moved to Vienna, where he had some success. He married Constance Weber and had two sons with her.

Mozart composed over 600 musical works, all of which are of the highest quality. The operas, The Marriage of Figaro, Don Giovanni, Cos fan tutte, and The Magic Flute; the symphonies in E-flat major, G minor, and C major ("Jupiter"); concertos for piano, violin, and various wind instruments; and numerous chamber pieces, and the Requiem are among his works. Along with Bach and Beethoven, Mozart is regarded as one of the greatest composers of all time.

There are several stories about Mozart's final illness and death, and it's difficult to know what happened. He was working on The Magic Flute, one of his best works and still a popular opera today. It is written in German rather than Italian, as are the majority of his other operas. It's similar to an English pantomime in some ways. At the same time, he was working on this, he was approached by a stranger and asked to compose a requiem. He was instructed to write this in private. Then he was commissioned to write the Italian opera La Clemenza di Tito, which premiered in Prague in September 1791. The Magic Flute received its first performance at the end of September. The Requiem was then a labor of love for Mozart. He must have realized that he was already gravely ill and that the Requiem (a mass for the dead) was for himself in some ways. He died in Vienna before completing it. Constanze commissioned another composer, Franz Xaver Süssmayr, to complete the work. Mozart was laid to rest in the St. Marx Cemetery.

1. When Mozart returned to Salzburg, he worked in the_____.
   a. Archbishop of Salzburg's court
   b. Salzburg's Music Store
   c. Archbishop High School

2. Mozart was an Austrian _____.
   a. composer, English teacher, singer
   b. science teacher, piano player and composer
   c. composer, instrumentalist, and music teacher

3. Mozart married _____ and had two sons with her.
   a. Constance Weber
   b. Courtney Webber
   c. Countesses Wilson

4. Mozart was laid to rest in the _____.
   a. Mozart family cemetery
   b. Dr. Mary Cemetery
   c. St. Marx Cemetery

10th Grade Spelling Words
Word Scramble

Look carefully at the jumbled words and unscramble the spelling words below.

1. eenegtl   _ _ n _ _ _ l

2. luieedbg   _ _ g _ _ _ e _

3. tramanel   _ _ _ e _ n _ _

4. ucmuevialt   c u _ _ _ _ t _ _ _

5. dandeut   _ _ _ n t _ _

6. lnarabmo   a _ _ _ _ m _ _

7. geossua   _ a _ _ o _ _

8. rirantpiopoap _ p _ _ _ r _ _ i _ _

9. iamlemd   _ i _ _ m _ _

10. lmaedu   m _ u _ _ _

11. iinnutoti   _ n _ _ _ _ i _ _

12. tiuneaecn   _ _ u _ c _ _ _ _

13. ioeaulgd   _ _ _ _ o _ u _

14. orecirtd   c _ _ _ i _ _ _

15. iietdcfne   d _ _ i _ _ _ _ _

16. lntceleie   _ l _ _ _ _ _ e

17. mtoidte   _ m i _ _ _ _

18. inoocslvun   _ _ _ _ u l _ _ _ n

19. ietlxpo   _ x _ l _ _ _

20. roancgi   o _ _ _ n _ _

10th Grade Spelling Words
Multiple Choice Quiz

Circle the best definition meaning for each spelling word provided below.

1. emboss

    a. to design with a sunken or recessed pattern

    b. to decorate with a raised pattern or design

    c. to print a material with flat pattern or design

2. perseverance

    a. the act or power of continuing to do something in spite of difficulties

    b. the act of giving up on something because it is difficult

    c. the act of being uninterested, unenthusiastic, or unconcerned

3. chagrin

    a. a feeling of being safe or protected

    b. a feeling of being annoyed by failure or disappointment

    c. a feeling of being sleepy and lethargic

4. mediocre

    a. not very often

    b. not very effective

    c. not very good

5. frugal

    a. careful, unwavering attention or persistent application

    b. careful in spending or using supplies

    c. careful in spending time and effort

6. benefactor

    a. someone who helps another especially by giving money

    b. someone who helps another find a job

    c. someone who helps another buy a house

7. personnel

    a. a group of kids who are members of a sports club

    b. a group of people employed in a business or an organization

    c. a group of elderly citizens that are members of senior social programs

8. journal

    a. a book in which we collect photographs

    b. a book in which you write down your personal experiences and thoughts

    c. a book in which map are compiled and collected

9. amphitheater

    a. a room built to enable an audience to hear and watch performances

    b. an arena with seats rising in curved rows around an open space

    c. a large room for public meetings or performances

10. horticulture

    a. the science and art of cultivating silkworms to produce silk

    b. the science and art of growing fruits, vegetables, flowers, or ornamental plants

    c. the science and art of cultivating plants and livestock

10th Grade Geometry Reading Comprehension

Score: _____

Date: _____

90-degree	segment	Acute	angles	Obtuse
directions	straight	halves	height	formulas

The study of shapes and space is known as geometry. It provides answers to size, area, and volume questions.

The earliest known geometry works date back to 2000 BC and are from Egypt. There were _____

for lengths, areas, and volumes, as well as one for pyramids. Thales of Miletus calculated the _____ of

pyramids in the 7th century BC, and the Greek mathematician Pythagoras proved the well-known Pythagorean

Theorem.

Euclid, another Greek mathematician, introduced Euclidean geometry around 300 BC by demonstrating how to

prove theorems using basic definitions and truths. We still use Euclidean geometry to prove theorems today.

Geometric terms include points, lines, and _____. A point is a non-dimensional object with no length or

width. A dot is commonly used to represent it. A line is an object that extends in both _____

without end. It is usually depicted with arrowheads to indicate that it continues indefinitely. A line

_____ is a section of a line that has two ends. A ray is one-half of a line with a single endpoint. Two

rays with the same endpoint form an angle. The angle is called a straight angle if the rays are the two

_____ of a single line. A straight angle is analogous to a book open flat on a desk. A right angle is

defined as an angle that is opened half that far.

Angles are expressed in degrees. A right angle is defined as a _____ angle. _____ angles

are those that are less than a right angle. _____ angles are those that are larger than a right angle but

smaller than a _____ angle.

10 Grade Math Algebraic Equation

Score: _____

Date: _____

Algebraic equations are made up of two algebraic expressions that are equal on either side of an equal sign. Constants, variables, and exponents are included, and they are also considered polynomial equations when the exponents are positive whole numbers.

1. An algebraic equation is the same thing as _____ being set equal to one another.
    a. three expressions
    b. 1 algebraic 2 expressions
    c. two algebraic expressions

2. The word equation is related to the word 'equal' meaning that there is___.
    a. an equal sign between the two expressions
    b. an equal sign between the x and y.
    c. an equal sign after y and x.

3. Polynomials are algebraic expressions that are created by ___,
    a. dividing by a variable
    b. combining negative exponents
    c. combining numbers and variables

4. A linear equation is one that usually only has two variables ____.
    a. 'x' and 'y'
    b. 'y' and 'z'
    c. 'x' and 'l'

5. Linear equations will only have ___line when graphed.
    a. two
    b. one
    c. three

6. A quadratic equation is an _____ equation of the second degree.
    a. coefficient
    b. polynomial
    c. quadratic equations

7. Linear equations sometimes can have ___ variables.
    a. zero
    b. only one
    c. one, two or three

8. When solving algebraic equations, the goal is to find out what number the ___ is representing.
    a. variable
    b. expression inside first
    c. figures

9. What type of equation is $-2x + 7 = 4$?
    a. proportional to
    b. linear equation
    c. integers

10. What type of equation is $7x^2 + 5x + 3 = 0$?
    a. cubic equation
    b. positive number
    c. quadratic equation

10th Grade Spelling Words
Word Search

Score: _____

Date: _____

Circle the 20 words listed below. Words appear straight across, back- word straight across, up and down.

V	B	U	E	T	A	R	U	S	N	E	M	M	O	C	E
C	F	P	M	D	R	S	U	O	I	C	A	L	L	A	F
K	D	H	M	S	I	E	E	T	N	E	S	B	A	H	D
A	M	Z	P	Y	S	G	L	J	W	E	G	N	M	A	I
Y	M	C	J	L	L	U	A	B	G	R	C	E	V	U	S
U	E	E	P	W	A	A	O	Z	I	O	J	T	X	V	E
E	D	Y	H	X	J	U	I	H	P	T	A	E	N	C	N
N	E	B	G	T	X	P	S	N	P	A	S	J	B	O	F
C	S	V	W	M	A	P	T	I	N	R	C	E	T	L	R
Y	J	H	S	I	D	N	A	R	B	E	O	H	M	L	A
C	O	N	S	U	L	T	A	N	T	L	I	M	O	O	N
L	N	B	E	L	V	E	D	E	R	E	E	B	A	Q	C
I	D	E	S	U	O	I	T	I	T	C	I	F	V	U	H
C	A	R	C	I	N	O	G	E	N	C	Y	M	F	I	I
A	Q	O	S	D	E	L	I	N	E	A	T	E	R	A	S
L	E	L	B	I	S	S	E	C	C	A	N	I	F	L	E

consultant	inaccessible	fictitious	brandish	plausible
absenteeism	accelerator	amorphous	anathema	belvedere
biennial	carcinogen	colloquial	comestible	commensurate
delineate	disenfranchise	encyclical	fallacious	gazpacho

10th Grade Spelling Test

Score: _____

Date: _____

Encircle the word with the correct spelling.

	A	B	C	D
1.	imperrturbible	imperrturbable	imperturbable	imperturbible
2.	largese	largesce	largece	largesse
3.	narcisus	narcissus	narciscus	narcisos
4.	neofyte	neophytte	neofytte	neophyte
5.	obstetricain	obstetrician	obsstetrician	obsstetricain
6.	elloquent	eloquent	eloqoent	elloqoent
7.	cryptic	criptic	crryptic	crriptic
8.	hypocrite	hypucrite	hypocrrite	hypucrrite
9.	assertive	acertive	ascertive	asertive
10.	parables	paribles	parribles	parrables
11.	assess	asess	asesc	ascess
12.	indisposed	indissposed	indispoused	indisspoused
13.	calloos	caloos	callous	calous
14.	ilustrious	ilustroius	illustrious	illustroius
15.	crredibiliti	credibility	crredibility	credibiliti
16.	allure	allore	alore	aeure
17.	pascive	passive	pasive	pasyve
18.	conscolidate	consolidate	conssolidate	cunsolidate
19.	percepsion	perception	perrception	perrcepsion
20.	obgecttivity	objectivity	objecttivity	obgectivity

TODY IS RESEARCH DAY!   GRADE_____

DATE_____   **RESEARCH: Andrew Jackson**

    Occupation _____

BORN DATE:_____   Nationality_____

DEATH DATE:_____   Education_____   #Children _____

Childhood and Family Background Facts

Work and Career Facts

Children, Marriage and or Significant Relationships

Friends, Social Life and Other Interesting Facts

Did you enjoy researching this person?

Give a Rating: ☆ ☆ ☆ ☆ ☆

TODAY IS RESEARCH DAY!

GRADE_____

DATE_____   RESEARCH: John F. Kennedy

Occupation _____

BORN DATE:_____ Nationality_____

DEATH DATE:_____ Education_____ #Children_____

Childhood and Family Background Facts

Work and Career Facts

Children, Marriage and or Significant Relationships

Friends, Social Life and Other Interesting Facts

Did you enjoy researching this person?

Give a Rating: ☆ ☆ ☆ ☆ ☆

GRADE_____

DATE_____   **RESEARCH: King Arthur**

Occupation _____

BORN DATE:_____   Nationality _____

DEATH DATE:_____   Education _____   #Children _____

Childhood and Family Background Facts

Work and Career Facts

Children, Marriage and or Significant Relationships

Friends, Social Life and Other Interesting Facts

Did you enjoy researching this person?

Give a Rating: ☆ ☆ ☆ ☆ ☆

GRADE_____

DATE_____

RESEARCH: Napoleon Bonaparte

Occupation _____

BORN DATE:_____ Nationality _____

DEATH DATE:_____ Education _____ #Children _____

Childhood and Family Background Facts

Work and Career Facts

Children, Marriage and or Significant Relationships

Friends, Social Life and Other Interesting Facts

Did you enjoy researching this person?

Give a Rating: ☆ ☆ ☆ ☆ ☆

GRADE_____

DATE_____

RESEARCH: Mother Teresa

Occupation _____

BORN DATE:_____ Nationality_____

DEATH DATE:_____ Education _____ #Children _____

Childhood and Family Background Facts

Work and Career Facts

Children, Marriage and or Significant Relationships

Friends, Social Life and Other Interesting Facts

Did you enjoy researching this person?

Give a Rating: ☆ ☆ ☆ ☆ ☆

10th Grade Biology: ANIMAL KINGDOM

Animals are the most numerous and diverse of the five kingdoms of living things. Over two million animal species have been identified so far. All animals share certain characteristics. Animals, unlike plants, obtain their energy from food. They are all made up of many cells, and many animals move quickly. Most reproduce sexually and have sense organs that allow them to respond rapidly to their environment.

Jellyfish, for example, has a relatively simple structure. They lack a skeleton, have few muscles, and move in an uncoordinated manner? They float along with the ocean currents. Jellyfish are classified as invertebrates because, like 98% of all animals, they lack a backbone.

Animals with backbones, such as these zebras, are known as vertebrates. Vertebrates include mammals, birds, fish, amphibians, and reptiles. Zebras are classified as mammals. Mammalian animals, which include humans, are the most complex in the animal kingdom.

1. What are 5 examples of a vertebrate?

2. What are 5 examples of invertebrates?

3. What exactly is a mammal?

4. Amphibians are a class of what cold-blooded vertebrates?

5. Reptiles use a variety of methods to defend themselves such as...

6. What are the 4 types of arthropods?

7. Oviparous animals lay eggs where?

8. An herbivore is an organism that mostly feeds on what?

9. A carnivore is an organism that mostly eats?

10. An omnivore is an organism that eats?

ARTS Vocabulary Terms 1

Choose the best answer to each question.

1	The arrangement of the parts of a work of art.		Binder	A
2	Coarse cloth or heavy fabric that must be stretched and primed to use for painting, particularly for oil paintings.		Chiaroscuro	B
3	The use of found objects or three-dimensional objects to create a work of art.		Assemblage	C
4	Colors next to each other on the color wheel.		Analogous colors	D
5	An arrangement of shapes adhered to a background.		Bisque	E
6	The organization of colors on a wheel. Used to help understand color schemes.		Canvas	F
7	The "glue" the holds pigment together and makes it stick to a surface.		Composition	G
8	Originally the study of beautiful things; currently refers to the study or understanding of anything that is visually pleasing or "works" within the boundaries of the principles of art.		Collagraph	H
9	A print made from a collage of assorted pasted materials such as papers, cardboards, string etc.		Collage	I
10	The art principle which refers to the arrangement of elements in an art work. Can be either formal symmetrical, informal asymmetrical or radial.		Balance	J
11	Italian word for "light-shade". The use and balance of light and shade in a painting, and in particular the use of strong .contrast.		Color wheel	K
12	Clay objects that have been fired one time. (unglazed).		Aesthetics	L

ARTS Vocabulary Terms 2

Choose the best answer to each question.

1	Computer art		Art made on a grand scale, involving the creation of a man-made environment such as architecture, sculpture, light or landscape.	A
2	Diptych		Painting, usually an altarpiece, made up of hinged panels.	B
3	Earth colors		Artwork based on the human form.	C
4	Eye-level		Art made with the use of a computer program.	D
5	Environmental art		Applying gold leaf to a painting or other surface.	E
6	Facade		The horizontal line that distinguishes the sky from the earth, or the ground from the wall. The eye-level of the artists view. Also, where the vanishing point lies in a perspective drawing.	F
7	Figurative		Dried clay forms that have not been fired.	G
8	Foreshortening		Pigments made using earth (dirt) that contain metal oxides mixed with a binder such as glue	H
9	Gilding		The front or face of a building.	I
10	Greenware		A binder used in watercolors made from the gum of an acacia tree.	J
11	Gum Arabic		The artists' view of where the perceived line or perspective came from.	K
12	Horizon line		A rule in perspective to create the illusion of coming forward or receding into space	L

ARTS Vocabulary Terms 3

Choose the best answer to each question.

1	India ink		A movement in the 19th century which bridged the "realist" tradition with the modern movements of the 20th century. The focus was on light and atmosphere.	A
2	Impressionism		A painting either on a wall or on a surface to be attached to a wall.	B
3	Kiln		Design, motif or symbol repeated over and over.	C
4	Linear perspective		French word for "small model". Used particularly by sculptors as a "sketch" of their work.	D
5	Marquette		A waterproof ink made from lampblack.	E
6	Medium		Light and dark tones of a singular color.	F
7	Monochrome		Oil based crayons.	G
8	Mural		Creating the illusion of depth on a picture plane with the use of lines and a vanishing point.	H
9	Newsprint		The surface used to dispense and mix paint on.	I
10	Oil pastel		A large "oven" used for firing clay work.	J
11	Palette		Newspaper stock used for sketching, preliminary drawings and printing.	K
12	Pattern		The process or material used in a work of art.	L

My First Resume

Tip: First, read the entire passage. After that, go back and fill in the blanks. You can skip the blanks you're unsure about and finish them later.

qualifications	potential	improvements	grammatical	freshman
intimidating	leadership	habits	contribute	regular

When you're a high school student, writing a résumé can be _____. The good news is that you probably have more work experience than you realize, even if this is your first résumé. Experiences such as childcare, yard work, and volunteerism all _____ to developing key work skills that companies seek. Simply because you have not held a position similar to the one you are seeking does not indicate you lack the requisite abilities to succeed.

Be sure to include any previous employment, especially if it was for pay. Other than that, you can consist of informal work such as pet sitting, cutting grass, snow shoveling, and any other tasks you've done for money. Although you may not have received a _____ income for your informal employment, your talents and reliability as an employee can still be shown via it.

Given that the majority of teenagers have not held many jobs, it is critical to draw on all elements of your life that prove you possess the attitude, willingness to work hard, competencies, and personality necessary for job success.

Please list any _____ positions you held (for example, a president of an organization or as team captain), as well as any honors or awards you have received. Include a list of your duties and accomplishments under each heading.

Employers are more concerned with your work _____ and attitude than anything else. Nobody expects you to be an expert in your field. When recounting an experience, you might use language to the effect that you have perfect or near-perfect attendance and are on time for school and other commitments.

Employers are looking for employees who have a history of positively impacting the company. Ask yourself whether there are any accomplishments that you can include from your time in school, your clubs, or your employment. Use verbs like "upgraded," "started," and "expanded" to describe what you've done if you want to illustrate what you've accomplished. To demonstrate to _____ employers that you are both bright and ambitious, include any demanding advanced academic assignments on your resume.

Keep it short: Keep it simple (But Include All Necessary Information). A single page is all you need. Contact information and previous work experience are both required in some way on every resume. On the other hand, you can exclude things like a career objective or summary.

Create a narrative. Match your talents and expertise to the job's requirements. For example, in the case of a cashier position, if you've never had a position with that precise title before, emphasize your customer service abilities, aptitude for mathematical calculations, work ethic, and ability to operate as part of a team. Examine the job description and make sure your _____ meet the requirements.

It is also appropriate to add information about your academic achievements, such as participation in organizations and the necessary curriculum you finished while producing a college _____ resume or a resume for a college application. Suppose you're applying for work as a front desk receptionist at a hotel. You could want to include the talents you gained while studying hospitality at a school.

Finally, be sure to double- or even triple-check your resume for typos and _____ errors. You may be tempted to send in your resume as soon as you finish it, but take a few minutes to review it.

As a last resort, ask for a second opinion on your resume from friends, family, or school teachers. Have them go it through to see if there's anything you missed or if you can make any _____.

PRACTICE ONLY

Employers use employment applications like this apart of their hiring process. It tells them about the potential employee.

Applicant

Name: Date:

Referral: Phone No.

Fax No.   Email:

Address:

Are You…

A U.S. Citizen?	☐ Yes	☐ No
Over 18 years old?	☐ Yes	☐ No
Licensed to drive?	☐ Yes	☐ No

Employment

Position: Department:

Type: ☐ Full-Time   ☐ Part-Time   ☐ Other (Seasonal/Temp):

Start Date: Starting Salary:

Current Employment: May we contact? ☐ Yes   ☐ No

Education History

Education	School	Location	Years	Graduated?	Degree(s)
High School					
College					
Graduate					
Other Training/Classes:					
Workshops/Certifications:					

Employment History

Employer	Address	Position	Dates	Reason for Leaving

References

Reference	Relationship	Phone	Email	Address

Applicant Signature   Date

Financial: Taxes

Tip: First, read the entire passage. After that, go back and fill in the blanks. You can skip the blanks you're unsure about and finish them later.

local	textbooks	public	fund	added
taxation	centuries	reside	compensation	construction

Every citizen pays taxes to the government to _____ critical services.

Have you ever been curious about how schools and parks are constructed? Or who is responsible for funding and maintaining roads? In a nutshell, you are! That is if you are of tax-paying age. The government uses taxes to raise funds for _____ services such as schools and roads.

Taxation has existed for _____, dating back to the earliest human civilizations. Animals or goods were used as tax payments in ancient Mesopotamia because the concept of paper money had not yet been developed. Over time, different types of money were made, and taxes were still being collected, but differently.

Consider the following scenario: you've just landed a fantastic job working at a video game store. You are aware that you earn $10 an hour and work ten hours per week after school. Because you're a math whiz, you're aware that 10 x 10 equals 100. Therefore, your initial _____ should be $100, correct? Sadly, you won't get $100 because the federal and state governments take a percentage of your earnings as tax.

So, you've got a great job, and you'd like to buy a car or a house when you're older. What do you imagine will happen? Automobiles and homes, too, are subject to _____. This is referred to as property tax, and it is frequently paid to local governments, such as the county in which you _____. Once you own a home, you are responsible for paying property taxes on it each year until you sell it.

Sales taxes are another method by which states and municipalities collect tax revenue. This means that when you purchase an item in a store or online, an additional charge in the form of a tax is _____. Different categories of goods are taxed differently, and the proceeds benefit the state and _____ governments.

While there may be numerous taxes, consider for a moment all of the public goods that taxes support. What about your educational institution? Taxes cover the cost of _____, desks, and even the building itself. What about your favorite teacher? They are compensated monthly with tax dollars. Taxes also fund the _____ and maintenance of roads and bridges, the employment of police officers to protect neighborhoods, and the operation of some parks and museums.

Geography: Time Zones

Score: _____

Date: _____

First, go over the entire message. Then go back and fill in the blanks. You can skip the blanks you're unsure about and come back to them later.

different	outside	message	shines	classmate
exist	clocks	time	ball	day

Have you ever tried to call or send a _____ to someone who was on the other side of the country or the world? It can be tough to reach a faraway location from you because the time of _____ may be different from your own. The purpose of time zones and why we have them will be discussed in this session.

Kim, Mike's _____ who recently relocated across the country, is texting him. After a short time, Kim sends Mike a text message saying that it is time for her to go to sleep for the night. The sun is beaming brightly _____, and Mike is confused about why Kim would choose this time of day to go to sleep. 'Can you tell me what _____ it is, please?' Mike asked. 'It's 9:00 p.m. now!' Kim replies.

What exactly is going on here? Was Mike able to travel back in time in some way?

What is happening to Mike and Kim is nothing more than a natural occurrence that occurs on our planet daily. Since Kim relocated across the country, she is now in a _____ time zone than she was previously.

A time zone is a geographical location on the planet with a fixed time that all citizens can observe by setting their _____ to that time. As you go from east to west (or west to east) on the globe's surface, you will encounter different time zones. The greater the distance traveled, the greater the number of time zones crossed.

Time zones are not something that arises in nature by chance. Humans created the concept of time zones and determined which regions of the world are located in which time zones.

Because of time zones, everyone experiences the same pattern of dawn in the early morning and sunset in the late afternoon. We require time zones because the earth is shaped like a _____ and therefore requires them. As the sun beams down on the planet, not every location receives the same amount of sunshine. The sun _____ on one side of the earth and brightens it during the day, while the other side is dark during the night (nighttime). If time zones didn't _____, many people worldwide would experience quite strange sunshine patterns during the day if there were no time zones.

One key skill that everyone should be able to perform is determining whether a location on earth is in a later or earlier time zone than they are. The general guideline is as follows:

If your friend lives in a location that is west of you, they are in a different time zone than you. If they live in a time zone later than yours, they are located east of you.

West is considered to be earlier, whereas the east is considered later.

The following are the primary time zones in the United States:
Eastern (New York, Georgia, Ohio, and other east coast states)
Central (Alabama, Iowa, Minnesota, and more)
Mountain (Arizona, Montana, Utah, and more)
Pacific (California, Nevada, and other west coast states)

Science: Albert Einstein

First, read the entire passage. After that, go back and fill in the blanks. You can skip the blanks you're unsure about and finish them later.

mathematics	boat	Nobel	overnight	top
experiment	paper	books	Germany	failed
pocket	marriage	missed	socks	door

Albert Einstein was born in _____ on March 14, 1879. Because he was Jewish, he fled to the United States to avoid Hitler and the Second World War.

When his grandmother first saw him, she said he was stupid! Little did she know!

He apparently didn't speak until he was four years old, and even then, he would repeat words and sentences until he was seven.

His father gave him a simple _____ compass when he was about five years old, and it quickly became his favorite toy!

He became obsessed with magnetism, which is basically all about magnets and how they work, from that day forward.

Young Einstein didn't like the way his grammar school taught him. He also wasn't particularly fond of authority. As a result, he was expelled from school quite a few times.

He developed an interest in _____ and science at the age of seven.

When Einstein was about ten years old, a much older friend gave him a large stack of science, mathematics, and philosophy _____.

He'd published his first scientific _____ by the age of sixteen. That is absolutely incredible!

Numerous reports have shown that Einstein _____ math in school, but his family has stated that this is not the case. They claimed he was always at the _____ of his class in math and could solve some challenging problems. He was obsessed with geometry and algebra, and no one taught him anything – he taught himself! He was also constantly attempting to prove various mathematical theories on his own.

Yes, he was brilliant.

Although he was not a top student in every subject in school, he certainly made up for it when he and his family moved to Switzerland when he was older.

He began teaching math and physics in 1900.

Einstein was a little disorganized. So, if you're feeling the same way, don't despair; there is still hope!

As an adult, he frequently _____ appointments, and because his mind was all over the place, his lectures were a little difficult to understand.

He didn't wear _____ and had uncombed hair! Even at posh dinners, he'd arrive unkempt, with crumpled clothes and, of course, no socks!

Despite the fact that he was all over the place, a little shabby, and a little difficult to understand, he rocked the world with his Theory of Relativity in 1915. An _____ in 1919 proved the theory correct. He became famous almost _____, and he suddenly received invitations to travel worldwide, as well as honors from all over the world!

In 1921, he was awarded the _____ Prize for Physics. He'd come a long way from the boy who was told he'd never amount to anything!

Today, his other discoveries enabled us to have things like garage _____ openers, televisions, and DVD players. Time magazine named him "Person of the Century" in 1999.

One of his favorite activities was to take a _____ out on a lake and take his notebook with him to think and write everything down. Perhaps this is what inspired him to create his inventions!

Einstein's first _____ produced two sons. His daughter, Lierserl, is believed to have died when she was young. He married twice, and she died before him.

On April 18, 1955, the great scientist died in America.

Government History: How Laws Are Made

Congress is the federal government's legislative branch, and it is in charge of making laws for the entire country. Congress is divided into two legislative chambers: the United States Senate and the United States House of Representatives. Anyone elected to either body has the authority to propose new legislation. A bill is a new law proposal.

People living in the United States and its territories are subject to federal laws.

Bills are created and passed by Congress. The president may then sign the bills into law. Federal courts may examine the laws to see if they are in accordance with the Constitution. If a court finds a law to be unconstitutional, it has the authority to overturn it.

The United States government has enacted several laws to help maintain order and protect the country's people. Each new law must be approved by both houses of Congress as well as the President. Before it becomes a new law in the nation, each law must go through a specific process.

The majority of laws in the United States begin as bills. An idea is the starting point for a bill. That thought could come from anyone, including you! The idea must then be written down and explained as the next step. A bill is the name given to the first draft of an idea. The bill must then be sponsored by a member of Congress. The sponsor is someone who strongly supports the bill and wishes to see it become law. A Senator or a member of the House of Representatives can be the sponsor.

The bill is then introduced in either the House or the Senate by the bill's sponsor. Once submitted, the bill is given a number and is officially recorded as a bill.

The bill is assigned to a committee after it is introduced. Committees are smaller groups of congress members who are experts in specific areas. For example, if the bill concerns classroom size in public schools, it would be referred to the Committee on Education. The committee goes over the bill's specifics. They bring in experts from outside Congress to testify and debate the bill's pros and cons.

The committee may decide to make changes to the bill before it is passed. If the committee finally agrees to pass the bill, it will be sent to the House or Senate's main chamber for approval.

If the bill was introduced in the House, it would first be considered by the House. The bill will be discussed and debated by the representatives. House members will then vote on the bill. If the bill is passed, it will be sent to the Senate for consideration.

The Senate will then follow the same procedure. It will discuss and debate the bill before voting. If the Senate approves the bill, it will be sent to the President.

The President's signature is the final step in a bill becoming law. When the President signs the bill, it becomes law.

The President has the option of refusing to sign the bill. This is known as a veto. The Senate and House can choose to override the President's veto by voting again. The bill must now be approved by a two-thirds majority in both the Senate and the House to override the veto.

A bill must be signed into law by the President within 10-days. If he does not sign it within 10-days, one of two things may occur:

1) It will become law if Congress is in session.

2) It will be considered vetoed if Congress is not in session (this is called a pocket veto).

1. If the Senate approves the bill, it will be sent to the ____.
   a. President
   b. House Representee

2. The _____ may decide to make changes to the bill before it is passed.
   a. governor
   b. committee

3. The bill must then be _____ by a member of Congress.
   a. signed
   b. sponsored

4. The President has the option of refusing to sign the bill. This is known as a ___.
   a. voted
   b. veto

5. **The Senate and House can choose to override the President's veto by ____again.**
   a. creating a new bill
   b. voting

6. **The bill is assigned to a committee after it is _____.**
   a. introduced
   b. vetoed

7. **Bills are created and passed by ____.**
   a. The House
   b. Congress

8. **A bill must be signed into law by the President within ___-days.**
   a. 10
   b. 5

9. **The President's ____ is the final step in a bill becoming law.**
   a. signature
   b. saying yes

10. **If the committee agrees to pass the bill, it will be sent to the House or Senate's main ___ for approval.**
    a. chamber
    b. state

Extra Credit: What are some of the weirdest laws in the world? List at least 5.

....

....

....

....

....

....

....

....

....

....

....

....

....

....

....

....

....

TODD IS RESEARCH DAY!

GRADE_____

DATE_____ RESEARCH: Warren Buffett

Occupation _____

BORN DATE: _____ Nationality_____

DEATH DATE: _____ Education _____ #Children _____

Childhood and Family Background Facts

Work and Career Facts

Children, Marriage and or Significant Relationships

Friends, Social Life and Other Interesting Facts

Did you enjoy researching this person?

Give a Rating: ☆ ☆ ☆ ☆ ☆

GRADE_____

DATE_____

RESEARCH: Nelson Mandela

Occupation _____

BORN DATE: _____ Nationality _____

DEATH DATE: _____ Education _____ #Children _____

Childhood and Family Background Facts

Work and Career Facts

Children, Marriage and or Significant Relationships

Friends, Social Life and Other Interesting Facts

Did you enjoy researching this person?

Give a Rating: ☆ ☆ ☆ ☆ ☆

GRADE_____

DATE_____

RESEARCH: Ruth Bader Ginsburg

Occupation _____

BORN DATE:_____ Nationality_____

DEATH DATE:_____ Education _____ #Children _____

Childhood and Family Background Facts

Work and Career Facts

Children, Marriage and or Significant Relationships

Friends, Social Life and Other Interesting Facts

Did you enjoy researching this person?

Give a Rating: ☆ ☆ ☆ ☆ ☆

GRADE_____

DATE_____

RESEARCH: Wild Bill Hickok

Occupation _____

BORN DATE:_____   Nationality _____

DEATH DATE:_____   Education _____   #Children _____

Childhood and Family Background Facts

Work and Career Facts

Children, Marriage and or Significant Relationships

Friends, Social Life and Other Interesting Facts

Did you enjoy researching this person?

Give a Rating: ☆ ☆ ☆ ☆ ☆

GRADE_____

DATE_____   **RESEARCH: Davy Crockett**

Occupation _____

BORN DATE:_____   Nationality _____

DEATH DATE:_____   Education _____   #Children _____

Childhood and Family Background Facts

Work and Career Facts

Children, Marriage and or Significant Relationships

Friends, Social Life and Other Interesting Facts

Did you enjoy researching this person?

Give a Rating: ☆ ☆ ☆ ☆ ☆

GRADE_____

DATE_____

RESEARCH: William Cullen

Occupation _____

BORN DATE: _____ Nationality _____

DEATH DATE: _____ Education _____ #Children _____

Childhood and Family Background Facts

Work and Career Facts

Children, Marriage and or Significant Relationships

Friends, Social Life and Other Interesting Facts

Did you enjoy researching this person?

Give a Rating: ☆ ☆ ☆ ☆ ☆

History: United States Armed Forces

The President of the United States is the Commander in Chief of the United States Armed Forces.

The United States, like many other countries, maintains a military to safeguard its borders and interests. The military has played an essential role in the formation and history of the United States since the Revolutionary War.

The **United States Department of Defense** (DoD) is in charge of controlling each branch of the military, except the United States Coast Guard, which is under the control of the Department of Homeland Security.

The Department of Defense is the world's largest 'company,' employing over 2 million civilians and military personnel.

The United States military is divided into six branches: the Air Force, Army, Coast Guard, Marine Corps, Navy, and Space Force.

The mission of the **United States Air Force** is to defend the country from outside forces. They also provide air support to other branches of the military, such as the Army and Navy.

The **United States Army** is responsible for defending against aggression that threatens the peace and security of the United States.

There are **Army National Guard** units in all 50 states, which their respective governments govern. The Constitution requires only one branch of the military. Members of the National Guard volunteer some of their time to keep the peace. They are not full-time soldiers, but they respond when called upon, for example, to quell violence when the police need assistance.

The primary concern of **the United States Coast Guard** is to protect domestic waterways (lakes, rivers, ports, etc.). The Coast Guard is managed by the United States Department of Homeland Security.

The **Marines** are a quick-response force. They are prepared to fight on both land and sea. The Marine Corps is a branch of the United States Navy. The Marine Corps conducts operations onboard warfare ships all over the world.

The **United States Navy** conducts its missions at sea to secure and protect the world's oceans. Their mission is to ensure safe sea travel and trade.

The **United States Space Force** is the newest branch of the military, established in December 2019. The world's first and currently only independent space force. It is in charge of operating and defending military satellites and ground stations that provide communications, navigation, and Earth observation, such as missile launch detection.

1. The United States military is divided into ___ branches.
    a. six
    b. five

2. _____ is managed by the United States Department of Homeland Security.
    a. The National Guard
    b. The Coast Guard

3. The _____ of the United States is the Commander in Chief of the United States Armed Forces.
    a. Governor
    b. President

4. The United States maintains a military to safeguard its _____ and interests.
    a. borders
    b. cities

5. DoD is in charge of controlling each _____ of the military.
    a. branch
    b. army

6. The Marines are prepared to fight on both land and ____.
    a. battlefield
    b. sea

7. The United States Space Force is in charge of operating and defending military _____ and ground stations.
    a. soldiers
    b. satellites

8. The mission of the _____ is to defend the country from outside forces.
    a. United States DoD Forces
    b. United States Air Force

9. There are _____ units in all 50 states.
   a. Army National Guard
   b. Armed Nations Guard

10. The United States Navy conducts its missions at sea to secure and protect the world's _____.
    a. oceans
    b. borders

11. The primary concern of the United States Coast Guard is to protect_____.
    a. domestic waterways
    b. domesticated cities

12. The United States military is: the Amy Force, Army, Coast Guard, Mario Corps, Old Navy, and Space Force.
    a. True
    b. False

Extra Credit: Has America ever been invaded?

_____

_____

_____

_____

_____

_____

_____

_____

_____

_____

_____

_____

_____

_____

_____

_____

Science: Water Cycle

On stormy days, water falls to the earth. The ground absorbs it. The movement of water is a component of the water cycle. The water cycle is critical to all living things on the planet!

Other cycles exist in your life. Your daily routine is a cycle that begins with you waking up. You attend classes. You take the bus back home. You leave for soccer practice. You eat your dinner. You retire to your bed. These occurrences are part of a cycle. Every weekday, this cycle is repeated. The water cycle is also a series of repeated events that occur repeatedly.

The water cycle is comprised of repeated events such as evaporation, condensation, precipitation, and collection. These occurrences occur regularly.

- Evaporation occurs when water is heated and turns into a gas.
- Condensation occurs when a gas of water cools and condenses back into a liquid.
- Precipitation occurs when water returns to the earth.
- Water is collected when stored in bodies of water such as lakes, rivers, oceans, soil, and rocks.

Observing the water cycle is a good way to see how water moves around the Earth and atmosphere on a daily basis. It is a complicated system with numerous processes. Liquid water evaporates into water vapor, condenses into clouds, and falls back to earth as rain and snow. Water in various phases circulates through the atmosphere (transportation). Runoff is the movement of liquid water across land, into the ground (infiltration and percolation), and through the ground (groundwater). Groundwater moves into plants (plant uptake) and evaporates into the atmosphere from plants (transpiration). Solid ice and snow can spontaneously decompose into gas (sublimation). When water vapor solidifies, the opposite can occur (deposition).

_____

Use the word bank to unscramble the words below.

molecule	pollutant	evaporation	radiation	groundwater	oceans
infiltration	nitrogen	deposition	environment	collection	sublimation
transpiration	hydrogen	condensation	organism	precipitation	oxygen
meltwater	movement	vapor	droplet	iceberg	weather
rainwater	glacier				

1. NMSALIITBOU   s u _ l _ _ _ _ _ _

2. IARTASRPONTIN   _ r _ _ _ _ _ _ _ _ i _ n

3. OMLLECUE   _ o _ e _ _ _ _

4. NEIRAVOTAOP   _ v _ _ _ _ a _ i _ _

5. ALEIGCR   _ l _ _ _ _ r

6. TONOINSNCEDA   c _ _ _ _ n s _ _ _ _ _

7. DARRWOGENTU   _ r o _ _ _ _ _ _ _ r

8. TUNLOPLAT   _ _ _ l _ _ n _

9. EPITITARINCPO   _ _ _ c _ _ _ t _ _ i _ _

10. ITNIOILRNFAT   _ n _ _ _ t _ _ _ _ o _

11. ODRLPET   _ r _ _ _ e _

12. NIEDTSOPIO   _ _ _ o _ _ t i _ _

13. WTAEERH   _ _ _ _ h _ r

14. EONNTIGR   n _ _ _ o _ _ _

15. RWANTREAI   r _ _ _ _ _ _ _ r

16. REBGICE   i _ e _ _ _ _

17. TNOAIADRI   _ _ _ _ a _ i _ _

18. EOXNGY   _ x y _ _ _

19. SGOMRNIA   _ _ g _ _ _ _ m

20. YNEDRHOG   _ _ _ r o _ _ _

21. EARTLWTME   _ _ _ _ _ a _ e _

22. COTNCLEOLI   _ o _ _ e _ t _ _ _

23. PAROV   v _ _ _ _

24. NEVOEMTM   _ _ _ _ _ e _ t

25. ORENINTNVEM   e n v _ _ _ _ _ _ _ _

26. OCSANE   _ c _ _ n _

Extra Credit: What is the process of the water cycle?

....

....

....

....

Prevent Food Poisoning

Tip: First, read the entire passage. After that, go back and fill in the blanks. You can skip the blanks you're unsure about and finish them later.

contaminated	digestive	electrolytes	pink	temperature
abdominal	spread	brush	hospitalizes	bloody

Did you know that approximately 1 in every 6 Americans will contract food poisoning this year? Food poisoning not only _____ 128,000 Americans each year, but it can also result in long-term health problems.

In general, a foodborne illness is defined as an infection of the _____ system caused by consuming food or beverages contaminated with harmful bacteria, parasites, or viruses. Disease-causing microorganisms are waiting for the right moment to get into your food. There are more than 200 of them. Salmonella, E. coli, and Listeria are three of the most common. Vomiting, diarrhea, _____ pain, fever, and chills are all symptoms of foodborne illnesses. Most foodborne illnesses are short-lived, meaning they come on quickly and last for only a few days.

At any point before consumption, your food can become _____ with dangerous microorganisms. The best way to avoid getting a foodborne illness is to store, cook and clean food properly.

Refrigerate or freeze perishable raw and cooked foods promptly. Make sure your refrigerator is set to the correct _____ to ensure proper storage. It's best to thaw frozen food in the refrigerator or microwave and then cook it right away.

Seafood, eggs, poultry, and meat should be cooked all the way through. Ensure that the juices from meat and poultry are clear, not _____. A meat thermometer can be used to check the internal temperature of foods. Boiling is a good idea for things like soups and stews.

Before eating, cutting, or cooking, wash fruits and vegetables under running water. If you want to clean fruits and vegetables with hard skin, you can use a produce _____. Hands should be washed in warm, soapy water for at least 20 seconds. It would help if you washed your hands before and after handling raw meats and poultry and after using the bathroom, changing diapers, or interacting with animals to prevent the _____ of bacteria. Before and after use, wash utensils and surfaces with hot, soapy water.

The majority of people recover completely from mild cases of foodborne illness. For mild foodborne illnesses, rehydrating and replenishing _____ like sodium, potassium, and chloride are the most common treatment. Anti-diarrhea medications are available over the counter. On the other hand, these medications should not be used if you have _____ diarrhea, as they may prolong your infection. If your symptoms persist for more than three days, you should seek medical attention.

Grammar: Adjectives Matching

Score: _____

Date: _____

Adjectives are words that describe people, places, and things, or nouns. Adjectives are words that describe sounds, shapes, sizes, times, numbers/quantity, textures/touch, and weather. You can remember this by saying to yourself, "an adjective adds something."

If you need to describe a friend or an adult, you can use words that describe their appearance, size, or age. When possible, try to use positive words that describe a person.

1	☐	disappointed		nothing frightens him/her	A
2	☐	anxious		everything is in order around him	B
3	☐	delighted		very pleased	C
4	☐	terrified		always arrives in time	D
5	☐	ashamed		loves being with people	E
6	☐	envious		very surprised and upset	F
7	☐	proud		very frightened	G
8	☐	shocked		wanting something another person has	H
9	☐	brave		feeling bad because you did sg wrong	I
10	☐	hard-working		uprightness and fairness	J
11	☐	organized		worried	K
12	☐	punctual		has 2 or more jobs	L
13	☐	honest		always supports his friends	M
14	☐	outgoing		feeling pleased and satisfied	N
15	☐	loyal		sad because something is worse than expected	O
16	☐	reliable		one can always count on him	P

Math: Arithmetic Refresher

Score: _____

Date: _____

Select the best answer for each question.

1. Use division to calculate 6/3. The answer is _____.
    a. 2
    b. 4
    c. 3.5

2. Fill in the blank 2 + √5 _____ 7 - √10
    a. >
    b. ≤
    c. ≥

3. Use division to calculate 50/10. The answer is _____.
    a. 5.5
    b. 8
    c. 5

4. Which family of numbers begins with the numbers 0, 1, 2, 3, ...?
    a. Integers
    b. Whole numbers
    c. Rational numbers

5. Use division to calculate 7/4. The answer is _____.
    a. 2 R4
    b. 1.5
    c. 1 R3

6. Which of the answer choices is an INCORRECT statement?
    a. 0 > -1
    b. -2 < -4
    c. 32 < -25x

7. Simplify: 7 * 5 - 2 + 11
    a. 44
    b. 23
    c. 21

8. -18 + (-11) = ?
    a. 28
    b. 32
    c. -29

9. 16 - (-7) = ?
    a. 20
    b. 23
    c. 19

10. -12 - (-9) = ?
    a. -3
    b.

11. Simplify: 37 - [5 + {28 - (19 - 7)}]
    a. 16
    b. 36
    c. 46

12. The numbers 1, 2, 3, 4, 5, 6, 7, 8, ..., i.e. natural numbers, are called____.
    a. Positive integers
    b. Rational integers
    c. Simplify numbers

13. _____ is the number you are dividing by.
    a. divisor
    b. equation
    c. dividend

14. _____ is the leftover amount when dividend doesn't divide equally.
    a. remainder
    b. quotient
    c. dividend

Math: Decimals Place Value

Our basic number system is decimals. The decimal system is built around the number ten. It is sometimes referred to as a base-10 number system. Other systems use different base numbers, such as binary numbers, which use base-2.

The place value is one of the first concepts to grasp when learning about decimals. The position of a digit in a number is represented by its place value. It determines the value of the number.

When the numbers 800, 80, and 8 are compared, the digit "8" has a different value depending on its position within the number.

8 - ones place
80 - tens place
800 - hundreds place

The value of the number is determined by the 8's place value. The value of the number increases by ten times as the location moves to the left.

Select the best answer for each question.

1. Which of the following is a decimal number?
   a. 1,852
   b. 1.123
   c. 15

2. For the number 125.928, what is in the tenths place?
   a. 9
   b. 2
   c. 5

3. For the number 359, which number is in the tens place?
   a. 3
   b. 5
   c. 9

4. Write the number 789.1 as an addition problem.
   a. 70 + 800 + 90 + 1
   b. 700 + 80 + 9 + 1 / 10
   c. 700 + 80 + 9+10

5. When we say 7 is in the hundreds place in the number 700, this is the same as 7x102.n.
   a. True
   b. False

6. For the number 2.14, what digit is in the hundredths place?
   a. 4
   b. 1
   c. 2

7. When you start to do arithmetic with decimals, it will be important to_____ properly.
   a. line up the numbers
   b. line up all like numbers
   c. line up numbers ending in 0

8. Depending upon the position of a digit in a number, it has a value called its_____.
   a. tenth place
   b. decimals place
   c. place value

9. The place value of the digit 6 in the number 1673 is 600 as 6 is in the hundreds place.
   a. True
   b. False

10. What is the place value of the digits 2 and 4 in the number 326.471?
    a. 2 is in the tens place. 4 is in the tenths place.
    b. 2 is in the tenths place. 4 is in the tens place.
    c. 2 is in the ones place. 4 is in the tenths place.

Math: Roman Numerals

The Ancient Romans used Roman numerals as their numbering system. We still use them every now and then. They can be found in the Super Bowl's numbering system, after king's names (King Henry IV), in outlines, and elsewhere. Roman numerals are base 10 or decimal numbers, just like the ones we use today. However, they are not entirely positional, and there is no number zero.

Roman numerals use letters rather than numbers. You must know the following seven letters:

I = 1

V = 5

X = 10

L = 50

C = 100

D = 500

M = 1000

Select the best answer for each question.

1. III = ___
   a. 33
   b. 30
   c. 3

2. XVI=___
   a. 60
   b. 61
   c. 16

3. IV = 5 - 1 =____
   a. 40
   b. 4
   c. 14

4. What number does the Roman numeral LXXIV represent?
   a. 79
   b. 74
   c. 70

5. Which of the following is the Roman numeral for the number 5?
   a. IV
   b. VI
   c. V

6. How many of the same letters can you put in a row in Roman numerals?
   a. 4 or more
   b. 3
   c. 2

7. Which of the following is the Roman numeral for the number 10?
   a. X
   b. IX
   c. XXI

8. What is the Roman numeral for 33?
   a. XXXIII
   b. XIII
   c. XVIII

9. Which of the following is the Roman numeral for the number 50?
   a. X
   b. L
   c. I

10. Which of the following is the Roman numeral for the number 100?
   a. C
   b. IVV
   c. LII

Nutrition: Reading Labels

Score: _____

Date: _____

Reading food labels can assist you in making educated food choices. Packaged foods and beverages—those in cans, boxes, bottles, jars, and bags—include extensive nutritional and food safety information on their labels or packaging. Keep an eye out for these items on the food label.

On certain foods you purchase, you may notice one of three types of product dates:

"Sell by" indicates how long the manufacturer recommends a store keep foods such as meat, poultry, eggs, or milk products on the shelf—buy them before this date.

The "use by" date indicates how long the food will remain fresh—if you purchase or consume it after that date, some foods may become stale or less tasty.

"Best if used by" (or "best if used before") indicates how long the food will retain its best flavor or quality—it does not suggest a purchase date.

The Food and Drug Administration (FDA) of the United States requires that most packaged foods and beverages bear a Nutrition Facts label. The total number of servings in the container and the food or beverage serving size are listed at the top of the Nutrition Facts label. The serving size indicated on the label is based on the amount of food that most people consume at one time and is not intended to be a guideline for how much to consume.

With permission, read the labels on the containers and answer the questions for each food item. If you do not have any of those items in your home, feel free to find the item online and use that to reference.

Egg carton

1. What store or farm are they from?

_____

2. Are the eggs free range?

_____

3. Where are the eggs produced or brand?

_____

4. When is the best before date?

_____

5. What is the display date if any?

6. How many calories?

7. Can you recycle the egg carton?

8. How much protein?

9. Should I keep the eggs in the fridge?

10. How many eggs were in the carton?

Water Bottle

1. What store is the water from and brand?

2. Does the water contains sodium? If so, how much?

3. What is the percent daily value?

4. Can I recycle the bottle?

5. What telephone number should I call if I have a problem?

6. What is the serving size?

7. How many days do I have to drink the water?

Milk

1. Which store does the milk come from and the brand name?

2. How many pints are in the milk?

3. The milk is ___ _____. A. **Semi-skimmed milk** B. **Whole Milk** C. **Half milk**

4. How much calcium is there?

5. When is the use-by date?

Juice

1. What store is the juice from?

2. How many **ml** are in one bottle?

3. Can I recycle the bottle?

4. What color is the bottle?

5. Should I keep the juice in the fridge?

TODAY IS RESEARCH DAY!   GRADE_____

DATE_____   **RESEARCH: Sally Ride**

Occupation _____

BORN DATE:_____   Nationality_____

DEATH DATE:_____   Education _____   #Children _____

Childhood and Family Background Facts

Work and Career Facts

Children, Marriage and or Significant Relationships

Friends, Social Life and Other Interesting Facts

Did you enjoy researching this person?

Give a Rating: ☆ ☆ ☆ ☆ ☆

TODAY IS RESEARCH DAY!   GRADE_____

DATE_____   **RESEARCH: Eli Whitney**

Occupation _____

BORN DATE:_____   Nationality_____

DEATH DATE:_____   Education_____   #Children_____

Childhood and Family Background Facts

Work and Career Facts

Children, Marriage and or Significant Relationships

Friends, Social Life and Other Interesting Facts

Did you enjoy researching this person?

Give a Rating: ☆ ☆ ☆ ☆ ☆

TODY IS RESEARCH DAY!   GRADE_____

DATE_____   RESEARCH: Nellie Bly

      Occupation _____

BORN DATE:_____ Nationality_____

DEATH DATE:_____ Education _____ #Children _____

Childhood and Family Background Facts

Work and Career Facts

Children, Marriage and or Significant Relationships

Friends, Social Life and Other Interesting Facts

Did you enjoy researching this person?

Give a Rating: ☆ ☆ ☆ ☆ ☆

TODAY IS RESEARCH DAY!   GRADE_____

DATE_____   **RESEARCH: Pope John Paul II**

    Occupation _____

BORN DATE:_____   Nationality _____

DEATH DATE:_____   Education _____   #Children _____

Childhood and Family Background Facts

Work and Career Facts

Children, Marriage and or Significant Relationships

Friends, Social Life and Other Interesting Facts

Did you enjoy researching this person?

Give a Rating: ☆ ☆ ☆ ☆ ☆

TODAY IS RESEARCH DAY!   GRADE_____

DATE_____   **RESEARCH: Nikola Tesla**

Occupation _____

BORN DATE:_____ Nationality_____

DEATH DATE:_____ Education _____ #Children _____

Childhood and Family Background Facts

Work and Career Facts

Children, Marriage and or Significant Relationships

Friends, Social Life and Other Interesting Facts

Did you enjoy researching this person?

Give a Rating: ☆ ☆ ☆ ☆ ☆

Social Skill Interests: Things To Do

A **hobby** is something that a person actively pursues relaxation and enjoyment. On the other hand, a person may have an **interest** in something because they are curious or concerned. Hobbies usually do not provide monetary compensation. However, a person's interests can vary and may lead to earning money or making a living from them. Hobbies are typically pursued in one's spare time or when one is not required to work. Interests can be followed in one's spare time or while working, as in the case of using one's passion as a source of income. A hobby can be a recreational activity that is done regularly in one's spare time. It primarily consists of participating in sports, collecting items and objects, engaging in creative and artistic pursuits, etc. The desire to learn or understand something is referred to as interest. If a person has a strong interest in a subject, he or she may pursue it as a hobby. However, an interest is not always a hobby. Hobbies such as stamp and flower collecting may not be a source of income for a person, but the items collected can sometimes be sold. Hobbies frequently lead to discoveries and inventions. Interests could be a source of income or something done for free. If a person is interested in cooking or enjoys creating dishes, he can do so at home or make it a career by becoming a chef.

_____

Put the words in the correct category.

pottery	card making	candle making	reading	weaving	knitting
gym	jewellery	chess	surfing	computer games	collecting
woodwork	Soccer	art	swimming	cooking	skateboarding
embroidery	skiing	gardening	writing	chatting	sewing
netball	stamp collecting	football	music	rugby	basketball

Sport (10)	Handcrafts (10)	Interests (10)

Health: Check Your Symptoms

Healthy habits aid in the development of happy and healthy children as well as the prevention of future health issues such as diabetes, hypertension, high cholesterol, heart disease, and cancer.

Chronic diseases and long-term illnesses can be avoided by leading a healthy lifestyle. Self-esteem and self-image are aided by feeling good about yourself and taking care of your health.

Maintain a consistent exercise schedule.

No, you don't have to push yourself to go to the gym and do tough workouts, but you should be as active as possible. You can maintain moving by doing simple floor exercises, swimming, or walking. You can also remain moving by doing some domestic chores around the house.

What matters is that you continue to exercise. At least three to five times a week, devote at least twenty to thirty minutes to exercise. Establish a regimen and make sure you get adequate physical activity each day.

Be mindful of your eating habits.

You must continue to eat healthily in order to maintain a healthy lifestyle. Eat more fruits and vegetables and have fewer carbs, salt, and harmful fat in your diet. Don't eat junk food or sweets.

Avoid skipping meals since your body will crave more food once you resume eating. Keep in mind that you should burn more calories than you consume.

1. I've got a pain in my head.
   a. Stiff neck
   b. headache

2. I was out in the sun too long.
   a. Sunburn
   b. Fever

3. I've got a small itchy lump or bump.
   a. Rash
   b. Insect bite

4. I might be having a heart attack.
   a. Cramps
   b. Chest pain

5. I've lost my voice.
   a. Laryngitis
   b. Sore throat

6. I need to blow my nose a lot.
   a. Runny nose
   b. Blood Nose

7. I have an allergy. I have a
   a. Rash
   b. Insect bite

8. My shoe rubbed my heel. I have a
   a. Rash
   b. Blister

9. The doctor gave me antibiotics. I have a/an
   a. Infection
   b. Cold

10. I think I want to vomit. I am
   a. Nauseous
   b. Bloated

11. **My arm is not broken. It is**
    a. Scratched
    b. Sprained

12. **My arm touched the hot stove. It is**
    a. Burned
    b. Bleeding

13. **I have an upset stomach. I might**
    a. Cough
    b. Vomit

14. **The doctor put plaster on my arm. It is**
    a. Sprained
    b. Broken

15. **If you cut your finger it will**
    a. Burn
    b. Bleed

16. **I hit my hip on a desk. It will**
    a. Burn
    b. Bruise

17. **When you have hay-fever you will**
    a. Sneeze
    b. Wheeze

18. **A sharp knife will**
    a. Scratch
    b. Cut

Grammar: 8 Parts of Speech Matching

Score: _____

Date: _____

- **NOUN**. used to identify any of a class of people, places, or things
- **PRONOUN**. a word (such as I, he, she, you, it, we, or they) that is used instead of a noun or noun phrase
- **VERB**. a word used to describe an action, state, or occurrence
- **ADJECTIVE**. modify or describe a noun or a pronoun
- **ADVERB**. word that modifies (describes) a verb (she sings loudly), adverbs often end in -ly
- **PREPOSITION**. word or phrase that connects a noun or pronoun to a verb or adjective in a sentence
- **CONJUNCTION**. word used to join words, phrases, sentences, and clauses
- **INTERJECTION**. word or phrase that expresses something in a sudden or exclamatory way, especially an emotion

#				
1	☐	Identify the noun.	verb	A
2	☐	Identify the verb.	mother, truck, banana	B
3	☐	What is an adjective?	Lion	C
4	☐	Three sets of nouns	conjunctions	D
5	☐	Three sets of adverbs	always, beautifully, often	E
6	☐	above, across, against	a word that describes nouns and pronouns	F
7	☐	but, and, because, although	preposition	G
8	☐	Wow! Ouch! Hurrah!	preposition	H
9	☐	Mary and Joe **are** friends.	barked	I
10	☐	Jane ran **around** the corner yesterday.	Interjection	J

Extra Credit: Write at least 3 examples of each: Interjection, Conjunction, Adverb & Preposition

....

....

....

....

Grammar:
Subjunctive Mood

Wishes, proposals, ideas, imagined circumstances, and assertions that are not true are all expressed in the subjunctive mood. The subjunctive is frequently used to indicate an action that a person hopes or wishes to be able to undertake now or in the future. In general, a verb in the subjunctive mood denotes a scenario or state that is a possibility, hope, or want. It expresses a conditional, speculative, or hypothetical sense of a verb.

When verbs of advice or suggestion are used, the subjunctive mood is utilized. After verbs of recommendation or advice, the subjunctive appears in a phrase beginning with the word -that.

Here are a few verbs that are commonly used in the subjunctive mood to recommend or advise.

- advise, ask, demand, prefer

1. Writers use the subjunctive mood to express ____ or ____conditions.
    a. imaginary or hoped-for
    b.

2. Which is NOT a common marker of the subjunctive mood?
    a.
    b. memories

3. Which is NOT an example of a hope-for verb?
    a. demand
    b. need

4. Subjunctive mood is used to show a situation is not _____.
    a. fictional or fabricated
    b. entirely factual or certain

5. Which of the below statements is written in the subjunctive mood?
    a. I wish I were a millionaire.
    b. What would you do with a million dollars?

6. The indicative mood is used to state facts and opinions, as in:
    a. My mom's fried chicken is my favorite food in the world.
    b. Smells, taste, chew

7. The imperative mood is used to give commands, orders, and instructions, as in:
    a. Eat your salad.
    b. I love salad!

8. The interrogative mood is used to ask a question, as in:
    a. Have you eaten all of your pizza yet?
    b. I ordered 2 slices of pizza.

9. The conditional mood uses the conjunction "if" or "when" to express a condition and its result, as in:
    a. Blue is my favorite color, so I paint with it often.
    b. If I eat too much lasagna, I'll have a stomach ache later.

10. The subjunctive mood is used to express wishes, proposals, suggestions, or imagined situations, as in:
    a. Yesterday was Monday, and I ate pizza.
    b. I prefer that my mom make pasta rather than tuna.

Proofreading Shakespeare: Romeo and Juliet

> There are **24** mistakes in this passage. 5 capitals missing. 3 unnecessary capitals. 4 unnecessary apostrophes. 3 punctuation marks missing or incorrect. 2 incorrect homophones. 7 incorrectly spelled words.

In 1597, William Shakespeare published "Romeo and Juliet" which would go on to become one of the world's most famous love stories. The plot of Shakespeare's pley takes place in Verona, where the two main characters romeo and Juliet, meet and fall in love Both are descended from two feuding families, the Capulets, and the Montagues. As a result, thay choose to keep their luve hidden and are married by Friar Laurence. Romeo gets into a fight with Juliet"s cousin Tybalt, whom he Kills in a Brawl despite his best efforts. Romeo is expelled from Verona and escapes to Mantua.

When juliet's parents press her to marry, she Seeks the assistance of Friar Laurence once more, who provides her with a sleeping potion designed to simulate her death. In a letter that never reaches Romeo, he explains his plan. Disgusted by the alleged death of his beloved Juliet, Rumeo returns to Verona and commits suicide at Juliet's open coffin. Juliet awakens from her slumber, sees what has happened, and decides to end her liphe. The two feuding families now recognize their complicity and reconcile at their children's graves.

The medieval old town of Verona is ideal for putting oneself in the shoes of Romeo and juliet. Every year, many loving couples and tourists come to walk in the footsteps of romeo and Juliet. A photograph of Juliet's famous balcony, a visit to Romeo's home, or sum queit time spent at Julia's grave. No matter were you look in the city, you wall find loving couple's who stick declarations of love and initials on small slips of paper to the walls or immortalize themselve's on the walls or stones of house's - often illegally.

Although Shakespeare's drama never corresponded to reality, verona has a unique charm, especially for lovers, who imagine they can feel the true story behind the literary work, almost as if Romeo and Juliet had really existed.

Proofreading Interpersonal Skills: Peer Pressure

Score: _____

Date: _____

In this activity, you'll see lots of grammatical *errors*. Correct all the grammar mistakes you see.

There are **30** mistakes in this passage. 3 capitals missing. 5 unnecessary capitals. 3 unnecessary apostrophes. 6 punctuation marks missing or incorrect. 13 incorrectly spelled words.

Tony is mingling with a large group of what he considers to be the school's cool kids. Suddenly, someone in the group begins mocking Tony's friend Rob, who walks with a limp due to a physical dasability.

They begin to imitate rob's limping and Call him 'lame cripple' and other derogatory terms. Although Tony disapproves of their behavior, he does not want to risk being excluded from the group, and thus joins them in mocking Rob.

Peer pressure is the influence exerted on us by member's of our social group. It can manifest in a variety of ways and can lead to us engaging in behaviors we would not normally consider such as Tony joining in and mocking his friend Rob.

However, peer pressure is not always detrimental. Positive peer pressure can motivate us to make better chioces, such as studying harder, staying in school, or seeking a better job. Whan others influence us to make poor Choices, such as smoking, using illicit drugs, or bullying, we succumb to negative peer pressure. We all desire to belong to a group and fit in, so Developing strategies for resisting peer pressure when necessary can be beneficial.

Tony and his friends are engaging in bullying by moking Rob. Bullying is defined as persistent, unwanted. aggressive behavior directed toward another person. It is moust prevalent in school-aged children but can also aphfect adults. Bullying can take on a variety of forms, including the following:

· Verbil bullying is when someone is called names, threatened, or taunted verbally.
· Bullying is physical in nature - hitting spitting, tripping, or poshing someone.
· Social Bullying is intentionally excluding Someone from activities spreading rumors, or embarrassing sumeone.

Credit Scores

A credit score is a number that is used to figure out how well someone manages their money. Lenders use credit scores to determine whether applicants will be able to repay the proposed loan amount. Many factors go into calculating an individual's creditworthiness, including the amount of money owed and how much money has been paid in the past. Credit scores typically range from 300 to 850 and provide lenders with information about the risk of extending credit to a potential applicant. Having a higher credit score benefits the borrower in several ways, most notably through the approval of loans or lines of credit and lower interest rates.

Lenders typically use one of three types of credit scores: the FICO® score, the VantageScore® score, or custom scores. The FICO® and VantageScore® credit scores are well-known, standardized models that lenders can utilize. On the other hand, numerous lenders use proprietary or internally developed custom scoring models. Custom scoring models are created for specific lenders and industries, so it's impossible to identify commonalities.

The majority of lenders use the Fair Isaac Corporation's FICO® score model. It is the most frequently used credit score model. The VantageScore® model was developed by VantageScore Solutions LLC, a company formed by the three major credit bureaus in the United States. Both of these models use the standard 300–850 range; however, their ranges of good versus poor scores differ slightly. Both models consider the same factors when calculating a score, but their treatment of each aspect may vary. There are many different versions of both models that lenders can use when deciding whether or not to give a person a credit card.

Experian, TransUnion, and Equifax are three credit reporting agencies that generate credit scores. Various factors affect credit scores, which means they may increase or decrease in response to specific changes in credit usage. In addition to the individual's payment history, debts owed, credit history length, credit mix, and new accounts are all factors that contribute to an individual's credit score score. Each type of information has a different weight depending on how important it is.

FICO® scores are used to generate credit ratings. They are calculated using the following values:

- 35% Payment History
- 30% Amounts Owed
- 15% Credit Length
- 10% Mix of Credit
- 10% New Credit

An individual's **payment history** is a record of the payments made to lenders. This is the most significant factor in calculating an individual's credit score, accounting for 35% of the total. This category of information indicates whether payments have been made on time and according to the loan terms. It can assist lenders in determining whether potential borrowers are financially capable of making their payments.

The **amount a person owes** to a lender reveals how much of their credit they've used. This factor contributes 30% to their credit score. Credit utilization measures how much credit an individual uses compared to the total credit available to them. Since it's expressed as a percentage, it's easy to see how much money you're borrowing from the financial institution. For instance, if a credit card has a $5,000 limit and the cardholder makes a $1,000 purchase, the credit utilization rate on that card will be 20%. This indicates that the cardholder has depleted 20% of their available credit. To improve a credit score, it is generally recommended to keep credit utilization at 30% or less.

How long an individual has been using and maintaining a credit card account is referred to as "**credit history length**." This accounts for 15% of a credit score and can help a credit score increase over time. For instance, a credit card account that has been open for several years will almost certainly have a positive effect on a credit score because it adds to the credit history.

When borrowers open **new lines of credit**, new credit is accounted for. This accounts for 10% of a credit score and can be used to determine whether a borrower is opening new accounts at an abnormally high rate. Lenders view those who open accounts frequently as riskier.

Credit mix refers to a credit profile with a variety of credit sources. For instance, a credit profile with a combination of loans, credit cards, and a mortgage results in a higher credit score than a credit profile with only one type of account. However, it is not recommended to apply for additional types of credit to boost a credit score, as this only accounts for 10% of the total score.

1. Credit scores typically range from 300 to
   _____.
   a. 850
   b. 800

2. Experian, _____, and _____ are three credit reporting agencies that generate credit scores.
   a. Fico, and TransCredit
   b. TransUnion, and Equifax

3. The majority of lenders use the Fair _____ Corporation's score model.
   a. Isaac
   b. Credit

4. A credit score is a number that is used to figure out how well someone manages their money.
   a. True
   b. False

5. An individual's payment history is a _____ of the payments made to lenders.
   a. contract agreement
   b. record

6. The VantageScore® model was developed by VantageScore Solutions LLC, a company formed by the _____ in the United States.
   a. three major credit bureaus
   b. federal reserve

7. The amount a person _____ to a lender reveals how much of their credit they've used.
   a. owes
   b. loaned

8. How long you been using and maintaining a credit card account is referred to as _____.
   a. credit score factor
   b. credit history length

9. _____ refers to a credit profile with a variety of credit sources.
   a. Credit maintaining
   b. Credit mix

10. A credit card account that has been open for several years will almost certainly have a positive effect on a credit score because it adds to the _____.
    a. credit history
    b. TransUnion score

Introvert vs. Extrovert

Introvert is a person who prefers calm environments, limits social engagement, or embraces a greater than average preference for solitude.

SYNONYMS:
brooder
loner
solitary

Extrovert is an outgoing, gregarious person who thrives in dynamic environments and seeks to maximize social engagement.

SYNONYMS:
character
exhibitionist
show-off
showboat

Fill in the blank with the correct word. [introvert, introverts, extrovert, extroverts]

1. Sue is the _____ in the family; opinionated, talkative and passionate about politics.

2. He was described as an _____, a reserved man who spoke little.

3. _____ are often described as the life of the party.

4. An _____ is often thought of as a quiet, reserved, and thoughtful individual.

5. _____ enjoy being around other people and tend to focus on the outside world.

6. Typically _____ tend to enjoy more time to themselves.

7. Jane is an _____ whose only hobby is reading.

8. I am still not as "outgoing" as an _____ is.

9. I had been a very _____ person, living life to the full.

10. I am an _____, I am a loner.

11. Because Pat is an _____ who enjoys chatting with others, she is the ideal talk show host.

12. She is basically an _____, uncomfortable with loud women and confrontations.

Dealing With Acne

Acne is a skin disorder that results in bumps. Whiteheads, blackheads, pimples, and pus-filled bumps are all sorts of blemishes. What's the source of these annoying bumps? Pores and hair follicles make up most of your skin's top layer. Sebum (pronounced "see-bum"), the natural oil that moisturizes hair and skin, is produced in the pores by oil glands.

Generally, the glands produce adequate sebum, and the pores are good. However, oil, dead skin cells, and bacteria can block a pore if they accumulate in it to an unhealthy level. Acne may result as a result of this.

Puberty-induced hormonal changes are to blame for acne in children. If your parent suffered from acne as a teen, you will likely as well because your pores may produce more sebum when under stress; stress may worsen acne. Acne is usually gone by the time a person reaches their twenties.

Here are a few tips for preventing breakouts if you suffer from acne:

- It would help if you washed your face with warm water and a light soap or cleanser in the morning before school and before bed.
- Avoid scrubbing your face. Acne can be exacerbated by irritating the skin, so scrubbing is not recommended.
- Makeup should be washed off at the end of the day if you wear it.
- Ensure to wash your face after a workout if you've been sweating heavily.
- Acne-fighting lotions and creams are readily available over-the-counter. Talk to your parents or doctor about the options available to you.

Make sure you follow the guidelines on any acne medication you use. If you're unsure whether you're allergic to the cream or lotion, use a small amount at first. If you don't notice results the next day, don't give up. Acne medication can take weeks or months to take effect. If you use more than recommended, your skin may become extremely dry and red.

Acne-suffering children can seek treatment from their doctor. Doctors can prescribe stronger medications than what you can get over the counter.

The following are some other factors to consider:

- Avoid touching your face if you can.
- Pimples should not be picked, squeezed, or popped.
- Long hair should be kept away from the face, and it should be washed regularly to reduce oil production.

It is possible to get pimples on the hairline by wearing headgear like baseball caps. Stay away from them if you suspect they're contributing to your acne problems.

Despite their best efforts, many children will get acne at some point in their lives. The situation isn't out of the ordinary.

If you suffer from acne, you now have several options for treating it. Remind yourself of this: You are not alone. Take a look around at your buddies and you'll notice that the majority of children and adolescents are dealing with acne, too!

1. Puberty _____ changes are to blame for acne in children.
   a. harmonic
   b. hormonal

2. Pores and hair _____ make up most of your skin's top layer.
   a. follicles
   b. folate

3. Avoid _____ your face.
   a. using cleanser
   b. scrubbing

4. _____ is the oil that moisturizes hair and skin, is produced in the pores by oil glands.
   a. Acne
   b. Sebum

Smart Ways to Deal With a Bully

First, read over the entire passage(s). Then go back and fill in the blanks. You can skip the blanks you're unsure about and come back to them later.

control	popular	confident	ground	society
threats	negative	skip	Fighting	mocking

One of the most serious issues in our _____ today is bullying. It's not uncommon for young people to experience a range of _____ emotions due to this. Bullies may use physical force (such as punches, kicks, or shoves) or verbal abuse (such as calling someone a name, making fun of them, or scaring them) to harm others.

Some examples of bullying include calling someone names, stealing from them and _____ them, or ostracizing them from a group.

Some bullies want to be the center of attention. As a strategy to be _____ or get what they want, they may believe bullying is acceptable. Bullies are usually motivated by a desire to elevate their own status. As a result of picking on someone else, they can feel more power and authority.

Bullies frequently target someone they believe they can _____. Kids who are easily agitated or have difficulty standing up for themselves are likely targets. Getting a strong reaction from someone can give bullies the illusion that they have the power they desire. There are times when bullies pick on someone who is more intelligent than them or who looks different from them somehow.

Preventing a Bully's Attack
Do not give in to the bully. Avoid the bully as much as possible. Of course, you aren't allowed to disappear or _____ class. However, if you can escape the bully by taking a different path, do so.

Bravely stand your _____. Scared people aren't usually the most courageous people. Bullies can be stopped by just showing courage in the face of them. Just how do you present yourself as a fearless person? To send a message that says, "Don't mess with me," stand tall. It is much easier to be brave when you are confident in yourself.

Don't Pay Attention to What the Bully Says or Does. If you can, do your best not to listen to the bully's _____. Act as though you aren't aware of their presence and immediately go away to a safe place. It's what bullies want: a big reaction to their teasing and being mean. If you don't respond to a bully's actions by pretending you don't notice or care, you may be able to stop them.

Defend your rights. Pretend you're _____ and brave. In a loud voice, tell the bully, "No! Stop it!" Then take a step back or even take off running if necessary. No matter what a bully says, say "no" and walk away if it doesn't feel right. If you do what a bully tells you to do, the bully is more likely to keep bullying you; kids who don't stand up for themselves are more likely to be targeted by bullies.

Don't retaliate by being a bully yourself. Don't fight back against someone who's bullying you or your pals by punching, kicking, or shoving them. _____ back only makes the bully happier, and it's also risky since someone can be injured. You're also going to be in a lot of trouble. It's essential to stick with your friends, keep safe, and seek adult assistance.

Inform a responsible adult of the situation. Telling an adult if you're being bullied is crucial. Find someone you can confide in and tell them what's going on with you. It is up to everyone in the school, from teachers to principals to parents to lunchroom assistants, to stop the bullies. As soon as a teacher discovers the bullying, the bully usually stops because they are worried that their parents will punish them for their behavior. Bullying is terrible, and everyone who is bullied or witnesses bullying should speak up.

Your Identity and Reputation Online

First, read over the entire passage(s). Then go back and fill in the blanks. You can skip the blanks you're unsure about and come back to them later.

persona	remarks	reputation	networking	repercussions
embarrassing	real-life	inappropriate	take-backs	derogatory

Your online identity grows every time you use a social network, send a text, or make a post on a website, for example. Your online _____ may be very different from your real-world persona – the way your friends, parents, and teachers see you.

One of the best things about having an online life is trying on different personas. If you want to change how you act and show up to people, you can. You can also learn more about things that you like. Steps to help you maintain control on the internet can be taken just like in real life.

Here are some things to think about to protect your online identity and reputation:

Nothing is temporary online. The worldwide web is full of opportunities to connect and share with other people. It's also a place with no "_____" or "temporary" situations. It's easy for other people to copy, save, and forward your information even if you delete it.

Add a "private" option for your profiles. Anyone can copy or screen-grab things that you don't want the world to see using social _____ sites. Use caution when using the site's default settings. Each site has its own rules, so read them to ensure you're doing everything you can to keep your information safe.

Keep your passwords safe and change them often. Someone can ruin your _____ by pretending to be you online. The best thing to do is pick passwords that no one can guess. The only people who should know about them are your parents or someone else who you can trust. Your best friend, boyfriend, or girlfriend should not know your passwords.

Don't put up pictures or comments that are _____ or sexually provocative. In the future, things that are funny or cool to you now might not be so cool to someone else, like a teacher or admissions officer. If you don't want your grandmother, coach, or best friend's parents to see it, don't post it. Even on a private page, it could be hacked or copied and sent to someone else.

Don't give in to unwanted advances. There are a lot of inappropriate messages and requests for money that teenagers get when they're on the web. These things can be scary, weird, or even

_____, but they can also be exciting and fun. Do not keep quiet about being bullied online. Tell an adult you trust right away if a stranger or someone you know is bullying you. It's never a good idea to answer. If you respond, you might say something that makes things even worse.

You can go to www.cybertipline.org to report bad behavior or other problems.

Avoid "flaming" by taking a break now and then. Do you want to send an angry text or comment to someone? Relax for a few minutes and realize that the _____ will be there even if you have cooled off or change your mind about them.

People may feel free to write hurtful, _____, or abusive remarks on the internet if they can remain anonymous. We can be painful to others if we share things or make angry comments when we aren't facing someone. If they find out, it could change how they see us. If you wouldn't say it, show it, or do it in person, don't do it online.

Make sure you don't break copyright laws. Don't upload, share, or distribute copyrighted photographs, sounds, or files. Be aware of copyright restrictions. Sharing them is great, but doing so illegally runs the risk of legal _____ down the road.

It's time for a self-evaluation. Take a look at your "digital footprint," which people can find out about you. When you search for your screen name or email address, see what comes up. That's one way to get a sense of what other people think of you online.

In the same way that your _____ identity is formed, your online identity and reputation are also formed. It's different when you're on the internet because you don't always have the chance to explain how you feel or what you mean. Thinking about what you're going to say and being responsible can help you avoid leaving an online trail that you'll later be sorry about.

Periodic Table Abbreviations

The Periodic Table is a method of organizing the elements. The table arranges elements according to the structure of their atoms. This includes the number of protons as well as the number of electrons in their outer shell. The elements are listed in the order of their atomic number, which is the number of protons in each atom, from left to right and top to bottom.

In the periodic table, each element has its own name and abbreviation. Some of the abbreviations, such as H for hydrogen, are simple to remember. Some are a bit harder, like Fe for iron or Au for gold.

Dmitri Mendeleev, a Russian chemist, proposed the periodic table in 1869. Mendeleev used the table to accurately predict the properties of many elements before they were discovered.

Write the correct element name to the abbreviation below. Need help? Try Google!

1. H ....

2. He ....

3. Li ....

4. Be ....

5. B ....

6. C ....

7. N ....

8. O ....

9. F ....

10. Ne ....

11. Na ....

12. Mg ....

13. Al ....

14. Si ....

15. P ....

16. S ....

17. Cl

18. Ar

19. K

20. Ca

21. Sc

22. Ti

23. V

24. Cr

25. Mn

26. Fe

27. Co

28. Ni

29. Cu

30. Zn

31. Ga

32. Ge

33. As

34. Se

35. Br

36. Kr

37. Rb

38. Sr

39. Y

40. Zr

41. Nb

42. Mo

This, That, These, and Those

This, that, these and those are demonstratives. We use this, that, these, and those to point to people and things. This and that are singular. These and those are plural.

1. _____ orange I'm eating is delicious.
    a. This
    b. These
    c. Those
    d. That

2. It is better than _____ apples from last week.
    a. that
    b. those
    c. these
    d. this

3. Let's exchange _____ bread for these crackers.
    a. those
    b. this
    c. these
    d. that

4. Let's try some of _____ freeze-dried steak.
    a. this
    b. this here
    c. them
    d. those there

5. Is _____ water boiling yet?
    a. these here
    b. that
    c. that there
    d. this here

6. _____ granola bars are tasty too.
    a. These
    b. This here
    c. Them
    d. These here

7. _____ mountains don't look that far away.
    a. This
    b. Those
    c. These
    d. That

8. I like _____ pictures better than those.
    a. this
    b. that
    c. those
    d. these

9. _____ car at the far end of the lot is mine.
    a. That
    b. This
    c. These
    d. Those

10. I like the feel of _____ fabric.
    a. those
    b. this here
    c. that there
    d. this

11. In _____ early days, space travel was a dream.
    a. that
    b. them
    c. those
    d. this

12. _____ days, we believe humans will go to Mars.
    a. These
    b. This
    c. Those
    d. That

HEALTH: Non-Communicable Disease Word Scramble

A non-communicable disease (NCD) is a noninfectious health condition lasting for a long period of time. This is also known as a chronic disease. NCD is a disease that is not transmissible directly from one person to another.

Traumatic Brain Injury	Liver Disease	Kidney Disease	Eczema	Ulcerative Colitis	Bipolar Disorder
Down Syndrome	Muscular Dystrophy	Seizure Disorder	Crohn's Disease	Epilepsy	Autism
Arthritis	Bell's Palsy	Psoriasis	Cerebral Palsy	Chronic Kidney Disease	

1. rtrshitai   _ r _ _ _ _ _ i _

2. atiums   _ _ _ i s _

3. s'blel lyasp   _ _ _ _ _ s _ a l _ _

4. orabipl rddoreis   _ _ p _ _ a _ _ _ _ _ _ _ e _

5. raeclrbe laysp   _ e r _ b _ _ _ _ a _ _ _

6. ocrnihc nekyid ieedssa   _ _ _ _ n _ c _ _ _ _ n _ _ D i _ e _ _ _

7. h'ocnsr sdieesa   _ _ _ _ n ' _ _ _ _ e a _ _

8. wodn ymedrson   D _ _ _ S _ n _ _ _ _ _

9. emzeac   E _ _ _ _ a

10. eielypsp   _ _ _ l _ _ s _

11. dikyen deiseas   _ _ d n e _ _ _ _ e _ _ _

12. ivrle asiesde   _ i v _ _ _ _ _ _ _ _ e

13. smuracul hposytdyr   M _ s c u _ _ _ _ _ s _ _ _ _ _ _

14. rpssisioa   _ _ _ r _ a _ _ _

15. euirsze dderirso   _ e _ _ _ r _ _ _ _ _ _ r _ _ _

16. micratuat inrba yrjinu   T r a _ m _ _ _ _ _ r _ _ _ _ _ _ u _ _

17. arvectluei osicitl   _ _ _ _ _ _ _ _ _ v e _ o _ _ t _ s

Write a definition for each word above:

GRADE_____

DATE_____

RESEARCH: Winston Churchill

Occupation _____

BORN DATE:_____ Nationality_____

DEATH DATE:_____ Education_____ #Children _____

Childhood and Family Background Facts

Work and Career Facts

Children, Marriage and or Significant Relationships

Friends, Social Life and Other Interesting Facts

Did you enjoy researching this person?

Give a Rating: ☆ ☆ ☆ ☆ ☆

GRADE_____

DATE_____   **RESEARCH:** Harriet Beecher Stowe

Occupation _____

BORN DATE:_____   Nationality_____

DEATH DATE:_____   Education _____   #Children _____

Childhood and Family Background Facts

Work and Career Facts

Children, Marriage and or Significant Relationships

Friends, Social Life and Other Interesting Facts

Did you enjoy researching this person?

Give a Rating: ☆ ☆ ☆ ☆ ☆

GRADE_____

DATE_____   **RESEARCH: Steve Jobs**

Occupation _____

BORN DATE:_____   Nationality _____

DEATH DATE:_____   Education _____   #Children _____

Childhood and Family Background Facts

Work and Career Facts

Children, Marriage and or Significant Relationships

Friends, Social Life and Other Interesting Facts

Did you enjoy researching this person?

Give a Rating:

GRADE_____

DATE_____

RESEARCH: Captain James Cook

Occupation _____

BORN DATE:_____ Nationality _____

DEATH DATE:_____ Education _____ #Children _____

Childhood and Family Background Facts

Work and Career Facts

Children, Marriage and or Significant Relationships

Friends, Social Life and Other Interesting Facts

Did you enjoy researching this person?

Give a Rating: ☆ ☆ ☆ ☆ ☆

TODAY IS RESEARCH DAY!

GRADE_____

DATE_____

RESEARCH: Dmitri Mendeleev

Occupation _____

BORN DATE:_____ Nationality_____

DEATH DATE:_____ Education _____ #Children _____

Childhood and Family Background Facts

Work and Career Facts

Children, Marriage and or Significant Relationships

Friends, Social Life and Other Interesting Facts

Did you enjoy researching this person?

Give a Rating: ☆ ☆ ☆ ☆ ☆

Test Your Mathematics Knowledge

Score: _____

Date: _____

1. To add fractions_____
   a. the denominators must be the same
   b. the denominators can be same or different
   c. the denominators must be different

2. To add decimals, the decimal points must be?
   a. column and carry the first digit(s)
   b. lined up in any order before you add the columns
   c. lined up vertically before you add the columns

3. When adding like terms_____
   a. the like terms must be same and they must be to the different power.
   b. the exponent must be different and they must be to the same power.
   c. the variable(s) must be the same and they must be to the same power.

4. The concept of math regrouping involves_____
   a. regrouping means that 5x + 2 becomes 50 + 12
   b. the numbers you are adding come out to five digit numbers and 0
   c. rearranging, or renaming, groups in place value

5. _____ indicates how many times a number, or algebraic expression, should be multiplied by itself.
   a. Denominators
   b. Division-quotient
   c. Exponent

6. _____is the numerical value of a number without its plus or minus sign.
   a. Absolute value
   b. Average
   c. Supplementary

7. Any number that is less than zero is called_____
   a. Least common multiple
   b. Equation
   c. Negative number

8. $2^3 = 2 \times 2 \times 2 = 8$, 8 is the
   a. third power of 2
   b. first power of 2
   c. second power of 2

9. -7, 0, 3, and 7.12223 are
   a. all real numbers
   b. all like fractions
   c. all like terms

10. How do you calculate 2 + 3 x 7?
    a. 2 + 3 x 7 = 2 + 21 = 23
    b. 2 + 7 x 7 = 2 + 21 = 35
    c. 2 + 7 x 3 = 2 + 21 = 23

11. How do you calculate (2 + 3) x (7 - 3)?

    a. (2 + 2) x (7 - 3) = 5 x 4 = 32
    b. (2 + 3) x (7 - 3) = 5 x 4 = 20
    c. (2 + 7) x (2 - 3) = 5 x 4 = 14

12. The Commutative Law of Addition says_____

    a. positive - positive = (add) positive
    b. that it doesn't matter what order you add up numbers, you will always get the same answer
    c. parts of a calculation outside brackets always come first

13. The Zero Properties Law of multiplication says_____

    a. that any number multiplied by 0 equals 0
    b. mathematical operation where four or more numbers are combined to make a sum
    c. Negative - Positive = Subtract

14. Multiplication is when you_____

    a. numbers that are added together in multiplication problems
    b. take one number and add it together a number of times
    c. factor that is shared by two or more numbers

15. When multiplying by 0, the answer is always_____

    a. 0
    b. -0
    c. 1

16. When multiplying by 1, the answer is always the _____

    a. same as the number multiplied by 0
    b. same as the number multiplied by -1
    c. same as the number multiplied by 1

17. You can multiply numbers in_____

    a. any order and multiply by 2 and the answer will be the same
    b. any order you want and the answer will be the same
    c. any order from greater to less than and the answer will be the same

18. Division is____

    a. set of numbers that are multiplied together to get an answer
    b. breaking a number up into an equal number of parts
    c. division is scaling one number by another

19. If you take 20 things and put them into four equal sized groups

    a. there will be 6 things in each group
    b. there will be 5 things in each group
    c. there will be 10 things in each group

20. The dividend is_____

    a. the number you are multiplied by
    b. the number you are dividing up
    c. the number you are grouping together

21. The divisor is _____

    a. are all multiples of 3
    b. the number you are dividing by
    c. common factor of two numbers

22. The quotient is _____

    a. the answer
    b. answer to a multiplication operation
    c. any number in the problem

23. When dividing something by 1_____
    a. the answer is the original number
    b. the answer produces a given number when multiplied by itself
    c. the answer is the quotient

24. Dividing by 0_____
    a. the answer will always be more than 0
    b. You will always get 1
    c. You cannot divide a number by 0

25. If the answer to a division problem is not a whole number, the number(s) leftover_____
    a. are called the Order Property
    b. are called the denominators
    c. are called the remainder

26. You can figure out the 'mean' by_____
    a. multiply by the sum of two or more numbers
    b. adding up all the numbers in the data and then dividing by the number of numbers
    c. changing the grouping of numbers that are added together

27. The 'median' is the_____
    a. last number of the data set
    b. middle number of the data set
    c. first number of the data set

28. The 'mode' is the number_____
    a. that appears equal times
    b. that appears the least
    c. that appears the most

29. Range is the_____
    a. difference between the less than equal to number and the highest number.
    b. difference between the highest number and the highest number.
    c. difference between the lowest number and the highest number

30. Please Excuse My Dear Aunt Sally: What it means in the Order of Operations is____
    a. Parentheses, Exponents, Multiplication and Division, and Addition and Subtraction
    b. Parentheses, Equal, Multiplication and Decimal, and Addition and Subtraction
    c. Parentheses, Ellipse, Multiplication and Data, and Addition and Subtraction

31. A ratio is_____
    a. a way to show a relationship or compare two numbers of the same kind
    b. short way of saying that you want to multiply something by itself
    c. he sum of the relationship a times x, a times y, and a times z

32. Variables are things_____
    a. that can change or have different values
    b. when something has an exponent
    c. the simplest form using fractions

33. Always perform the same operation to_____of the equation.
    a. when the sum is less than the operation
    b. both sides
    c. one side only

34. The slope intercept form uses the following equation:
    a. $y = mx + b$
    b. $y = x + ab$
    c. $x = mx + c$

35. The point-slope form uses the following equation:

    a. $y - y1 = m(y - x2)$

    b. $y - y1 = m(x - x1)$

    c. $x - y2 = m(x - x1)$

36. Numbers in an algebraic expression that are not variables are called____

    a. Square

    b. Coefficient

    c. Proportional

37. A coordinate system is _____

    a. a type of cubed square

    b. a coordinate reduced to another proportion plane

    c. a two-dimensional number line

38. Horizontal axis is called_____

    a. h-axis

    b. x-axis

    c. y-axis

39. Vertical axis is called____

    a. v-axis

    b. y-axis

    c. x-axis

40. Equations and inequalities are both mathematical sentences____

    a. has y and x variables as points on a graph

    b. reduced ratios to their simplest form using fractions

    c. formed by relating two expressions to each other

Step 1: Double-check that the bottom numbers (the denominators) are the same.
Step 2: Add the top numbers (the numerators), then place that answer over the denominator

Step 3: Reduce the fraction to its simplest form (if possible)

Score : _____

Date : _____

Adding Fractions

1) $\dfrac{5}{7} + \dfrac{4}{7} = \dfrac{9}{7} = 1\dfrac{2}{7}$

2) $\dfrac{2}{8} + \dfrac{5}{8} =$

3) $\dfrac{6}{7} + \dfrac{4}{7} =$

4) $\dfrac{5}{4} + \dfrac{3}{4} =$

5) $\dfrac{1}{8} + \dfrac{3}{8} =$

6) $\dfrac{2}{6} + \dfrac{5}{6} =$

7) $\dfrac{2}{6} + \dfrac{2}{6} =$

8) $\dfrac{5}{4} + \dfrac{3}{4} =$

9) $\dfrac{8}{8} + \dfrac{6}{8} =$

10) $\dfrac{3}{7} + \dfrac{5}{7} =$

11) $\dfrac{7}{9} + \dfrac{1}{9} =$

12) $\dfrac{3}{9} + \dfrac{6}{9} =$

13) $\dfrac{2}{7} + \dfrac{4}{7} =$

14) $\dfrac{3}{6} + \dfrac{2}{6} =$

15) $\dfrac{3}{6} + \dfrac{5}{6} =$

The factors of a number are the numbers that add up to the original number when multiplied together. Factors of 8, for example, could be 2 and 4 because 2 * 4 equals 8.

Find the Greatest Common Factor for each number pair.

1) 15 , 3 __3__

2) 24 , 12 _____

3) 10 , 4 _____

4) 40 , 4 _____

5) 8 , 40 _____

6) 10 , 4 _____

7) 12 , 20 _____

8) 5 , 20 _____

9) 8 , 2 _____

10) 24 , 40 _____

11) 6 , 8 _____

12) 10 , 3 _____

13) 8 , 6 _____

14) 24 , 10 _____

15) 24 , 12 _____

16) 40 , 24 _____

17) 8 , 10 _____

18) 10 , 20 _____

19) 2 , 3 _____

20) 6 , 12 _____

Step 1: List or write ALL the factors of each number.

Step 2: Identify the common factors.

Step 3: After identifying the common factors, select or choose the number which has the largest value. This number will be your Greatest Common Factor (GCF).

Example:
12, 18

Factors of 12: 1, 2, 3, 4, 6, 12
Factors of 18: 1, 2, 3, 6, 9, 18

What is the Greatest Common Factor?
The GCF of 12 and 18 is 6. That's it!

The factors of a number are the numbers that add up to the original number when multiplied together. Factors of 8, for example, could be 2 and 4 because 2 * 4 equals 8.

Score : _____

Date : _____

List All of the Prime Factors for each number.

1) 38   **2, 19** _____

2) 49   _____

3) 35   _____

4) 25   _____

5) 15   _____

6) 44   _____

7) 32   _____

8) 48   _____

9) 22   _____

10) 21   _____

11) 30   _____

12) 20   _____

13) 39   _____

14) 14   _____

15) 12   _____

16) 26   _____

17) 46   _____

18) 40   _____

19) 24   _____

20) 10   _____

The term "prime factorization" refers to the process of determining which prime numbers multiply to produce the original number.

Step 1 : Divide the given number in two factors.

Step 2 : Now divide these two factors into other two multiples.

Step 3 : Repeat the step 2 until we reach all prime factors.

Step 4 : All the prime factors so obtained collectively known as prime factors of given number. In order to cross check; multiply all the prime factors, you must get the given number.

Find the Prime Factors of the Numbers

1)

27

3   9

3   3

Prime Factors

_ x _ x _ = 27

2)

52

Prime Factors

_ x _ x _ = 52

3)

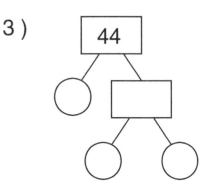

44

Prime Factors

_ x _ x _ = 44

4)

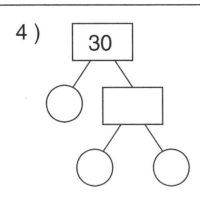

30

5)

24

6)

28

Prime Factors

_ x _ x _ = 30

Prime Factors

_ x _ x _ x _ = 24

Prime Factors

_ x _ x _ = 28

TIME

What time is on the clock? _____

What time was it 1 hour ago? _____

What time was it 3 hours and 40 minutes ago? _____

What time will it be in 4 hours and 20 minutes? _____

What time is on the clock? _____

What time was it 2 hours ago? _____

What time will it be in 3 hours ? _____

What time will it be in 4 hours and 20 minutes? _____

What time is on the clock? _____

What time was it 1 hour ago? _____

What time was it 3 hours and 20 minutes ago? _____

What time will it be in 2 hours ? _____

What time is on the clock? _____

What time will it be in 3 hours and 20 minutes? _____

What time was it 2 hours ago? _____

What time was it 1 hour ago? _____

Visually Adding Simple Fractions

1)

$$\frac{1}{11} + \frac{7}{11} = \rule{2cm}{0.4pt}$$

2)

$$\frac{1}{10} + \frac{7}{10} = \rule{2cm}{0.4pt}$$

3)

$$\frac{1}{5} + \frac{3}{5} = \rule{2cm}{0.4pt}$$

4)

$$\frac{2}{11} + \frac{6}{11} = \rule{2cm}{0.4pt}$$

5)

$$\frac{3}{7} + \frac{3}{7} = \rule{2cm}{0.4pt}$$

Matching Pictographs to Charts

Determine which pictograph best represents the information in the chart.

1)

Month	Cats Sold
June	56
July	32
August	24
September	40
October	80

2)

Month	Cats Sold
June	24
July	56
August	8
September	32
October	40

3)

Month	Cats Sold
June	16
July	8
August	56
September	48
October	24

4)

Month	Cats Sold
June	48
July	40
August	24
September	32
October	64

5)

Month	Cats Sold
June	24
July	80
August	48
September	56
October	32

6)

Month	Cats Sold
June	32
July	48
August	80
September	16
October	8

A.

Month	Cats Sold
June	🐱🐱🐱🐱🐱
July	🐱🐱🐱🐱🐱
August	🐱🐱🐱
September	🐱🐱🐱🐱
October	🐱🐱🐱🐱🐱🐱🐱🐱

Each 🐱 = 8 cat

B.

Month	Cats Sold
June	🐱🐱🐱
July	🐱🐱🐱🐱🐱🐱🐱
August	🐱
September	🐱🐱🐱🐱
October	🐱🐱🐱🐱🐱

Each 🐱 = 8 cat

C.

Month	Cats Sold
June	🐱🐱
July	🐱
August	🐱🐱🐱🐱🐱🐱🐱
September	🐱🐱🐱🐱🐱🐱
October	🐱🐱🐱

Each 🐱 = 8 cat

D.

Month	Cats Sold
June	🐱🐱🐱
July	🐱🐱🐱🐱🐱🐱🐱🐱🐱
August	🐱🐱🐱🐱🐱🐱
September	🐱🐱🐱🐱🐱🐱🐱
October	🐱🐱🐱🐱

Each 🐱 = 8 cat

E.

Month	Cats Sold
June	🐱🐱🐱🐱
July	🐱🐱🐱🐱🐱🐱
August	🐱🐱🐱🐱🐱🐱🐱🐱🐱🐱
September	🐱🐱
October	🐱

Each 🐱 = 8 cat

F.

Month	Cats Sold
June	🐱🐱🐱🐱🐱🐱🐱
July	🐱🐱🐱🐱
August	🐱🐱🐱
September	🐱🐱🐱🐱🐱
October	🐱🐱🐱🐱🐱🐱🐱🐱🐱🐱

Each 🐱 = 8 cat

Examining Number Value by Place Value

Solve each problem.

1) What is the value of the 6 in the number 154,637?

2) What is the value of the 1 in the number 417,298?

3) What is the value of the 9 in the number 97?

4) What is the value of the 3 in the number 9,673,824?

5) What is the value of the 4 in the number 14,697?

6) What is the value of the 4 in the number 42?

7) What is the value of the 1 in the number 29,158?

8) What is the value of the 1 in the number 268,514?

9) What is the value of the 7 in the number 3,576?

10) What is the value of the 5 in the number 3,956,728?

11) What is the value of the 1 in the number 4,781,392?

12) What is the value of the 4 in the number 734,168?

13) What is the value of the 6 in the number 68,435?

14) What is the value of the 2 in the number 51,627?

15) What is the value of the 2 in the number 235?

16) What is the value of the 3 in the number 31,475?

17) What is the value of the 5 in the number 9,536?

18) What is the value of the 7 in the number 37,681?

19) What is the value of the 6 in the number 3,264,871?

20) What is the value of the 1 in the number 76,183?

Finding Ten More & Ten Less

Fill in the blanks for each problem.

SCORE:_____
DATE:_____

What is 10 more than 59?_____

What is 10 more than 2?_____

What is 10 more than 87?_____

What is 10 more than 25?_____

What is 10 more than 85?_____

What is 10 more than 72?_____

What is 10 more than 79?_____

What is 10 more than 1?_____

What is 10 more than 39?_____

What is 10 more than 27?_____

What is 10 more than 86?_____

What is 10 more than 7?_____

What is 10 more than 69?_____

What is 10 more than 60?_____

What is 10 more than 31?_____

What is 10 more than 11?_____

What is 10 more than 12?_____

What is 10 more than 63?_____

What is 10 more than 97?_____

What is 10 more than 41?_____

What is 10 more than 99?_____

What is 10 more than 92?_____

What is 10 more than 67?_____

What is 10 more than 51?_____

What is 10 more than 16?_____

What is 10 less than 13?_____

What is 10 less than 15?_____

What is 10 less than 17?_____

What is 10 less than 19?_____

What is 10 less than 21?_____

What is 10 less than 23?_____

What is 10 less than 25?_____

What is 10 less than 27?_____

What is 10 less than 29?_____

What is 10 less than 31?_____

What is 10 less than 33?_____

What is 10 less than 35?_____

What is 10 less than 37?_____

What is 10 less than 39?_____

What is 10 less than 41?_____

What is 10 less than 43?_____

What is 10 less than 45?_____

What is 10 less than 47?_____

What is 10 less than 49?_____

What is 10 less than 51?_____

What is 10 less than 53?_____

What is 10 less than 55?_____

What is 10 less than 57?_____

What is 10 less than 59?_____

What is 10 less than 61?_____

Math Terms Crossword

Solve the puzzle below with the correct math vocabulary word.

Across

1. A unit of measure equal to 1000 meters.
4. A six-sided and six-angled polygon.
6. Quotient, Goes Into, How Many Times
8. Multiply, Product, By, Times, Lots Of
9. Minus, Less, Difference, Decrease, Take Away, Deduct
10. A value that does not change.

Down

3. The process of breaking numbers down into all of their factors.
4. A graph that uses bars that equal ranges of values.
5. Two rays sharing the same endpoint (called the angle vertex).
7. Sum, Plus, Increase, Total

MULTIPLICATION
HEXAGON   KILOMETER
CONSTANT   ANGLE
FACTORING   DIVISION
SUBTRACTION
HISTOGRAM   ADDITION

Math Terms Matching

Score: _____

Date: _____

Match each math term to the correct meaning.

1	☐	Rectangle		A parallelogram with four right angles.	A
2	☐	Negative Number		The measure of how heavy something is.	B
3	☐	Triangle		A three-sided polygon.	C
4	☐	X		The Roman numeral for 10.	D
5	☐	X-Axis		A straight infinite path joining an infinite number of points in both directions.	E
6	☐	Weight		The ____ is a list of numbers are the values that occur most frequently.	F
7	☐	Like Fractions		A number less than zero.	G
8	☐	Like Terms		A point that is exactly halfway between two locations.	H
9	☐	Mode		The top number in a fraction.	I
10	☐	Midpoint		The sum of two or more monomials.	J
11	☐	Line		____ with the same variable and same exponents/powers.	K
12	☐	Numerator		The solution to a division problem.	L
13	☐	Octagon		Fractions with the same denominator.	M
14	☐	Logic		Sound reasoning and the formal laws of reasoning.	N
15	☐	Outcome		Used in probability to refer to the result of an event.	O
16	☐	Polynomial		The horizontal axis in a coordinate plane.	P
17	☐	Quotient		A polygon with eight sides.	Q
18	☐	Proper Fraction		A fraction whose denominator is greater than its numerator.	R

- The **mean** is the average, and this is a simple way to remember that. The mean can be calculated by adding all of the numbers in the set and then dividing by the number of numbers in the set.
- The **median** is the middle number of the data set. It is referred to as the "middle number" in a set of data. To calculate the median, the data must first be organized.
- The **mode** is the number that appears the most. All you have to do is figure out which value in a set appears the most.

Mean, Mode, Median

1) 2, 2, 3, 4, 4, 9, 4

Mean _____ Median _____ Mode _____

6) 9, 7, 4, 4, 4, 2

Mean _____ Median _____ Mode _____

2) 7, 7, 9, 7, 2, 8, 3, 6, 4, 7

Mean _____ Median _____ Mode _____

7) 8, 8, 4, 3, 4, 7, 9, 4, 7

Mean _____ Median _____ Mode _____

3) 8, 4, 2, 7, 5, 6, 2, 3, 4, 9

Mean _____ Median _____ Mode _____

8) 2, 4, 6, 2, 5, 2, 9, 2

Mean _____ Median _____ Mode _____

4) 7, 7, 3, 2, 6

Mean _____ Median _____ Mode _____

9) 6, 5, 8, 2, 9

Mean _____ Median _____ Mode _____

5) 5, 6, 6, 7, 6, 5, 6, 7, 6

Mean _____ Median _____ Mode _____

10) 6, 3, 3, 5, 8, 1, 9

Mean _____ Median _____ Mode _____

Examining Number Value by Place Value   SCORE:

Solve each problem.

Answers

1) What is the value of the 6 in the number 154,637?

2) What is the value of the 1 in the number 417,298?

3) What is the value of the 9 in the number 97?

4) What is the value of the 3 in the number 9,673,824?

5) What is the value of the 4 in the number 14,697?

6) What is the value of the 4 in the number 42?

7) What is the value of the 1 in the number 29,158?

8) What is the value of the 1 in the number 268,514?

9) What is the value of the 7 in the number 3,576?

10) What is the value of the 5 in the number 3,956,728?

11) What is the value of the 1 in the number 4,781,392?

12) What is the value of the 4 in the number 734,168?

13) What is the value of the 6 in the number 68,435?

14) What is the value of the 2 in the number 51,627?

15) What is the value of the 2 in the number 235?

16) What is the value of the 3 in the number 31,475?

17) What is the value of the 5 in the number 9,536?

18) What is the value of the 7 in the number 37,681?

19) What is the value of the 6 in the number 3,264,871?

20) What is the value of the 1 in the number 76,183?

1. _____
2. _____
3. _____
4. _____
5. _____
6. _____
7. _____
8. _____
9. _____
10. _____
11. _____
12. _____
13. _____
14. _____
15. _____
16. _____
17. _____
18. _____
19. _____
20. _____

- Start by naming the number to the left of the decimal.
- Use the word "and" to indicate the decimal point.
- Then name the number to the right of the decimal point as if it were a whole number.

Score : _____

Date : _____

Write the Names for the Decimal Numbers.

1) 3.48 _____

2) 8.20 _____

3) 2.19 _____

4) 2.38 _____

5) 9.47 _____

6) 3.51 _____

7) 2.25 _____

8) 9.47 _____

9) 6.76 _____

10) 3.28 _____

Each digit within a number has a place. The
place of a number can be the ones, tens,
hundreds, or thousands.

Score : _____

Date : _____

Find the Mystery Numbers

1) The mystery number has ...

A 2 in the Thousands place.
A 8 in the Tens place.
A 2 in the Hundreds place.
A 3 in the Ones place.

What is the mystery number ?   _____

2) The mystery number has ...

A 1 in the Tens place.
A 6 in the Hundreds place.
A 1 in the Thousands place.
A 7 in the Ones place.

What is the mystery number ?   _____

3) The mystery number has ...

A 7 in the Thousands place.
A 1 in the Hundreds place.
A 3 in the Tens place.
A 2 in the Ones place.

What is the mystery number ?   _____

4) The mystery number has ...

A 5 in the Ones place.
A 1 in the Thousands place.
A 4 in the Hundreds place.
A 7 in the Tens place.

What is the mystery number ?   _____

5) The mystery number has ...

A 1 in the Ones place.
A 8 in the Hundreds place.
A 8 in the Tens place.
A 6 in the Thousands place.

What is the mystery number ?   _____

7m + 14m - 6n - 5n + 2m

Step 1: Organize your like terms. You can use a highlighter, shapes, or just rewrite the problem so that the like terms are next to each other.

7m + 14m - 6n - 5n + 2m

Step 2: Combine the coefficients.

(7 + 14 + 2)m + (-6 + -5)n

23m - 11n

"Like terms" are terms whose variables are the same. Terms whose variables (such as x or y) with any exponents (such as the 2 in x^2) are the same.

Combining Like Terms

1) 8 + 13y - 15y

2) 14 - 6y + 3

3) -11 + 2 - 14y - 4y

4) -14(5 - 2f) - 8

5) 12n + 6n

6) 13k + k

7) 16(-14z - 4) - 3

8) -19(16 + 13s)

9) 3 + 9r - 7r + 6

10) 14(-19c + 8)

Look It Up! Pop Quiz

Learn some basic vocabulary words that you will come across again and again in the course of your studies in algebra. By knowing the definitions of most algebra words, you will be able to construct and solve algebra problems much more easily.

Find the answer to the questions below by *looking up each word. (The wording can be tricky. Take your time.)*

1. improper fraction
   a. a fraction that the denominator is equal to the numerator
   b. a fraction in which the numerator is greater than the denominator, is always 1 or greater

2. equivalent fraction
   a. a fraction that has a DIFFERENT value as a given fraction
   b. a fraction that has the SAME value as a given fraction

3. simplest form of fraction
   a. an equivalent fraction for which the only common factor of the numerator and denominator is 1
   b. an equivalent fraction for which the only least factor of the denominator is -1

4. mixed number
   a. the sum of a whole number and a proper fraction
   b. the sum of a variable and a fraction

5. reciprocal
   a. a number that can be divided by another number to make 10
   b. a number that can be multiplied by another number to make 1

6. percent
   a. a percentage that compares a number to 0.1
   b. a ratio that compares a number to 100

7. sequence
   a. a set of addition numbers that follow a operation
   b. a set of numbers that follow a pattern

8. arithmetic sequence
   a. a sequence where EACH term is found by adding or subtracting the exact same number to the previous term
   b. a sequence where NO term is found by multiplying the exact same number to the previous term

9. geometric sequence
   a. a sequence where each term is found by multiplying or dividing by the exact same number to the previous term
   b. a sequence where each term is solved by adding or dividing by a different number to the previous term

10. order of operations
   a. the procedure to follow when simplifying a numerical expression
   b. the procedure to follow when adding any fraction by 100

11. variable expression
   a. a mathematical phrase that contains variables, numbers, and operation symbols
   b. a mathematical phrase that contains numbers and operation symbols

12. absolute value
   a. the distance a number is from zero on the number line
   b. the range a number is from one on the number line

13. integers
   a. a set of numbers that includes whole numbers and their opposites
   b. a set of numbers that includes equal numbers and their difference

14. x-axis
   a. the horizontal number line that, together with the y-axis, establishes the coordinate plane
   b. the vertical number line that, together with the y-axis, establishes the coordinate plane

15. y-axis

    a. the vertical number line that, together with the x-axis, establishes the coordinate plane

    b. the horizontal number line that, together with the x-axis, establishes the coordinate plane

16. coordinate plane

    a. plane formed by one number line (the horizontal y-axis and the vertical x-axis) intersecting at their -1 points

    b. plane formed by two number lines (the horizontal x-axis and the vertical y-axis) intersecting at their zero points

17. quadrant

    a. one of two sections on the four plane formed by the intersection of the x-axis

    b. one of four sections on the coordinate plane formed by the intersection of the x-axis and the y-axis

18. ordered pair

    a. a pair of numbers that gives the location of a point in the coordinate plane. Also known as the "coordinates" of a point.

    b. a pair of equal numbers that gives the range of a point in the axis plane. Also known as the "y-axis" of a point.

19. x-coordinate

    a. the number that indicates the position of a point to the left or right of the y-axis

    b. the number that indicates the range of a point to the left ONLY of the y-axis

20. y-coordinate

    a. the number that indicates the position of a point above or below the x-axis

    b. the number that indicates the value of a point only above the x-axis

21. inverse operations

    a. operations that equals to each other

    b. operations that undo each other

22. inequality

    a. a math sentence that uses a letter (x or y) to indicate that the left and right sides of the sentence hold values that are different

    b. a math sentence that uses a symbol ($<, >, \leq, \geq, \neq$) to indicate that the left and right sides of the sentence hold values that are different

23. perimeter

    a. the distance around the outside of a figure

    b. the distance around the inside of a figure

24. circumference

    a. the distance around a circle

    b. the range around a square

25. area

    a. the number of square units inside a 2-dimensional figure

    b. the number of circle units inside a 3-dimensional figure

26. volume

    a. the number of cubic units inside a 3-dimensional figure

    b. the number of cubic squared units inside a 2-dimensional figure

27. radius

    a. a line segment that runs from the middle of the circle to end of the circle

    b. a line segment that runs from the center of the circle to somewhere on the circle

28. chord

    a. a line segment that runs from somewhere on the circle to another place on the circle

    b. a circle distance that runs from somewhere on the far left to another place on the circle

29. diameter

    a. a chord that passes through the center of the circle

    b. a thin line that passes through the end of the circle

30. mean

    a. the sum of the data items added by the number of data items minus 2

    b. the sum of the data items divided by the number of data items

31. median

    a. the first data item found after sorting the data items in descending order

    b. the middle data item found after sorting the data items in ascending order

32. mode

    a. the data item that occurs most often

    b. the data item that occurs less than two times

33. range
   a. the difference between the highest and the lowest data item
   b. the difference between the middle number and the lowest number item

34. outlier
   a. a data item that is much higher or much lower than all the other data items
   b. a data item that is much lower or less than all the other data items

35. ratio
   a. a comparison of two quantities by multiplication
   b. a comparison of two quantities by division

36. rate
   a. a ratio that has equal quantities measured in the same units
   b. a ratio that compares quantities measured in different units

37. proportion
   a. a statement (ratio) showing five or more ratios to be equal
   b. a statement (equation) showing two ratios to be equal

38. outcomes
   a. possible results of action
   b. possible answer when two numbers are the same

39. probability
   a. a ratio that explains the likelihood of the distance and miles between to places
   b. a ratio that explains the likelihood of an event

40. theoretical probability
   a. the probability of the highest favorable number of possible outcomes (based on what is not expected to occur).
   b. the ratio of the number of favorable outcomes to the number of possible outcomes (based on what is expected to occur).

41. experimental probability
   a. the ratio of the number of times by 2 when an event occurs to the number of times times 2 an experiment is done (based on real experimental data).
   b. the ratio of the number of times an event occurs to the number of times an experiment is done (based on real experimental data).

42. distributive property
   a. a way to simplify an expression that contains a equal like term being added by a group of terms.
   b. a way to simplify an expression that contains a single term being multiplied by a group of terms.

43. term
   a. a number, a variable, or probability of an equal number and a variable(s)
   b. a number, a variable, or product of a number and a variable(s)

44. Constant
   a. a term with no variable part (i.e. a number)
   b. a term with no variable + y part (i.e. 4+y)

45. Coefficient
   a. a number that divides a variable
   b. a number that multiplies a variable

GRADE_____

DATE_____   **RESEARCH: Robert E. Lee**

Occupation _____

BORN DATE:_____ Nationality_____

DEATH DATE:_____ Education _____ #Children _____

Childhood and Family Background Facts

Work and Career Facts

Children, Marriage and or Significant Relationships

Friends, Social Life and Other Interesting Facts

Did you enjoy researching this person?

Give a Rating: ☆ ☆ ☆ ☆ ☆

TODAY IS RESEARCH DAY!   GRADE_____

DATE_____   **RESEARCH:**

    Occupation _____

BORN DATE:_____   Nationality _____

DEATH DATE:_____   Education _____   #Children _____

Childhood and Family Background Facts

Work and Career Facts

Children, Marriage and or Significant Relationships

Friends, Social Life and Other Interesting Facts

Did you enjoy researching this person?

Give a Rating: ☆ ☆ ☆ ☆ ☆

TODAY IS RESEARCH DAY!   GRADE_____

DATE_____   **RESEARCH: Elizabeth I of England**

    Occupation _____

BORN DATE:_____   **Nationality**_____

DEATH DATE:_____   **Education**_____   **#Children**_____

Childhood and Family Background Facts

Work and Career Facts

Children, Marriage and or Significant Relationships

Friends, Social Life and Other Interesting Facts

Did you enjoy researching this person?

Give a Rating: ☆ ☆ ☆ ☆ ☆

TODAY IS RESEARCH DAY!   GRADE_____

DATE_____   RESEARCH: Charles Darwin

       Occupation _____

BORN DATE:_____ Nationality_____

DEATH DATE: _____ Education _____ #Children _____

Childhood and Family Background Facts

Work and Career Facts

Children, Marriage and or Significant Relationships

Friends, Social Life and Other Interesting Facts

Did you enjoy researching this person?

Give a Rating: ☆ ☆ ☆ ☆ ☆

GRADE_____

DATE_____

RESEARCH: Louis XIV of France

Occupation _____

BORN DATE:_____ Nationality _____

DEATH DATE:_____ Education _____ #Children _____

Childhood and Family Background Facts

Work and Career Facts

Children, Marriage and or Significant Relationships

Friends, Social Life and Other Interesting Facts

Did you enjoy researching this person?

Give a Rating: ☆ ☆ ☆ ☆ ☆

GRADE_____

DATE_____

RESEARCH: Ludwig van Beethoven

Occupation _____

BORN DATE:_____ Nationality_____

DEATH DATE:_____ Education_____ #Children _____

Childhood and Family Background Facts

Work and Career Facts

Children, Marriage and or Significant Relationships

Friends, Social Life and Other Interesting Facts

Did you enjoy researching this person?

Give a Rating: ☆ ☆ ☆ ☆ ☆

Polynomial Understanding Quiz

Need help? Try Google.

1. A polynomial is an expression consisting of_____.
   a. variables and coefficients
   b. variables and constant

2. A polynomial can have____.
   a. constants, variables, exponents
   b. terms, variables, exponents

3. To add polynomials you simply_____.
   a. add any like terms together
   b. divide any like terms together

4. If the variable in a term is multiplied by a number, then this number is called?
   a. polynomial
   b. coefficient

5. The exponent on the variable portion of a term tells you the _____ of that term.
   a. the degree
   b. the term

6. The "poly-" prefix in "polynomial" means many
   a. few
   b. many

7. Monomial
   a. is a one-term polynomial
   b. is a two-term polynomial

8. Linear
   a. is a first-degree polynomial
   b. is a second-degree polynomial

9. Cubic
   a. is a third/fourth-degree polynomial
   b. is a third-degree polynomial

10. Binomial
   a. is a one-term polynomial
   b. is a two-term polynomial

11. Quadratic
   a. is a zero-degree polynomial
   b. is a second-degree polynomial

12. Trinomial
   a. is a three-term polynomial
   b. is a two-term polynomial

13. The degree of a polynomial is the degree of the_____.
   a. term with the smallest degree
   b. term with the largest degree

14. Quintic
   a. is a fifth-degree polynomial
   b. is a fifth/sixth-degree polynomial

15. Quartic
   a. is a fourth-degree polynomial
   b. is a fifth-degree polynomial

16. What is a polynomial with 4 terms?
   a. trinomial
   b. quadrinomial

17. A polynomial is the sum or _____.
   a. difference of monomials
   b. difference of exponent

18. The degree of a monomial is the sum of the?
   a. degree of the variables
   b. exponents of the variables

19. Leading coefficient is the____.
   a. term with the smallest degree
   b. term with the largest degree

20. Standard Form of a polynomial is the list of the monomials in order from?
   a. smaller to largest degree
   b. largest to smaller degree

10th Grade Geometry Reading Comprehension

segment	Obtuse	90-degree	straight	halves
directions	Acute	height	formulas	angles

The study of shapes and space is known as geometry. It provides answers to size, area, and volume questions. The earliest known geometry works date back to 2000 BC and are from Egypt. There were _____ for lengths, areas, and volumes, as well as one for pyramids. Thales of Miletus calculated the _____ of pyramids in the 7th century BC, and the Greek mathematician Pythagoras proved the well-known Pythagorean Theorem.

Euclid, another Greek mathematician, introduced Euclidean geometry around 300 BC by demonstrating how to prove theorems using basic definitions and truths. We still use Euclidean geometry to prove theorems today.

Geometric terms include points, lines, and _____. A point is a non-dimensional object with no length or width. A dot is commonly used to represent it. A line is an object that extends in both _____ without end. It is usually depicted with arrowheads to indicate that it continues indefinitely. A line _____ is a section of a line that has two ends. A ray is one-half of a line with a single endpoint. Two rays with the same endpoint form an angle. The angle is called a straight angle if the rays are the two _____ of a single line. A straight angle is analogous to a book open flat on a desk. A right angle is defined as an angle that is opened half that far.

Angles are expressed in degrees. A right angle is defined as a _____ angle. _____ angles are those that are less than a right angle. _____ angles are those that are larger than a right angle but smaller than a _____ angle.

10 Grade Biology: Reading Comprehension Viruses

When we catch a cold or get the flu, we are dealing with the effects of a viral infection. Viruses, despite sharing some characteristics with living organisms, are neither cellular nor alive. The presence of cells, the ability to reproduce, the ability to use energy, and the ability to respond to the environment are all important characteristics of living organisms. A virus cannot perform any of these functions on its own.

A virus, on the other hand, is a collection of genetic material encased in a protective coat, which is typically made of proteins. Viruses are obligate parasites because they must replicate on the host. To replicate itself, a virus must first attach to and penetrate a host cell, after which it will go through the various stages of viral infection. These stages are essentially the virus lifecycle. A virus can enter the host cell via one of several methods by interacting with the surface of the host cell. The virus can then replicate itself by utilizing the host's energy and metabolism.

Bacteriophages, viruses that infect bacteria, either use the lysogenic cycle, in which the host cell's offspring carry the virus, or the lytic cycle, in which the host cell dies immediately after viral replication. Once viral shedding has occurred, the virus can infect additional hosts. Viral infections can be productive in the sense that they cause active infection in the host, or they can be nonproductive in the sense that they remain dormant within the host. These two types of infection can result in chronic infections, in which the host goes through cycles of illness and remission, as well as latent infections, in which the virus remains dormant for a period of time before causing illness in the host.

1. A virus is encased in a protective coat, which is typically made of ____.
   a. proteins
   b. molecules
   c. cells

2. To replicate itself, a virus must first attach to and penetrate a ___ cell.
   a. healthy
   b. living atom
   c. host

3. Viruses are neither cellular nor __.
   a. alive
   b. moving
   c. a threat

4. The virus can replicate itself by utilizing the host's ___and ___.
   a. cells and DNA
   b. molecules and cell
   c. energy and metabolism

5. A virus can remain _____ for a period of time before causing illness in a host.
   a. metabolized
   b. dormant
   c. infected

Match Politics Terms

Learn how to *look up* words in a *Spanish-English dictionary or online. Write the* corresponding letter(s).

1	Campaign		la diplomacia	A
2	Candidate		el político	B
3	Coalition		la libertad de expresión	C
4	Coup		el/la portavoz	D
5	Democracy		la oposición	E
6	Demonstration		la democracia	F
7	Demonstrator		electoral	G
8	Deputy, Representative		el golpe de Estado	H
9	Dictatorship		el diputado	I
10	Diplomacy		el presidente	J
11	Elections		el candidato	K
12	Electoral		el ministro	L
13	Foreign Policy		la campaña	M
14	Freedom Of Speech		el/la manifestante	N
15	Government		la minoría	O
16	Internal Affairs		las elecciones	P
17	Majority		la manifestación	Q
18	Minister		el voto	R

19	[ ]	Ministry		la coalición	S
20	[ ]	Minority		el primer ministro	T
21	[ ]	Movement		el gobierno	U
22	[ ]	Opposition		el partido	V
23	[ ]	Parliament		el ministerio	W
24	[ ]	Party		el estado	X
25	[ ]	Politician		la mayoría	Y
26	[ ]	President		la dictadura	Z
27	[ ]	Prime Minister		la política interior	AA
28	[ ]	Referendum		el parlamento	AB
29	[ ]	Spokesperson		el plebiscito/referendo	AC
30	[ ]	State		el movimiento	AD
31	[ ]	Vote		la política exterior	AE

Pick 7 politics Spanish words from above and work on arranging them in order alphabetically:

_____

_____

_____

_____

_____

_____

Score: _____

Date:_____

No Answer Key

Periodic Table Abbreviations

The Periodic Table is a method of organizing the elements. The table arranges elements according to the structure of their atoms. This includes the number of protons as well as the number of electrons in their outer shell. The elements are listed in the order of their atomic number, which is the number of protons in each atom, from left to right and top to bottom.

In the periodic table, each element has its own name and abbreviation. Some of the abbreviations, such as H for hydrogen, are simple to remember. Some are a bit harder, like Fe for iron or Au for gold.

Dmitri Mendeleev, a Russian chemist, proposed the periodic table in 1869. Mendeleev used the table to accurately predict the properties of many elements before they were discovered.

Write the correct element name to the abbreviation below. Need help? Try Google!

1. H _____

2. He _____

3. Li _____

4. Be _____

5. B _____

6. C _____

7. N _____

8. O _____

9. F _____

10. Ne _____

11. Na _____

12. Mg _____

13. Al _____

14. Si _____

15. P _____

16. S _____

17. Cl

18. Ar

19. K

20. Ca

21. Sc

22. Ti

23. V

24. Cr

25. Mn

26. Fe

27. Co

28. Ni

29. Cu

30. Zn

31. Ga

32. Ge

33. As

34. Se

35. Br

36. Kr

37. Rb

38. Sr

39. Y

40. Zr

41. Nb

42. Mo

The History of the Calendar

Is there a calendar in your family's home? Every day, the majority of households use a calendar. Calendars help us stay organized. Using a calendar, you can keep track of the passing of time and plan ahead. The ancients based their calendars on the most apparent regular events they were aware of—the Sun, Moon, and stars changing positions. These calendars assisted them in determining when to plant and harvest their crops. Different groups of people developed other calendars over time based on their own needs and beliefs.

The Gregorian calendar is used by people all over the world. In 1752, the world switched to the Gregorian calendar. Otherwise, different calendars were used by people all over the world.

Julius Caesar first introduced the 12 months of the calendar as we know them today on January 1st, 45 BC.

The previous Roman calendar had the year begin in March and end in December. Romulus, Rome's legendary first king, had used it since 753 BC. Because it only accounted for 304 days in a year, this calendar was later modified.

To account for the missing days, Rome's second king, Numa Pompilius, added two months at the end of the calendar, Januarius and Februarius. He also put in place an intercalary month that fell after Februarius in some years. These years were nicknamed "leap years." In addition, he deleted one day from each month with 30 days, making them 29 days instead.

This resulted in 355 days in a regular year and 377 days in a leap year. The leap years were declared at the king's discretion. Despite its instability, the calendar was in use for 700 years.

However, it became highly perplexing because the seasons and calendars did not correspond. It wreaked havoc on the farmers.

So, in 45 BC, Julius Caesar, with the help of his astronomers, decided to change the calendar and make it more stable. The seasons finally had a chance to catch up.

Since 1752, when the Gregorian calendar was adopted worldwide to synchronize it with the English and American colonies, the same calendar had been in use. Since Caesar's time, the world and its boundaries have expanded dramatically! The Gregorian calendar corrected the Julian calendar error of calculating one revolution of the earth around the sun to account for 365.2422 days.

That's all there is to it! Julius Caesar was the first to institute the 12-month calendar we have today!

Unscramble the calendar words.

Tuesday	Saturday	November	February	Monday	March
Friday	weekend	May	Wednesday	Sunday	January
weekday	October	June	September	December	August
April	Thursday	July			

1. rauanjy   _ a _ _ _ _ y

2. uraeybfr   _ e _ _ u _ _ _

3. macrh   _ _ _ _ h

4. iralp   _ p _ _ _

5. yma   _ a _

6. nuej   J _ _ _

7. luyj   J _ _ _

8. suagut   A _ _ u _ _

9. ebpmeetrs   _ e _ _ _ m _ _ _

10. btcreoo   _ c _ _ _ e _

11. vmbeneor   _ o _ _ _ b _ _

12. eedcrmbe   D e _ _ _ _ _ _

13. dmnyoa   _ o _ _ a _

14. saetudy   _ _ _ _ d a _

15. deeawysnd   W _ d _ _ _ _ _ _

16. shtayudr   _ h _ r _ _ _ _

17. rdayfi   _ _ _ _ a y

18. yuartdas   _ _ _ _ _ d _ y

19. ydsaun   S _ _ _ a _

20. eenekwd   _ _ _ _ e n _

21. kaewedy   _ _ _ _ d a _

April
28

Write the Dates Practice

Score : _____

Date : _____

Short Format: Month, Day, Year | **Example**: May 10, 1998

Long Format: Month, Day, Year | **Example**: Wednesday, May 29, 2019

Numerical Format: month/day/year | **Example**: 3/15/2013 or 3-15-2013

1. The day you were born - *Write Short Format*

2. Yesterday's date - *Write Short Format*

3. Tomorrow's date - *Write Long Format*

4. Today's date - *Write Long Format*

5. January 10, 2006 - *Write Numerical Format*

6. September 18, 1980 - *Write Numerical Format*

7. 11/12/1999 - *Write Long Format*

8. 5/2/2005 - *Write Short Format*

9. Sept 16 2014 - *Write Numerical Format*

10. Jul 4 1776 - *Write Long Format*

Write the next 4 days in the *long format*.

1.

2.

3.

4.

Acronym

Name: _____

Date: _____

A common way to make an acronym is to use the first letter of each word in a phrase to make a word that can be spoken. This is a great way to make a longer, more complicated phrase easier to say and shorter.

Carefully choose the acronym for each word or phrase.

1. Also Known As
   a. AKA
   b. KAA

2. Central Standard Time
   a. CST
   b. TCS

3. Doing Business As
   a. DBA
   b. ASDOING

4. Do Not Disturb
   a. NOTDN
   b. DND

5. Electronic Data Systems
   a. SDE
   b. EDS

6. End of Day
   a. EOD
   b. ENDDAY

7. Eastern Standard Time
   a. EST
   b. TSE

8. Estimated Time of Arrival
   a. ET
   b. ETA

9. Human Resources
   a. HRS
   b. HR

10. Masters of Business Administration
    a. MOBA
    b. MBA

11. MST - Mountain Standard Time
    a. MST
    b. MSTS

12. Overtime
    a. OTIME
    b. OT

13. Point Of Service
    a. POS
    b. POOS

14. Pacific Standard Time
    a. PST
    b. PSTE

15. Anti-lock Braking System
    a. LOCKBS
    b. ABS

16. Attention Deficit Disorder
    a. ADD
    b. ATTDD

17. Attention Deficit Hyperactivity Disorder
    a. ADHP
    b. ADHD

18. Acquired Immune Deficiency Syndrome
    a. ACQIMDEF
    b. AIDS

19. Centers for Disease Control and Prevention
    a. CDC
    b. CDCP

20. Dead On Arrival
    a. DONA
    b. DOA

21. Date Of Birth
    a. DOB
    b. DOFB

22. Do It Yourself
    a. DIY
    b. DIYO

23. Frequently Asked Questions
    a. FAQA
    b. FAQ

24. Graphics Interchange Format
    a. GIF
    b. GIFF

25. Human Immunodeficiency Virus
    a. HIV
    b. HIMMV

26. Medical Doctor
    a. MD
    b. MED

27. Over The Counter
    a. OTC
    b. OTHEC

28. Pay Per View
    a. PPV
    b. PAYPPV

29. Sound Navigation And Ranging
    a. SONAR
    b. SONAVR

30. Sports Utility Vehicle
    a. SPOUV
    b. SUV

GRADE_____

DATE_____

RESEARCH: Benedict Arnold

Occupation _____

BORN DATE:_____ Nationality _____

DEATH DATE:_____ Education _____ #Children _____

Childhood and Family Background Facts

Work and Career Facts

Children, Marriage and or Significant Relationships

Friends, Social Life and Other Interesting Facts

Did you enjoy researching this person?

Give a Rating: ☆ ☆ ☆ ☆ ☆

GRADE_____

DATE_____

RESEARCH: Molly Pitcher

Occupation _____

BORN DATE:_____ Nationality _____

DEATH DATE:_____ Education _____ #Children _____

Childhood and Family Background Facts

Work and Career Facts

Children, Marriage and or Significant Relationships

Friends, Social Life and Other Interesting Facts

Did you enjoy researching this person?

Give a Rating: ☆ ☆ ☆ ☆ ☆

TODAY IS RESEARCH DAY!   GRADE_____

DATE_____   **RESEARCH: Dwight D. Eisenhower**

Occupation _____

BORN DATE:_____   Nationality_____

DEATH DATE:_____   Education_____   #Children _____

Childhood and Family Background Facts

Work and Career Facts

Children, Marriage and or Significant Relationships

Friends, Social Life and Other Interesting Facts

Did you enjoy researching this person?

Give a Rating: ☆ ☆ ☆ ☆ ☆

TODAY IS RESEARCH DAY!

GRADE_____

DATE_____   **RESEARCH: Eleanor Roosevelt**

Occupation _____

BORN DATE: _____   Nationality_____

DEATH DATE: _____   Education_____   #Children _____

Childhood and Family Background Facts

Work and Career Facts

Children, Marriage and or Significant Relationships

Friends, Social Life and Other Interesting Facts

Did you enjoy researching this person?

Give a Rating: ☆ ☆ ☆ ☆ ☆

GRADE_____

DATE_____

RESEARCH: Texas Jack Omohundro

Occupation _____

BORN DATE:_____ Nationality _____

DEATH DATE:_____ Education _____ #Children _____

Childhood and Family Background Facts

Work and Career Facts

Children, Marriage and or Significant Relationships

Friends, Social Life and Other Interesting Facts

Did you enjoy researching this person?

Give a Rating: ☆ ☆ ☆ ☆ ☆

GRADE_____

DATE_____   **RESEARCH: Francis Beaufort**

Occupation _____

BORN DATE:_____   Nationality_____

DEATH DATE:_____   Education_____   #Children _____

Childhood and Family Background Facts

Work and Career Facts

Children, Marriage and or Significant Relationships

Friends, Social Life and Other Interesting Facts

Did you enjoy researching this person?

Give a Rating: ☆ ☆ ☆ ☆ ☆

GRADE_____

DATE_____

RESEARCH: Alan Archibald Campbell-Swinton

Occupation _____

BORN DATE:_____ Nationality_____

DEATH DATE:_____ Education _____ #Children _____

Childhood and Family Background Facts

Work and Career Facts

Children, Marriage and or Significant Relationships

Friends, Social Life and Other Interesting Facts

Did you enjoy researching this person?

Give a Rating: ☆ ☆ ☆ ☆ ☆

GRADE_____

DATE_____

RESEARCH: Nicolaus Copernicus

Occupation _____

BORN DATE: _____ Nationality _____

DEATH DATE: _____ Education _____ #Children _____

Childhood and Family Background Facts

Work and Career Facts

Children, Marriage and or Significant Relationships

Friends, Social Life and Other Interesting Facts

Did you enjoy researching this person?

Give a Rating: ☆ ☆ ☆ ☆ ☆

GRADE_____

DATE_____   **RESEARCH:** Friedrich Clemens Gerke

Occupation _____

BORN DATE:_____ Nationality_____

DEATH DATE:_____ Education _____ #Children _____

Childhood and Family Background Facts

Work and Career Facts

Children, Marriage and or Significant Relationships

Friends, Social Life and Other Interesting Facts

Did you enjoy researching this person?

Give a Rating: ☆ ☆ ☆ ☆ ☆

The Life of Benjamin Franklin

1. Franklin first published Poor Richard's Almanack in 1742.
   - a. True in 1742 and 1745
   - b. False in 1732

2. Benjamin Franklin was the publisher of the Pennsylvania _____.
   - a. Gazette
   - b. Philadelphian

3. Benjamin Franklin was born in Boston, Massachusetts.
   - a. True
   - b. False

4. Ben dropped out of school when he was 12 years old to work with his father.
   - a. True
   - b. False

5. _____ was the founder of Philadelphia and the State of Pennsylvania.
   - a. Richard Saunders
   - b. William Penn

6. Franklin came up with the idea of the First _____ Congress in ____.
   - a. Founding, 1772
   - b. Continental, 1774

7. The ____, signed in 1783, put an end to the Revolutionary War.
   - a. Treaty of Paris
   - b. Treaty of America

8. When it came to winning the war, the United States relied heavily on its partnership with ____.
   - a. France
   - b. Spain

9. Franklin helped put pen to paper on what would become America's first ____ and was its first _____ general.
   - a. congressional, founder
   - b. constitution, postmaster

10. Ben Franklin also invented bifocals, the Franklin stove, a carriage ___, and the ___ harp
    - a. the dollar bill, metal
    - b. odometer, glass

11. Ben was the President of the state of Pennsylvania.
    - a. True
    - b. False

12. Ben was the only founding father to sign the Declaration of Independence and the ____Treaty, Paris Treaty, and United States Constitution all at the same time.
    - a. Law, Congress
    - b. Alliance, Constitution

Alice & The Rabbit-Hole

ALICE was growing tired of sitting beside her sister on the bank and having nothing to do: she had peeped into the book her sister was reading once or twice, but it was lacking pictures or words; "and what use is a book," Alice argued, "without pictures or conversations?"

Thus, she was wondering in her mind (as best she could, given how sleepy and foolish she felt due to the heat) whether the pleasure of creating a cute daisy chain was worth the difficulty of getting up and gathering the daisies when a white Rabbit with pink eyes darted nearby her.

There was nothing remarkable about that; nor did Alice consider it strange to hear the Rabbit exclaim to itself, "Oh no! Oh no! I will arrive too late!" (On reflection, she should have been surprised, but at the time, it seemed perfectly natural). Still, when the Rabbit actually removed a watch from its waistcoat-pocket, examined it, and then hurried on, Alice jumped to her feet , for it flashed across her mind that she had never seen a rabbit with either a waistcoat-pocket or a watch to remove from it, and burning with curiosity, she ran across the field after it. Alice saw the Rabbit go down a hole under the hedge. Alice followed it down in a hurry , never once thinking how she would get out again.

The rabbit-hole continued straight ahead like a tunnel for some distance and then suddenly dipped down, so quickly that Alice had no time to think about stopping herself before falling into what appeared to be a very deep well.

Either the well was really deep, or she dropped very slowly, as she had plenty of time to look around her and ponder on what might happen next. She first attempted to glance down and see what she was approaching, but it was too dark to see anything; then, she discovered the sides of the well were lined with cupboards and bookcases; here and there, she observed maps and images hung on hooks. She removed a jar from one of the shelves as she passed; it was labeled "ORANGE MARMALADE," but it was empty; she did not want to drop the jar for fear of killing someone beneath, so she managed to stuff it into one of the cupboards as she passed it.

"Perfect!" Alice exclaimed to herself. "After such a tumble, I shall have no worries about falling downstairs! How courageous they will all believe I am at home!

History: United States Armed Forces

1. The United States military is divided into ___ branches.
   - a. six
   - b. five

2. _____ is managed by the United States Department of Homeland Security.
   - a. The National Guard
   - b. The Coast Guard

3. The _____ of the United States is the Commander in Chief of the United States Armed Forces.
   - a. Governor
   - b. President

4. The United States maintains a military to safeguard its _____ and interests.
   - a. borders
   - b. cities

5. DoD is in charge of controlling each _____ of the military.
   - a. branch
   - b. army

6. The Marines are prepared to fight on both land and ____.
   - a. battlefield
   - b. sea

7. The United States Space Force is in charge of operating and defending military ____ and ground stations.
   - a. soldiers
   - b. satellites

8. The mission of the _____ is to defend the country from outside forces.
   - a. United States DoD Forces
   - b. United States Air Force

9. There are _____ units in all 50 states.
   - a. Army National Guard
   - b. Armed Nations Guard

10. The United States Navy conducts its missions at sea to secure and protect the world's _____.
    - a. oceans
    - b. borders

11. The primary concern of the United States Coast Guard is to protect_____.
    - a. domestic waterways
    - b. domesticated cities

12. The United States military is: the Amy Force, Army, Coast Guard, Mario Corps, Old Navy, and Space Force.
    - a. True
    - b. False

Extra Credit: Has America ever been invaded? (Independent student research answer)

[Student worksheet has a 19 line writing exercise here.]

Geography: Time Zones

Have you ever tried to call or send a message to someone who was on the other side of the country or the world? It can be tough to reach a faraway location from you because the time of day may be different from your own. The purpose of time zones and why we have them will be discussed in this session.

Kim, Mike's classmate who recently relocated across the country, is texting him. After a short time, Kim sends Mike a text message saying that it is time for her to go to sleep for the night. The sun is beaming brightly outside , and Mike is confused about why Kim would choose this time of day to go to sleep. 'Can you tell me what time it is, please?' Mike asked. 'It's 9:00 p.m. now!' Kim replies.

What exactly is going on here? Was Mike able to travel back in time in some way?

What is happening to Mike and Kim is nothing more than a natural occurrence that occurs on our planet daily. Since Kim relocated across the country, she is now in a different time zone than she was previously.

A time zone is a geographical location on the planet with a fixed time that all citizens can observe by setting their clocks to that time. As you go from east to west (or west to east) on the globe's surface, you will encounter different time zones. The greater the distance traveled, the greater the number of time zones crossed.

Time zones are not something that arises in nature by chance. Humans created the concept of time zones and determined which regions of the world are located in which time zones.

Because of time zones, everyone experiences the same pattern of dawn in the early morning and sunset in the late afternoon. We require time zones because the earth is shaped like a ball and therefore requires them. As the sun beams down on the planet, not every location receives the same amount of sunshine. The sun shines on one side of the earth and brightens it during the day, while the other side is dark during the night (nighttime). If time-zones didn't exist , many people worldwide would experience quite strange sunshine patterns during the day if there were no time zones.

History: Darius the Great

Many stories have appeared on the news about conflicts in the Middle East from Egypt to Iran.

Darius the Great, the Persian Empire's most famous ruler, ruled during the empire's height of power and size.

Darius had his biography and accomplishments carved into the face of a mountain for them to be remembered and respected.

Darius overthrew the emperor's son and became the new ruler of Persia with the assistance of six other nobles.

Following that, he led his army into Scythia, the northern part of the Black Sea and a vital trading region.

He is renowned for decorating his palace hall with images of happy people throughout the empire rather than conflict and war.

Darius attempted to make peace with the Greeks at first but ultimately decided it would be easier to conquer them with his gigantic army .

However, he began to experience significant difficulties. The first was a massive storm that destroyed 200 of his ships and possibly 30,000 of his soldiers.

Following that, Darius' army fought and lost against the Greeks at the Battle of Marathon.

Science: Dolphins Life Cycle

You may have seen dolphins on __television__ or in person, but did you know they are among the most intelligent animals on the planet or that baby dolphins are referred to as calves?

While the idea of a dolphin socializing may seem silly, dolphins are incredibly sociable and __friendly__ creatures.

Following mating, the male dolphin occasionally swims in pretty patterns and produces noises with his __blowhole__ to alert other male dolphins in the area that he has mated with a female dolphin.

Calves are the term used to refer to dolphin __infants__ .

Their milk is highly nutritious, and the dolphin calf feeds exclusively on its mother's __milk__ for six months to two years, depending on the species.

This includes fish and crustaceans for dolphins. Crustaceans, such as lobsters and shrimp, are __small__ sea animals with several legs, a sectioned body, and a hard shell.

Sometimes pods are composed of multiple species of dolphins, or they may consist of a single male, a female, and a group of baby dolphins, much like a __family__ . Dolphins can live to be 50 years old; however, their average __lifespan__ is about 30 years; however, if they are captured and not allowed to dwell in their natural habitats, their lifespans are typically shorter.

This is advantageous for dolphin survival since it enables them to __protect__ and hunt.

Dolphins die for various reasons, but some of the more prevalent ones include __old__ age, heart illness, parasites, and viruses.

Science: Mars

1. **Mars is the color_____.**

   a. red

   b. orange

2. **Mars is coated in red dust and rocks composed of _____ and oxygen.**

   a. iron

   b. metal

3. **Mars is not a habitable planet for humans.**

   a. True

   b. False

4. **Mars has _____seasons.**

   a. four

   b. three

5. **Mar is covered in ____, gorges, plateaus, flatlands, and mountains.**

   a. sand

   b. canyons

6. **Mars lacks ____.**

   a. energy

   b. oxygen

7. **Mars' thin atmosphere is dense with toxic ____.**

   a. carbon dioxide

   b. minerals carbon

8. **Mars has tremendous ____ storms.**

   a. dust

   b. rain

Geography: Rivers

1. Rivers vary in _____.
   - a. height
   - b. size

2. A river is a moving, flowing _____ of water.
   - a. body
   - b. streams

3. A river is a body of primarily _____ that flows across the land's surface.
   - a. freshwater
   - b. biome

4. When one stream meets another, they_____.
   - a. cross over
   - b. merge

5. When a river comes to an end, it's known as the _____.
   - a. mouth
   - b. lake

6. A large number of _____ form a river.
   - a. tributaries
   - b. oceans

7. A river expands as it _____ more and more water from its tributaries.
   - a. collects
   - b. decreases

8. The _____ runs for 4,135 miles.
   - a. Nile River
   - b. Mississippi River

9. _____ flows through several countries on the South American continent, including Brazil.
   - a. Amazon River
   - b. Antarctica River

10. _____ and _____ systems form the longest river system in North America.
    - a. Mississippi River and Missouri River
    - b. Mississippi River and Michigan River

Extra Credit: Answer The Following 3 Questions: (1.) Where is majority of all water located on Earth? (2.) What is all the water on earth called? (3.) Why the Earth is called Blue planet?

NO ANSWERS- INDEPENDENT RESEARCH QUESTIONS

Grammar: Homophones vs Homographs vs. Homonyms

1. 'there,' 'their,' or 'they're' are examples of _____.

    a. Homophones

    b. Homographs

2. _____ are words that have the same spelling or pronunciation but different meanings.

    a. Homonyms

    b. Hemograms

3. Choose the correct homophone for this sentence: Please don't drop and _____ that bottle of hand sanitizer!

    a. brake

    b. break

4. Homographs are two or more words that have the same spelling but different _____.

    a. ending sounds

    b. meanings

5. Current (A flow of water / Up to date) is both homograph and homophone.

    a. True

    b. False

6. To, two and too are _____.

    a. Homonyms

    b. Homagraphs

7. The candle filled the _____ with a delicious scent.

    a. air

    b. heir

8. Kim drove _____ the tunnel.

    a. threw

    b. through

9. John wants to go to _____ house for dinner, but they don't like her, so _____ going to say no.

    a. there, they're

    b. their, they're

10. We won a $95,000 _____!

    a. check

    b. cheque

11. For example, a pencil is not really made with _____.

    a. led

    b. lead

12. Choose the correct homophone for this sentence: Timmy was standing _____ in line.

    a. fourth

    b. forth

13. Homophones are two words that sound the same but have a different meaning.

    a. True

    b. False

14. The word ring in the following two sentences is considered what? She wore a ruby ring. | We heard the doorbell ring.

    a. hologram

    b. homograph

15. A Homograph is a word that has more than one meaning and doesn't have to sound the same.

    a. True

    b. False

16. Homophones occur when there are multiple ways to spell the same sound.

    a. True

    b. False

17. **Select the correct homophone: I have very little (patience/patients) when students do not follow directions.**

    a. patience
    b. patients

18. **The correct homophone (s) are used in the sentence: Personally, I hate the smell of read meet.**

    a. True
    b. False

19. **The correct homophone(s) is used in the sentence: We saw a herd of cattle in the farmer's field.**

    a. True
    b. False

20. **What is NOT an example of a homograph?**

    a. or, oar
    b. live, live

21. **I love my _____ class.**

    a. dear
    b. deer

22. **We will go _____ after we finish our lesson.**

    a. there
    b. their

23. **Please grab _____ jacket for recess.**

    a. you're
    b. your

24. **There is _____ more water at the concession stand.**

    a. no
    b. know

Life Skills: Internet Safety

Internet __safety__ is the act of making one's self safer while surfing the web.

You may enjoy going online to watch __videos__, play games, and communicate with friends and family.

Because you are becoming more independent online and may go online __unsupervised__, you face more internet safety risks than younger children.

You __protect__ yourself from potentially harmful or inappropriate content and activities when you take practical internet safety precautions.

1. Unless my parents have given me permission, I will not give out __personal__ information such as my home address, phone number, or my parents' work address/phone number.

2. If I come across something that makes me __uncomfortable__, I will immediately notify my parents.

3. I will never __agree__ to meet someone I "met" online without first discussing with my parents. If my parents agree to the meeting, I will make sure that it is held in a public location and bring a parent with me.

4. If my parents think a picture of me or someone else online is __inappropriate__, I will discuss the issue with them and refrain from posting it.

5. I will not respond to any __hurtful__ messages or make me feel uncomfortable in any way. I don't believe that it is my fault if I receive such a message. If I do, I will immediately notify my parents.

6. Without their __permission__, I will not be able to access other areas or break these rules.

7. Other than my parents, I will not share my __passwords__ with anyone else (even if they are my best friends).

8. I will consult with my parents before __downloading__ or installing software or doing anything else that could potentially harm our computer or mobile device or that could compromise my family's privacy.

9. I will responsibly conduct myself on the internet, refraining from doing anything that is harmful to others or in __violation__ of the law.

10. I will educate my parents on how I have fun and learn new __skills__ online and teach them about the internet, computers, and other technology.

Extra Credit: Answer These 2 questions: 1. What is meant by Internet safety? 2. How can you stay safe on the Internet?

[NO ANSWERS. INDEPENDENT RESEARCH.]

Life Skills: Making Friends

People find it difficult to believe, but I used to **walk** around school by myself.

I spent all of my energy attempting to **persuade** other students that I was interesting.

Being interested in others was the key to **opening** the door to making friends for me.

A smile may appear to be such a simple thing to do, but it can start a lot of **friendships**.

Now, I'm not suggesting that you walk around with a **grin** on your face all day because people will think you're weird.

Everyone wishes to be heard. It's easy to believe that the best way to make friends is to **brag** about how cool you are.

Everyone wants to feel like they are the most **important** person in the room.

I used to **dream** about being so well-known that I didn't have time to do anything other than saying "hi" to people as I walked by.

You will have a much happier school life if you have a few good friends rather than a tight connection to the **entire** school. What you are interested in is reflected in your friends.

Knowing who you allow you to be yourself. Perhaps you enjoy watching silly stuff on YouTube, riding your **bike**, or cooking Tacos every Tuesday.

Extra Credit: Answer These 2 questions: 1. What are 3 ways to make friends? 2. What is the difference between acquaintance and friend?

[NO ANSWERS. INDEPENDENT RESEARCH]

Science: All About Beavers

Beavers are mammals well-known for their building abilities.

Beavers are rodents , which are a type of animal.

Beavers are slow on land, but their webbed back feet help them swim.

Beavers are herbivores, which means they eat plants .

The beaver's large front teeth never stop growing .

Beavers have a translucent third eyelid (called a nictitating membrane) that covers and protects their

eyes while still allowing some sight underwater .

Even in the wee hours of the morning, Beavers have a hard time keeping their hands off the

 hammer .

Beavers will slap the water with their broad, scaly tail to warn other beavers in the area that a

predator is approaching.

However, due to hunting for its fur and glands for medicine, as well as the beavers' tree-felling and

damming affecting other land uses, the population has declined to around 12 million.

Beavers can live in the wild for up to 24 years.

Extra Credit: Answer These 3 questions: 1. Are beavers friendly? 2. Why are beavers' teeth orange? 3. How many beavers live in a dam?

[NO ANSWERS. INDEPENDENT RESEARCH.]

Science: Helium

1. **Helium is an ___, ___, and colorless gas at room temperature.**
   a. orderly, tasteful
   b. odorless, tasteless

2. **Helium is one of the _____ elements in the universe.**
   a. heaviest
   b. lightest

3. **Helium is classified as an inert or _____ gas.**
   a. noble
   b. odor

4. **_____Pierre Janssen discovered helium for the first time in 1868.**
   a. Scientist
   b. Astronomer

5. **Helium is used to make _____ and airships float.**
   a. kites
   b. balloons

6. **The internal cores of _____ are constantly producing helium.**
   a. stars
   b. the sun

7. **Helium protects divers from being poisoned by too much _____.**
   a. oxygen
   b. gas

8. **Helium can be found trapped underground in _____ gas reservoirs as a result of radioactive decay.**
   a. natural
   b. minerals

Extra Credit: Answer The Following 3 Questions: 1. What is helium made from? 2. Can you make a balloon float without helium? 3. Why did my helium balloons sink overnight?

[NO ANSWERS. INDEPENDENT RESEARCH]

Science: The First Moon Walk Part II

1. NASA is currently working on sending humans to another planet: _____.

   a. Saturn

   b. Mars

2. On _____, the Apollo 11 crew returned to Earth.

   a. July 24, 1969

   b. July 25, 1967

3. The _____ is a space research station.

   a. US International Center Moon

   b. International Space Station

4. Armstrong took the lead as mission _____ and became the first person to set foot on the moon.

   a. commander

   b. scientist

5. The astronauts saw a _____ reading that stated they "came in peace for all mankind,".

   a. written letter

   plaque

The last moon mission took place in _____.

   1972

   1975

Extra Credit: Answer The Following 3 Questions: 1. How old was Neil Armstrong when he landed on the moon? 2. Is the flag still on the moon? 3. What was the first animal in space?

[No Answers. Independent Reseach]

Science: The Moon Walk

On July 20, 1969, a record-breaking event occurred when millions of people gathered around their television sets to witness two American astronauts accomplish something no one had ever done before. Neil Armstrong and Edwin "Buzz" Aldrin became the first humans to walk on the moon, wearing bulky spacesuits and oxygen backpacks.

Armstrong famously said after the two stepped onto the lunar surface, "That's one small step for a man, one giant leap for mankind."

Russia launched the first artificial satellite, Sputnik 1, into space in 1957. Following that, the United States launched several satellites of its own. Both countries wanted to be the first to send a person into space.

It wasn't until 1961 that a person went into space: Russian Yuri Gagarin became the first on April 12, 1961. Alan Shepard of the United States became the first American in space less than a month later. Following these achievements, President John F. Kennedy challenged the National Aeronautics and Space Administration (NASA) to land a man on the moon in ten years or less.

NASA got right to work. On July 16, 1969, the Apollo 11 spacecraft was preparing to launch three astronauts into space.

As part of the selection process for the Apollo 11 astronauts, officials from NASA chose Neil Armstrong, Buzz Aldrin, and Michael Collins. The spacecraft approached the moon's surface just four days after taking off from Florida's Kennedy Space Center.

The three men separated before landing. Collins boarded Apollo 11's command module, the Columbia, from which he would remain in lunar orbit. Armstrong and Aldrin boarded the Eagle, Apollo 11's lunar module, and began their descent to the moon's surface.

The Eagle made a daring landing in a shallow moon crater known as the Sea of Tranquility, which was a risky move. Most people who watched the landing on television were unaware that the Eagle had only 20 seconds of landing fuel remaining at this point in the flight.

1. Neil _____ and Edwin "Buzz" _____ became the first humans to walk on the moon.
   a. Armstrong and Aldrin
   b. Armadale and Aladdin

2. Russia launched the first artificial satellite called _____.
   a. Spank 1.0
   b. Sputnik 1

3. The Eagle made a daring landing in a shallow moon crater known as the _____.
   a. Sea of Tranquility
   b. U.S.A Sea of Trinity

4. On _____, the Apollo 11 spacecraft was preparing to launch three astronauts into space.
   a. July 16, 1989
   b. July 16, 1969

5. Russian _____ became the first person in space on April 12, 1961
   a. Yuri Gagarin
   b. Yari Kim Jun

6. Armstrong and Aldrin boarded the _____, Apollo 11's lunar module, and began their descent to the moon's surface.
   a. Eagle
   b. Black Bird

Geography
Vocabulary Crossword

Complete the crossword by filling in a word that fits each clue. Fill in the correct answers, one letter per square, both across and down, from the given clues. There will be a gray space between multi-word answers.

Tip: Solve the easy clues first, and then go back and answer the more difficult ones.

Across

1. a bowl-shaped vessel used for holding food or liquids
9. water that has condensed on a cool surface overnight
10. droplets of water vapor suspended in the air near the ground
11. ice crystals forming a white deposit
12. a slowly moving mass of ice
16. a shelter serving as a place of safety or sanctuary
17. a relatively flat highland
18. an extensive plain without trees
20. topographic study of a given place
21. a long steep-sided depression in the ocean floor
23. A circular, spiral, or helical motion in a fluid
24. a low area where the land is saturated with water

Down

2. an indentation of a shoreline smaller than a gulf
3. a large cave or a large chamber in a cave
4. a steep rock face
5. the shore of a sea or ocean
6. the territory occupied by a nation
7. an open valley in a hilly area
8. arid land with little or no vegetation
13. precipitation of ice pellets
14. a large frozen mass floating at sea
15. a thin fog with condensation near the ground
18. air pollution by a mixture of smoke and fog
23. a valley
25. a slight wind

GLACIER   ZEPHYR   ICEBERG
DESERT   FROST   DALE   HAIL
SMOG   BASIN   VALE   BAY
OASIS   COUNTRY   COAST
TOPOLOGY   WETLAND   MIST
STEPPE   VORTEX   PLATEAU
FOG   DEW   CLIFF   TRENCH
CAVERN

Geography: Castles in Germany

1. _____ is now the seat of the local government and an art museum.
   a. Schwerin Castle
   b. Swaziland Castle

2. Hohenzollern Castle is situated on the _____ of Mount Hohenzollern.
   a. crest
   b. end

3. The architecture of German castles consists of a combination of towers and _____.
   a. beautiful curtains
   b. fortified walls

4. German castles evolved during the "_____ Ages".
   a. Century
   b. Medieval

5. This castle was built as a residence rather than a fortress.
   a. Eltz Castle
   b. Schwerin Castle

6. Castles are now iconic symbols of magnificence and _____ tales.
   a. real life
   b. mythical

7. _____ has inspired poets for centuries.
   a. Schloss Heidelberg
   b. Steven Spielberg

8. _____ Castle is located in the Bavarian Alps near the town of Füssen.
   a. Norwegian
   b. Neuschwanstein

Life Skills: Peer Pressure

Almost all of us will come into contact with the apparent problem of peer pressure or the feeling that we have to do something because our friends or __classmates__ think it is cool. Peer pressure can be a serious issue, whether we're talking about first-graders being pressured to play games, they don't want to play, or college students being pressured to smoke or __drink__ alcohol. As you get older, you'll realize you're responsible for the peer pressure you're subjected to and inadvertently exert on others. Though you can never completely eliminate peer pressure, you can mitigate some of its negative effects.

Peers have an __impact__ on your life, even if you are unaware of it, simply by spending time with you. You learn from them, and they do the same for you. It's only natural to listen to and learn from people your own age.

Peers can have a __positive__ impact on one another. Perhaps another student in your science class taught you an easy way to remember the planets in the solar system, or someone on your soccer team taught you a cool ball trick. You might look up to a friend who is always a good sport and try to emulate him or her. Perhaps you piqued the interest of others in your new favorite book, and now everyone is reading it. These are examples of how peers positively __influence__ one another daily.

Peers can have a __negative__ influence on one another. For example, a few kids at school may try to persuade you to skip class with them, a soccer friend may try to convince you to be mean to another player and never pass the ball to her, or a kid in the neighborhood may try to persuade you to shoplift with him.

It is common for kids to fall __victim__ to the pressure of their peers because they want to be liked, to fit in, or because they are afraid that other kids will make fun of them if they don't follow suit. Others join in because they want to try something new that others are doing. The notion that "everyone is doing it" can lead some children to disregard their better judgment or common sense.

You've probably heard your parents or teachers tell you to "pick your friends wisely." Peer pressure is a major reason for this. If you choose friends who don't do drugs, skip class, smoke cigarettes, or lie to their parents, you're less likely to do the same, even if other kids do. Try to assist a friend who is __struggling__ to resist peer pressure. It can be powerful for one child to simply say, "I'm with you - let's go."

Even if you're alone and subjected to peer pressure, there are things you can do. You can __avoid__ peers who put you under pressure to do things you know are wrong. You can say "no" and walk away. Even better, find other friends and classmates to hang out with.

If you continue to experience peer pressure and find it challenging to deal with, talk to someone you __trust__. If you've made a mistake or two, don't feel bad about it. Talking to a parent, teacher, or school counselor can make you feel much better and prepare you for peer pressure the next time you are subjected to it.

Science: The Seasons

Our __planet__ has four seasons each year: autumn, winter, spring, and __summer__ .

The Earth spins in a slightly tilted position as it orbits the sun (on an axis tilted 23.5 degrees from a straight-up, vertical position). Because different parts of the planet are angled towards or away from the sun's light throughout the year, this tilt causes our seasons. More or less sunlight and heat influence the length of each day, the average daily temperature, and the amount of rainfall in different seasons.

The tilt has two major effects: the sun's angle to the Earth and the length of the days. The Earth is tilted so that the __North__ Pole is more pointed towards the sun for half of the year. The South Pole is pointing at the sun for the other half. When the North Pole is angled toward the sun, the days in the northern hemisphere (north of the equator) receive more sunlight, resulting in longer days and shorter nights. The northern hemisphere __heats__ up and experiences summer as the days lengthen. As the year progresses, the Earth's tilt shifts to the North Pole points away from the sun, resulting in winter.

As a result, seasons north of the equator are opposed to seasons south of the equator. When Europe and the United States are experiencing winter, Brazil and Australia will be experiencing summer.

We discussed how the length of the day changes, but the angle of the sun also changes. In the summer, the sun __shines__ more directly on the Earth, providing more energy to the surface and heating it. In the winter, sunlight strikes the Earth at an angle. This produces less energy and heats the Earthless.

The longest day in the Northern Hemisphere is __June__ 21st, while the longest night is December 21st. The opposite is true in the Southern Hemisphere, where December 21st is the longest day, and June 21st is the longest night. There are only two days a year when the day and night are the same. These are September 22nd and March 21st.

The amount of time it is light for decreases in autumn, and the __leaves__ begin to change color and fall off the trees. In the United States of America, autumn is referred to as Fall.

Winter brings colder weather, sometimes snow and __frost__ , no leaves on the trees, and the amount of daylight during the day are at its shortest.

The weather usually warms up in the spring, trees begin to sprout leaves, plants begin to bloom, and young animals such as __chicks__ and lambs are born.

The weather is usually warm in the summer, the trees have entire __green__ leaves, and the amount of daylight during the day is extended.

Storytime Reading: The Wolf & 7 Kids

The story goes that once upon a time, an old Goat had seven little Kids and adored them with all the affection a mother would have for her children.

She wanted to go into the forest and get some food one day. So she called up all seven children to her and said, "Dear Children, I must go into the forest." Keep an eye out for the Wolf. If he gets in, he'll eat you whole-skin, hair, and all. The wretch frequently disguises himself, but you'll recognize him right away by his rough voice and black feet."

"Dear Mother, we will take good care of ourselves," the children said. You may leave without wariness."

It wasn't long before someone knocked on the door and yelled, "Open the door, dear Children! Your mother has arrived, and she has brought something for each of you."

The little Kids, however, recognized the Wolf by his rough voice. "We will not open the door," they cried, "because you are not our mother." Your voice is rough, whereas hers is soft and pleasant. "You are Wolf!"

However, the Wolf had placed his black paws against the window, and when the children saw them, they cried out, "We will not open the door; our mother does not have black feet like you." "You are Wolf!"

The Wolf then dashed over to a baker and said, "I've hurt my feet; rub some dough over them for me."

After rubbing his feet, the baker ran to the miller and said, "Strew some white meal over my feet for me." "The Wolf wants to deceive someone," the miller reasoned, and he refused. "If you don't do it," the Wolf said, "I will devour you." The miller became terrified and whitened his paws for him. Yes, and so are men!

Now, for the third time, the wretch went to the house-door, knocked, and said, "Open the door for me, Children!" Your dear little mother has returned home, and she has brought something from the forest for each of you."

Then he inserted his paws through the window. When the kids saw they were white, they believed everything he said and opened the door. But who else but the Wolf should enter?

They were terrified and wished to remain hidden. One jumped under the table , another into the bed, a third into the stove, a fourth into the kitchen, a fifth into the cupboard, a sixth into the washing bowl, and a seventh into the clock case. But the Wolf found them all and swallowed them down his throat one after the other. The only one he didn't find was the youngest in the clock case.

When the Wolf had satisfied his hunger , he exited the building, sat down under a tree in the green meadow outside, and fell asleep.

Soon after, the old Goat returned from the forest. What a sight she saw over there! The front door was wide open. The table, chairs, and benches were thrown to the ground, the washing bowl was shattered, and the quilts and pillows were yanked from the bed.

She took the Kid out, and it informed her that the Wolf had arrived and devoured all the others. You can only imagine how she cried over her poor children!

In her grief, she eventually went out, and the youngest Kid followed her. When they arrived at the meadow, the Wolf by the tree was snoring so loudly that the branches shook. She examined him from every angle and noticed that something was moving and struggling in his stomach. "Ah!" she exclaimed, "is it possible that my poor children, whom he has devoured for his supper, are still alive?"

The Kid then had to dash home to get scissors , a needle and thread, and the Goat to cut open the monster's stomach. She had barely made one cut when a little Kid thrust its head out, and when she had cut further, all six sprang out one after the other, all still alive and unharmed, because the monster had swallowed them whole in his greed.

There was a lot of joy! They ran up to their mother and jumped like a tailor at his wedding. "Now go and look for some big stones," the mother said. We'll stuff them into the wicked beast's stomach while he's sleeping."

When the Wolf awoke from his slumber, he rose to his feet, and because the stones in his stomach were making him thirsty, he desired to go to a well to drink. When he started walking and moving around, the stones in his stomach knocked against each other and rattled . Then he cried out:

And as he approached the well, stooped over the water , and was about to drink, the heavy stones caused him to fall in. There was no way to save him, so he had to drown!

Art: Abstract Art

1. Who splatters and dribbles paint directly from the can onto the canvas?
   a. Mark Rothko
   b. Jackson Pollock

2. Abstract Art consists solely of lines, ____, and colors.
   a. pictures
   b. shapes

3. Abstract Expressionism movement began in the 1940s in _____.
   a. Washington
   b. New York City

4. _____ created many large color blocks in his paintings.
   a. Mark Rothko
   b. John Mondrian

5. The main feature of abstract art is that it lacks a _____ subject.
   a. recognizable
   b. colorful

6. _____ paintings are filled with precision and geometric shapes.
   a. Mondrian's
   b. Rothko

7. The Abstract Expressionism movement began in the ____.
   a. The 1940s
   b. The 1840s

8. Based on what you read, what do you think is the main idea of abstract art?
   a. Not to tell a story, but to encourage involvement and imagination.
   b. Tell a true story and show emotions.

9. Who painted the first true Abstract Art in the early 1900s?
   a. Walter Kondiskny
   b. Wassily Kandinsky

10. Some abstract artists painted with emotion and ____.
   a. randomness
   b. black lines and dots

FOOD CHAIN ANSWERS

1. In ecology, it is the sequence of transfers of matter and energy in the form of food from organism to organism.
   a. Food Sequencing
   b. Food Transport
   c. Food Chain

2. _____ can increase the total food supply by cutting out one step in the food chain.
   a. Birds
   b. Animals
   c. People

3. Plants, which convert solar energy to food by photosynthesis, are the _____.
   a. secondary food source
   b. tertiary food source
   c. primary food source

4. _____ help us understand how changes to ecosystems affect many different species, both directly and indirectly.
   a. Food Transport
   b. Food Chain
   c. Food Web

5. _____ eat decaying matter and are the ones who help put nutrients back into the soil for plants to eat.
   a. Decomposers
   b. Consumers
   c. Producers

6. _____ are producers because they produce energy for the ecosystem.
   a. Animals
   b. Decomposers
   c. Plants

7. Each organism in an ecosystem occupies a specific _____ in the food chain or web.
   a. trophic level
   b. space
   c. place

8. What do you call an organism that eats both plants and animals?
   a. Omnivores
   b. Herbivores
   c. Carnivores

9. Carnivore is from the Latin word that means _____.
   a. "flesh devourers"
   b. "eats both plants and animals"
   c. "plant eaters"

10. A food web is all of the interactions between the species within a community that involve the transfer of energy through _____.
    a. consumption
    b. reservation
    c. adaptation

11. Why are animals considered consumers?
    a. because they produce energy for the ecosystem
    b. because they don't produce energy, they just use it up
    c. because they only produce energy for themselves

12. How do plants turn sunlight energy into chemical energy?
    a. through the process of photosynthesis
    b. through the process of adaptation
    c. through the process of cancelation

13. Grass produces its own food from_____,
    a. animals
    b. sunlight
    c. soil

14. Each of these living things can be a part of _____ food chains.
    a. zero
    b. multiple
    c. only one

15. When an animal dies, _____ breaks down its body.
    a. bacteria
    b. grass
    c. sunlight

Geography: The North Pole

historians	cold	frozen	solar	survive
Frederick	Arctic	bears	axis	fish

What is the world's most northern location? You may be familiar with it as the location of Santa's workshop, but let's take a look at the North Pole's history, environment, and wildlife. It is situated in the middle of the __Arctic__ Ocean, which is almost entirely __frozen__ all year. The only direction you could travel if you stood precisely on the North Pole is south!

For hundreds of years, explorers have attempted to reach the North Pole. Many exploration trips ended in disaster or with the explorers turning around and returning home due to inclement weather. __Frederick__ Cook was an American explorer who claimed to have discovered the North Pole for the first time in 1908. A year later, another American explorer, Robert Peary, made the same claim. Scientists and __historians__ have not been able to back up these claims. There are currently numerous expeditions to the North Pole, many traveling by airplane, boat, or submarine.

We all know the North Pole is __cold__, but compared to the South Pole, the weather is like summer. That is if you consider average winter temperatures of -22 degrees Fahrenheit to be comparable to summer temperatures! Summer temperatures hover around 32 degrees Fahrenheit on average. Pack your shorts and flip-flops for a trip to the North Pole!

There aren't many animals that can __survive__ in this environment because it's so cold all year. Many people believe that polar __bears__ live in the North Pole, but they do not travel that far north. Several bird species, including the Arctic snow bunting and the Arctic tern, travel to the North Pole. Every year, the tern travels to and from the South and North Poles!

Sealife is also scarce. Scientists discovered shrimp and __fish__, including Arctic cod, in the Arctic Ocean near the North Pole. Many sea animals, however, do not travel far enough north to reach the North Pole.

At the North Pole, day and night are very different. Because the Earth's __axis__ is tilted and the North Pole is at the top of the world, there is only one sunrise and one sunset each year. In the winter, there is constant darkness, whereas, in the summer, there is daylight all day and night!

An aurora is a unique event that occurs in polar areas, both north and south. These are brilliant colorful flashes of light in the night sky that are commonly referred to as polar lights. Auroras are caused by __solar__ winds and electromagnetic activity in the atmosphere.

Multiple Choice Quiz: Fiji

Select the best answer for each question.

1. Fiji, officially the Republic of Fiji, is an island country in the _____.
   a. Arctic Ocean
   b. North Pacific Ocean
   c. South Pacific Ocean

2. Bula, which means _____ in Fijian, is the first word you'll need to learn because you'll hear it everywhere.
   a. Hello
   b. Welcome
   c. Good day

3. What is the capital and largest city of Fiji?
   a. Suva
   b. Lautoka
   c. Nadi

4. What is the climate in Fiji?
   a. Dry
   b. Temperate continental
   c. Tropical marine

5. _____, _____, and _____ are the official languages of Fiji.
   a. English, Fijian, and Samoan
   b. Fijian, Māori, and Rotuman
   c. English, Fijian, and Hindustan

6. The native Fijians are mostly _____ and the Indo-Fijians are mostly Hindu.
   a. Christians
   b. Buddhist
   c. Catholics

7. The traditional cooking method in Fiji is called _____.
   a. lovo
   b. ahima'a
   c. uma

8. After 96 years of British rule, Fiji became independent in _____ but remained part of the British Commonwealth.
   a. May 10, 1977
   b. October 10, 1970
   c. June 11, 1970

9. The original settlers of Fiji were _____ and _____ peoples who have lived on the islands for thousands of years.
   a. Austronesian, Micronesian
   b. Polynesian and Micronesian
   c. Polynesian, Melanesian

10. _____ is a Fijian military leader who led a 2006 coup that resulted in his becoming acting president (2006–07) and later acting prime minister (2007–14) of Fiji.
    a. Ratu Epeli Nailatikau
    b. Frank Bainimarama
    c. Laisenia Qarase

11. Fiji was ruled by one military coup after another until a democratic election was held in _____.
    a. November of 2014
    b. October of 2014
    c. September of 2014

12. What are Fiji's two largest islands?
    a. Viti Levu & Vanua Levu
    b. Kadavu & Mamanuca
    c. Rotuma & Lomaiviti

Reading Comprehension:
Marco Polo

Marco Polo was a merchant and explorer who spent much of his life traveling throughout the Far East and China. For many years, his stories were the foundation of what much of Europe knew about Ancient China. He lived between 1254 and 1324.

Marco was born in 1254 in Venice, Italy. Marco's father was a merchant in Venice, a prosperous trading city.

The Silk Road was a network of trade routes that connected major cities and trading posts from Eastern Europe to Northern China. The Silk Road was named because silk cloth was China's main export. Few people completed the entire route. Trading was mostly done between cities or small sections of the route, and goods would slowly make their way from one end to the other, changing hands several times along the way. Marco Polo's father and uncle desired to try something new. They intended to travel all the way to China and return the goods to Venice. They believed that by doing so, they would be able to make a fortune. It took them nine years, but they eventually returned home.

Marco left for China for the first time when he was 17 years old. He accompanied his father and uncle on the trip. During their first trip to China, his father and uncle met the Mongol Emperor Kublai Khan and promised him they would return. At the time, Kublai was the ruler of all of China.

Marco Polo traveled to China for three years. Along the way, he visited many great cities and sites, including the holy city of Jerusalem, the Hindu Kush mountains, Persia, and the Gobi Desert. He met a wide range of people and had numerous adventures.

Marco spent many years in China, where he learned the language. As a messenger and spy for Kublai Khan, he traveled throughout China. He even went as far south as Myanmar and Vietnam are today. He learned about different cultures, foods, cities, and people during these visits. He saw places and things that no European had ever seen before.

Marco was captivated by the wealth and luxury of Chinese cities and the court of Kublai Khan. It was nothing like what he had seen in Europe. Kinsay's capital city was large but well-organized and clean. Wide roads and massive civil engineering projects like the Grand Canal were far beyond what he had seen back home. Everything was new and exciting, from the food to the people to the animals, such as orangutans and rhinos.

1. The _____ Road was a network of trade routes that connected major cities and trading posts.
   a. Reddit
   b. Silk
   c. Forest

2. Who intended to travel all the way to China and return the goods to Venice?
   a. Marco Polo's father and uncle
   b. Marco Polo
   c. Marco Polo mother and aunt

3. Marco Polo was a merchant and _____.
   a. artist
   b. explorer
   c. painter

4. Marco was born in 1254 in _____, Italy
   a. Vincent
   b. Vance
   c. Venice

5. Marco left for China for the first time when he was _____.
   a. seventeen years old
   b. eighteen years old.
   c. 21 years old

6. The Silk Road was named because silk _____ was China's main export.
   a. cloth
   b. curtains
   c. shoes

7. _____ was the ruler of all of China.
   a. Kubilla
   b. Kublai
   c. Kyle

8. How many year Marco Polo traveled to China?
   a. for four years.
   b. for 3 years.
   c. for 5 years.

Science Multiple Choice Quiz: Coral Reef Biome

Select the best answer for each question.

1. _____ is a ring of land surrounding a pool of water called a lagoon.
   a. A Fringe reef
   b. An Atoll
   c. A Coral reef

2. Most of the reef of an atoll is _____.
   a. on the shore
   b. underwater
   c. above the water

3. The _____ in the Indian Ocean and the _____ in the Pacific are countries made up of atolls and other islands.
   a. Maldives, Marshall Islands
   b. Marshall Islands, Boracay
   c. Valley Indonesia, Maldives

4. How many percent of the known marine species live in coral reefs?
   a. Greater than 50%
   b. Around 25 %
   c. Less than 10%

5. How many different types of coral reefs are there?
   a. 3
   b. 7
   c. 4

6. _____ are the primary makers of reefs and come in a variety of shapes and sizes.
   a. Seaweeds
   b. Coral polyps
   c. Sea grass

7. The majority of the plants living on the coral reef are various species of _____, _____, and _____.
   a. seaweeds, crabs, fishes
   b. crabs, shrimps, sea horse
   c. sea grass, seaweed, algae

8. Large reefs grow at a rate of _____ per year.
   a. 5 to 6 cm
   b. 1 to 2 cm
   c. 3 to 4 cm

9. It is a ridge or hummock formed in shallow ocean areas by algae and the calcareous skeletons of certain coelenterates.
   a. Shore
   b. River
   c. Coral reef

10. The coral reef can be divided by?
    a. Barriers
    b. Water
    c. Zones

11. Coral reefs have been called _____.
    a. "the rain forests of the seas"
    b. "the underwater garden of the seas"
    c. "the Amazon rainforest of the seas"

12. Corals live with algae in a type of relationship called _____.
    a. apodosis
    b. symbiosis
    c. amaurosis

Science:
Tyrannosaurus

First, read the entire passage. After that, go back and fill in the blanks. You can skip the blanks you're unsure about and finish them later.

fossils	Mexico	teeth	walk	Jurassic
meat	skull	largest	scientists	museums

Tyrannosaurus Rex, one of the most famous and notable dinosaurs, is a theropod dinosaur. Many Tyrannosaurus _fossils_ have been discovered, allowing scientists to learn more about how big it was, how it hunted, and how it lived.

Tyrannosaurus rex was a land predator dinosaur that was one of the _largest_. The T-rex could grow to be 43 feet long and weigh up to 7.5 tons. Because of its size and overall fearsome image, the dinosaur is frequently used in movies and films such as _Jurassic_ Park.

Tyrannosaurus rex was a two-legged dinosaur. This means it could _walk_ and run on two legs. These two legs were large and strong enough to support the dinosaur's massive weight. The T-arms, rex's on the other hand, were relatively small. However, it is believed that the small arms were powerful to hold onto prey.

The Tyrannosaurus' massive _skull_ and large _teeth_ are among its most terrifying features. T-rex skulls as long as 5 feet have been discovered! Other evidence suggests that the Tyrannosaurus had a powerful bite that allowed it to crush other dinosaurs' bones easily when combined with sharp teeth.

The Tyrannosaurus Rex ate _meat_ from other animals and dinosaurs. Still, it is unclear whether it was a predator (hunted and killed its own food) or a scavenger (meaning it stole food from other predators). Many _scientists_ believe the dinosaur did both. Much is dependent on how fast the dinosaur was. Some claim that the T-Rex was fast and capable of catching its own prey. Others argue that the dinosaur was slow and used its fearsome jaws to frighten off other predators and steal their prey.

There are numerous significant Tyrannosaurus specimens in _museums_ around the world. "Sue" at the Field Museum of Natural History in Chicago is one of the largest and most comprehensive. "Stan," another significant T-Rex specimen, can be found at the Black Hills Museum of Natural History Exhibit in Hill City, South Dakota. Also on display at the American Museum of Natural History in New York, paleontologist Barnum Brown's largest Tyrannosaurus find (he discovered five in total).

The only known Tyrannosaurus Rex track can be found at Philmont Scout Ranch in New _Mexico_.

Spelling: Unscramble

Unscramble the spelling words below.

Tip: Unscramble the words you are sure about first.

sailor	misunderstand	heroes	decision	remarkable	ambulance
intermission	sentence	shampoo	creative	discussion	forgiveness
roam	recently	performance	remind	minus	comfortable

1. ytcleenr   r e c e n t l y

2. psomhao   s h a m p o o

3. eiacrvte   c r e a t i v e

4. nriuadmsetsnd   m i s u n d e r s t a n d

5. deinmr   r e m i n d

6. aomr   r o a m

7. nceulbama   a m b u l a n c e

8. rmbaeekral   r e m a r k a b l e

9. vegofsnries   f o r g i v e n e s s

10. boreoftcmla   c o m f o r t a b l e

11. lsioar   s a i l o r

12. misnu   m i n u s

13. enetcsen   s e n t e n c e

14. incsoied   d e c i s i o n

15. sdoicisuns   d i s c u s s i o n

16. esoerh   h e r o e s

17. ferpenmroac   p e r f o r m a n c e

18. tireiinosmsn   i n t e r m i s s i o n

Sentence Vocabulary

1. Amy painted a __colorful__ picture of a rainbow.

2. We have a __reasonable__ amount of time to study for our test.

3. Doesn't the night sky look __peaceful__ with all the stars shining so brightly?

4. The dishes that Mrs. Price bought were not __breakable__ .

5. Our bus driver is one of the most __cheerful__ people I know.

6. The situation isn't __hopeless__ ; we can find a solution.

7. Cynthia enjoys writing __creative__ stories and reading them to her family.

8. Wow! Every room in your house looks __spotless__ !

9. The young figure skater performed an __impressive__ routine at her first state competition.

10. Krishna ran __around__ the backyard with his dog.

11. One __careless__ camper could be responsible for an enormous forest fire.

12. The school bus comes to Lizzie's house at a __predictable__ time each morning.

13. Rhett did an __honorable__ thing by turning in the wallet he found to his teacher.

14. This is the most __wonderful__ cake I've ever tasted!

15. Steven wrote __thoughtful__ thank-you notes to everyone who came to his birthday party.

16. There were __thousands__ of people at the art festival last weekend.

17. Jamie's family moves around a lot, so she has learned to become __adaptable__ .

18. Running outside in the freezing temperature made Nora feel __breathless__ .

19. Tia's most __memorable__ holiday was the year her baby sister was born on Christmas Day.

20. Have you ever seen a cat __destroy__ a roll of toilet paper?

21. A __massive__ boulder fell from the side of the mountain and blocked the hiking trail.

22. Mrs. Dobmire, the lunch lady, is one of the most __likable__ people you'll ever meet.

23. The fact that the local newspaper is one of the oldest in the country is __remarkable__ .

AREA 51 WORDSEARCH

Area 51, a classified United States Air Force military installation near Groom Lake in southern Nevada. Edwards Air Force Base in southern California is in charge of it. The facility has been the subject of numerous conspiracies involving **extraterrestrial life**, despite the fact that its only confirmed use is as a flight testing facility.

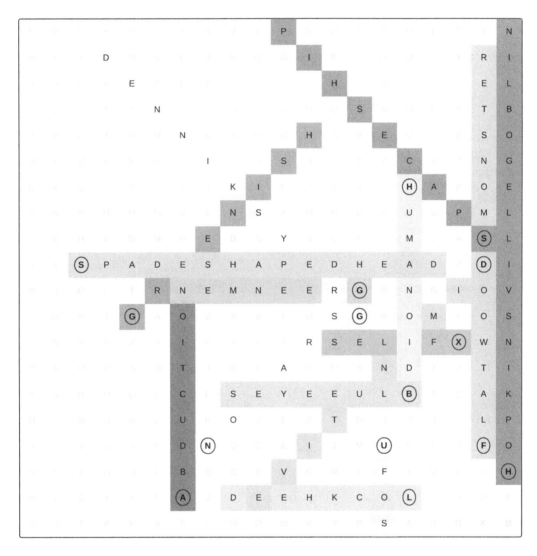

Humanoid ↓ Spade Shaped Head → Flatwoods Monster ↑ No Ears ↗ Grey Skinned ↖ Xfiles ←

Ufos ↓ Greenish ↗ Hopkinsville Goblin ↑ Green Men ← Spaceship ↖ Diminutive ↙ Abduction ↑

Blue Eyes ← Lockheed ←

15 words in Wordsearch: 5 vertical, 5 horizontal, 5 diagonal. (10 reversed.)

Fictional vs. Fictitious vs. Fictive

Fictional is invented as part of a work of fiction

SYNONYMS:
Fabricated
Imaginary

Fictitious is created, taken, or assumed for the sake of concealment; not genuine; false

SYNONYMS:
Bogus
Counterfeit

Fictive - fictitious; imaginary. pertaining to the creation of fiction
- is capable of imaginative creation.

SYNONYMS:

Make-believe
Fabricated

1. He dismissed recent rumors about his private life as _____.
  a. fictitious
  b. fictional
  c. fictive

2. I have the impression that this _____ marriage of ours is like a ghost in a play.
  a. fictional
  b. fictitious
  c. fictive

3. The setting is a _____ island in the Chesapeake River.
  a. fictitious
  b. fictional
  c. fictive

4. The writer has _____ talent.
  a. fictitious
  b. fictional
  c. fictive

5. Almost all _____ detectives are unreal.
  a. fictitious
  b. fictional
  c. fictive

6. The names of the shops are entirely _____.
  a. fictive
  b. fictional
  c. fictitious

How It's Made: Money

1. **The _____ agency is in charge of money creation.**
   a. federal
   b. government

2. **The United States Mint produces coins and dollar bills.**
   a. True - coins and dollar bills
   b. False - only coins

3. **Each side of a sheet of banknotes must dry for ___ hours.**
   a. 72
   b. 24

4. **Dollar bills and computer paper don't have the same _____ and feel.**
   a. design
   b. weight

5. **The metal sheets are fed into a machine that punches out _____.**
   a. coins
   b. silver dollars

6. **United States Bureau of _____ produces dollar notes.**
   a. Engraving and Printing
   b. Engravers and Commission

7. **The Secretary of the _____ selects one of the designs submitted by the designers for production.**
   a. Treasury
   b. Bank

8. **Coins in the United States are created from a combination of ____.**
   a. metals and alloys
   b. silver and nickels

9. **Before being stamped with the design, the blank coins are _____.**
   a. heated and cleaned
   b. shined and reserved

10. **Paper money is created from a particular _____ blend, it is more difficult to forge.**
    a. parcel and green dye
    b. cotton and linen

Introvert vs. Extrovert

Introvert is a person who prefers calm environments, limits social engagement, or embraces a greater than average preference for solitude.

SYNONYMS:
brooder
loner
solitary

Extrovert is an outgoing, gregarious person who thrives in dynamic environments and seeks to maximize social engagement.

SYNONYMS:
character
exhibitionist
show-off
showboat

Fill in the blank with the correct word. [introvert, introverts, extrovert, extroverts]

1. Sue is the extrovert in the family; opinionated, talkative and passionate about politics.

2. He was described as an introvert , a reserved man who spoke little.

3. Extroverts are often described as the life of the party.

4. An introvert is often thought of as a quiet, reserved, and thoughtful individual.

5. Extroverts enjoy being around other people and tend to focus on the outside world.

6. Typically introverts tend to enjoy more time to themselves.

7. Jane is an introvert whose only hobby is reading.

8. I am still not as "outgoing" as an extrovert is.

9. I had been a very extrovert person, living life to the full.

10. I am an introvert , I am a loner.

11. Because Pat is an extrovert who enjoys chatting with others, she is the ideal talk show host.

12. She is basically an introvert , uncomfortable with loud women and confrontations.

Quiz: Famous Entrepreneurs

Match the well-known entrepreneurs below to the correct company or industry.

Need help? Try Google.

1. Arianna Huffington
   a. CNN reporter
   b. [Huffington Post]

2. Sergey Brin and Larry Page
   a. Yahoo
   b. [Google]

3. Elon Musk
   a. Mercedes
   b. [Tesla]

4. Mark Zuckerberg
   a. [Facebook]
   b. Twitter

5. Estee Lauder
   a. [cosmetics]
   b. fashion

6. Richard Branson
   a. [media, aviation, banking]
   b.

7. Weili Dai
   a. Walmart Chief Executive
   b. [Marvell Technologies (semi-conductors)]

8. Coco Chanel
   a. [fashion]
   b. chocolate

9. Steve Jobs
   a. Samsung
   b. [Apple Inc.]

10. Bill Gates
   a. [Microsoft]
   b. Snap Chat

11. Kiran Mazumdar-Shaw
   a. [Biocon (biotech)]
   b. Instagram

12. JK Rowling
   a. Hello Kitty empire
   b. [Harry Potter empire]

13. Jack Ma Yun
   a. eBay
   b. [Alibaba]

14. Jeff Bezos
   a. [Amazon]
   b. Esty

15. Ken Kutaragi
   a. Xbox
   b. [PlayStation]

16. Vivian Horner
   a. [Nickelodeon]
   b. Disney

Dealing With Acne

Acne is a skin disorder that results in bumps. Whiteheads, blackheads, pimples, and pus-filled bumps are all sorts of blemishes. What's the source of these annoying bumps? Pores and hair follicles make up most of your skin's top layer. Sebum (pronounced "see-bum"), the natural oil that moisturizes hair and skin, is produced in the pores by oil glands.

Generally, the glands produce adequate sebum, and the pores are good. However, oil, dead skin cells, and bacteria can block a pore if they accumulate in it to an unhealthy level. Acne may result as a result of this.

Puberty-induced hormonal changes are to blame for acne in children. If your parent suffered from acne as a teen, you will likely as well because your pores may produce more sebum when under stress; stress may worsen acne. Acne is usually gone by the time a person reaches their twenties.

Here are a few tips for preventing breakouts if you suffer from acne:

- It would help if you washed your face with warm water and a light soap or cleanser in the morning before school and before bed.
- Avoid scrubbing your face. Acne can be exacerbated by irritating the skin, so scrubbing is not recommended.
- Makeup should be washed off at the end of the day if you wear it.
- Ensure to wash your face after a workout if you've been sweating heavily.
- Acne-fighting lotions and creams are readily available over-the-counter. Talk to your parents or doctor about the options available to you.

Make sure you follow the guidelines on any acne medication you use. If you're unsure whether you're allergic to the cream or lotion, use a small amount at first. If you don't notice results the next day, don't give up. Acne medication can take weeks or months to take effect. If you use more than recommended, your skin may become extremely dry and red.

Acne-suffering children can seek treatment from their doctor. Doctors can prescribe stronger medications than what you can get over the counter.

The following are some other factors to consider:

- Avoid touching your face if you can.
- Pimples should not be picked, squeezed, or popped.
- Long hair should be kept away from the face, and it should be washed regularly to reduce oil production.

It is possible to get pimples on the hairline by wearing headgear like baseball caps. Stay away from them if you suspect they're contributing to your acne problems.

Despite their best efforts, many children will get acne at some point in their lives. The situation isn't out of the ordinary.

If you suffer from acne, you now have several options for treating it. Remind yourself of this: You are not alone. Take a look around at your buddies and you'll notice that the majority of children and adolescents are dealing with acne, too!

1. Puberty _____ changes are to blame for acne in children.
   a. harmonic
   b. hormonal

2. Pores and hair _____ make up most of your skin's top layer.
   a. follicles
   b. folate

3. Avoid _____ your face.
   a. using cleanser
   b. scrubbing

4. _____ is the oil that moisturizes hair and skin, is produced in the pores by oil glands.
   a. Acne
   b. Sebum

Smart Ways to Deal With a Bully

One of the most serious issues in our _society_ today is bullying. It's not uncommon for young people to experience a range of _negative_ emotions due to this. Bullies may use physical force (such as punches, kicks, or shoves) or verbal abuse (such as calling someone a name, making fun of them, or scaring them) to harm others.

Some examples of bullying include calling someone names, stealing from them and _mocking_ them, or ostracizing them from a group.

Some bullies want to be the center of attention. As a strategy to be _popular_ or get what they want, they may believe bullying is acceptable. Bullies are usually motivated by a desire to elevate their own status. As a result of picking on someone else, they can feel more power and authority.

Bullies frequently target someone they believe they can _control_. Kids who are easily agitated or have difficulty standing up for themselves are likely targets. Getting a strong reaction from someone can give bullies the illusion that they have the power they desire. There are times when bullies pick on someone who is more intelligent than them or who looks different from them somehow.

Preventing a Bully's Attack
Do not give in to the bully. Avoid the bully as much as possible. Of course, you aren't allowed to disappear or _skip_ class. However, if you can escape the bully by taking a different path, do so.

Bravely stand your _ground_. Scared people aren't usually the most courageous people. Bullies can be stopped by just showing courage in the face of them. Just how do you present yourself as a fearless person? To send a message that says, "Don't mess with me," stand tall. It is much easier to be brave when you are confident in yourself.

Don't Pay Attention to What the Bully Says or Does. If you can, do your best not to listen to the bully's _threats_. Act as though you aren't aware of their presence and immediately go away to a safe place. It's what bullies want: a big reaction to their teasing and being mean. If you don't respond to a bully's actions by pretending you don't notice or care, you may be able to stop them.

Defend your rights. Pretend you're _confident_ and brave. In a loud voice, tell the bully, "No! Stop it!" Then take a step back or even take off running if necessary. No matter what a bully says, say "no" and walk away if it doesn't feel right. If you do what a bully tells you to do, the bully is more likely to keep bullying you; kids who don't stand up for themselves are more likely to be targeted by bullies.

Don't retaliate by being a bully yourself. Don't fight back against someone who's bullying you or your pals by punching, kicking, or shoving them. _Fighting_ back only makes the bully happier, and it's also risky since someone can be injured. You're also going to be in a lot of trouble. It's essential to stick with your friends, keep safe, and seek adult assistance.

Inform a responsible adult of the situation. Telling an adult if you're being bullied is crucial. Find someone you can confide in and tell them what's going on with you. It is up to everyone in the school, from teachers to principals to parents to lunchroom assistants, to stop the bullies. As soon as a teacher discovers the bullying, the bully usually stops because they are worried that their parents will punish them for their behavior. Bullying is terrible, and everyone who is bullied or witnesses bullying should speak up.

The Human Bones

1. A baby's body has about _____ bones.
   a. 320
   b. 300

2. The _____, which is like a bowl, holds the spine in place.
   a. pelvis
   b. spinal cord

3. A _____ is where two bones meet.
   a. legs
   b. joint

4. At what age is there no more room for growth?
   a. 25
   b. 18

5. Adults have how many bones?
   a. 206
   b. 200

6. The _____ lets you twist and bend.
   a. hip bones
   b. spine

7. Your skull protects your what?
   a. brain
   b. joints

8. Your ribs protect your what?
   a. Heart, spine, and arms
   b. heart, lung, and liver

9. The _____ connects to a large triangular bone on the upper back corner of each side of the ribcage.
   a. shoulder blade
   b. joints blade

10. You have _____ bones in your arm.
    a. two
    b. three

US Government: Running for Office

When running for public office, candidates must persuade voters that they are the best candidate for the position. Running for office is a term for this type of endeavor. Running for office can be a full-time job in some cases, such as the presidential race. When running for office, there are a lot of things to do.

To run for office, the first step is to ensure that you meet all of the requirements . For example, one must be at least 18 years of age and a US citizen in order to apply.

Almost everyone joins a political party to run for public office these days. The primary election, in which they run to represent that party, is frequently the first election they must win. The Democratic Party and the Republican Party are the two most influential political organizations in the United States today.

Without money, it's challenging to run for office. Candidates frequently use billboards, television commercials, and travel to give speeches to promote their campaigns. All of this comes at a price. The people who want to help a candidate win the election provide them with money. As a result, the budget is established. This is critical, as the person with the most significant financial resources may be able to sway the greatest number of voters, ultimately leading to their victory.

A candidate's campaign staff should be assembled as well. These are people who will assist the candidate in their bid for the presidency. They coordinate volunteers, manage funds, plan events, and generally assist the candidate in winning the election. It is the campaign manager's responsibility to lead the campaign team.

Many candidates attempt to stand out from the crowd by creating a memorable campaign slogan. This is a catchy phrase that will stick in voters' minds as they cast their ballots. Calvin Coolidge and Dwight Eisenhower both had memorable campaign slogans, "I Like Ike" for Eisenhower and "Keep Cool with Coolidge" for Coolidge.

At some point, the candidate will begin a public campaign. A lot of "shaking hands and hugging babies" is involved in the process of running for office. There are a lot of speeches they give outlining what they plan to do when they get into the White House. It's their job to explain why they're better than their rivals.

When a candidate runs for office, they usually take a position on several issues relevant to the position for which they are running. A wide range of topics, such as education, clean water, taxation, war, and healthcare , are examples.

The debate is yet another aspect of running for office. At a debate, all of the candidates for a particular office sit down together to discuss their positions on a specific issue. Candidates take turns speaking and responding to each other's arguments during the debate. The outcome of a debate between two candidates can mean the difference between victory and defeat.

After months of campaigning, the election is finally upon us. They'll cast their ballots and then get right back to work. Attending rallies or shaking hands with strangers on the street may be part of their campaign strategy . All the candidates can do is wait until the polls close. Family, friends, and campaign members usually gather to see how things turn out. If they are successful, they are likely to deliver a victory speech and then go to a party to celebrate.

Becoming Class President

Start working toward your goal of becoming class or high school president as soon as possible if you want to one day hold that position.

If you want to get involved in student government your freshman year, go ahead and join, but don't hold your breath waiting to be elected president. Elections for the freshman class council are frequently a complete disaster. Since freshman elections are held within a month of the start of school, no one has had a chance to get to know one another. The person elected president is usually the one whose name has been mentioned the most by other students. A lot of the time, it's not based on competence or trust.

Building trust and rapport with your classmates is essential from the beginning of the school year. This is the most crucial step in the process of becoming a Class Officer President.

Electing someone they like and trust is a top priority for today's college students. Be a role model for your students. In order to demonstrate your competence, participate in class discussions and get good grades. Avoid being the class clown or the laziest or most absent-minded member of the group.

Become a part of the students' lives. Attend lunch with a variety of people from various backgrounds. Ask them about their worries and their hopes for the school's future.

Make an effort to attend student council meetings even if you aren't currently a member. If you're interested in joining the student council, you may be able to sit in on their meetings, or you may be able to attend an occasional meeting where non-council members can express their concerns and ideas.

Reading Comprehension
Alphabetical Order

1. Which word follows "engage" in the dictionary?

   a. encounter

   b. erase

   c. energy

   d. emigrant

2. Which word would follow "honor" in the dictionary?

   a. hiccup

   b. hesitate

   c. humble

   d. hideout

3. Which word would follow "linoleum" in the dictionary?

   a. literature

   b. lightning

   c. lilac

   d. liberty

4. Which word would follow "minute" in the dictionary?

   a. method

   b. mimic

   c. misery

   d. minister

5. Which word would follow "pleasure" in the dicitonary?

   a. pliers

   b. photo

   c. platinum

   d. place

6. What word follows "proceed" in the dictionary?

   a. product

   b. program

   c. probable

   d. priority

7. What word follow "respiration" in the dictionary?

   a. resound

   b. resign

   c. resort

   d. respond

8. What word follows "sneeze" in the dictionary?

   a. slumber

   b. snarl

   c. snatch

   d. snorkel

9. What word follows "territory" in the dictionary?

   a. textile

   b. terrific

   c. telescope

   d. tarnish

10. What word follows "curtain" in the dictionary?

   a. crumble

   b. curse

   c. cube

   d. customer

Understanding Questions-
Answer Relationship

The question-answer relationship (QAR) strategy helps students understand the different types of questions. By learning that the answers to some questions are "Right There" in the text, that some answers require a reader to "Think and Search," and that some answers can only be answered "On My Own," students recognize that they must first consider the question before developing an answer.

Throughout your education, you may be asked four different types of questions on a quiz:

Right There Questions: Literal questions with answers in the text. The words used in the question are frequently the same as those found in the text.

Think and Search Questions: Answers are obtained from various parts of the text and combined to form meaning.

The Author and You: These questions are based on information from the text, but you must apply it to your own experience. Although the answer is not directly in the text, you must have read it in order to respond to the question.

On My Own: These questions may require you to do some research outside of reading the passage. You can use primary sources to help such as online research articles, books, historical documents, and autobiographies.

Why is the question-answer relationship used?

It has the potential to improve your reading comprehension.
It teaches you how to ask questions about what you're reading and where to look for answers.
It encourages you to think about the text you're reading as well as beyond it.
It motivates you to think creatively and collaboratively, while also challenging you to use higher-level thinking skills.

1. Literal questions with answers in the text are_____.
   a. Right There Questions
   b. Right Here Questions

2. These questions are based on information from the text, but you must apply it to your own
   a. The Teacher and You
   b. The Author and You

3. Answers are obtained from various parts of the text.
   a. Think and Search Questions
   b. Check Your Knowledge Questions

4. These questions may require you to do some research outside of reading the passage.
   a. On My Own
   b. Find The Author

Weather Vocabulary Words
Match Up

The weather is simply the state of the atmosphere at any given time, which includes temperature, precipitation, air pressure, and cloud cover. Winds and storms cause daily changes in the weather. Seasonal changes are caused by the Earth's rotation around the sun.

The sun's rays do not fall evenly on the land and oceans because the Earth is round rather than flat. The sun shines more directly near the equator, bringing more warmth to these areas. On the other hand, the polar regions are at such an angle to the sun that they receive little or no sunlight during the winter, resulting in colder temperatures. These temperature differences cause a frantic movement of air and water in great swirling currents, distributing heat energy from the sun across the planet. When the air in one region is warmer than air in another, it becomes less dense and begins to rise, drawing more air in beneath it. Cooler, denser air sinks elsewhere, pushing air outward to flow along the surface and complete the cycle.

Match to the correct answer.

1	H	Anemometer	→	meteorological instrument used to measure wind speed
2	F	Barometer	→	meteorological instrument used to measure the atmospheric pressure
3	I	Blizzard	→	snow storm that has winds of 35 miles per hour or more
4	B	Cloud	→	tiny water droplets floating in the atmosphere that you can see
5	G	Coriolis effect	→	It affects weather patterns - affects an object that's moving over something that's rotating
6	A	Flash flood	→	something that happens quickly usually due to heavy rain
7	D	High-pressure system	→	A region with high air pressure and cool, dry air
8	J	Hurricane	→	tropical cyclone that formed in the North Atlantic Ocean
9	E	Isobar	→	line on a weather map that represents a given barometric pressure
10	C	Low-pressure system	→	A region with low air pressure and warm, moist air

Word Problems

1) There are sixteen pencils in the drawer. Sandy placed forty - one more
pencils in the drawer. How many pencils are now there in total ?   57 pencils

2) Tom had 77 pennies in his bank. He spent 37
of his pennies. How many pennies does he have now ?   40 pennies

3) There are 33 oak trees currently in the park. Park workers will plant
44 more oak trees today. How many oak trees will the park have
when the workers are finished ?   77 oak trees

4) Dan picked thirty - three lemons and Jessica picked sixty - one lemons from the lemon tree.
How many lemons were picked in all ?   94 lemons

5) Tom has 63 books. Nancy has 22 books.
How many books do they have together ?   85 books

6) Mary has 89 black marbles, she gave Sally 73 of the marbles.
How many black marbles does she now have ?   16 black marbles

7) Nancy found 67 seashells on the beach, she gave Sandy 37 of
the seashells. How many seashells does she now have ?   30 seashells

8) Keith has ninety - eight Pokemon cards. Sally bought fifty - two of Keith's
Pokemon cards. How many Pokemon cards does Keith have now ?   46 Pokemon cards

9) Sally grew thirteen carrots. Tom grew seventy - six carrots. How many
carrots did they grow in all ?   89 carrots

10) Joan's high school played eighty - four hockey games this year. She attended
thirteen games. How many hockey games did Joan miss ?   71 games

Word Problems

1) Dan was at the beach for five days and found eight seashells every day.
How many seashells did Dan find during the beach trip ?   40 seashells

2) Sam goes out to lunch with Fred and Keith. Each person orders the
$9 lunch special. Sam agrees to pay the bill. How much will he have to pay ? 27 dollars

3) Melanie worked 2 hours for 6 days.
How many hours did she work in total ?   12 hours

4) A restaurant sold 5 sandwiches every day for a week.
How many sandwiches were sold during the week ?   35 sandwiches

5) Melanie goes fishing with Sally. Melanie catches nine trout. Sally
catches twice as many trout as Melanie. How many trout did Sally catch ?   18 trout

6) Nancy has 9 black balloons. Melanie has 3 times more
black balloons than Nancy. How many black balloons does Melanie have now ?
                                                                27 black balloons

7) Sally has nine five dollars bills. How much money does she have ?
                                        45 dollars

8) Jessica, Mike, and Sally each have 6 rulers.
How many rulers do they have have in all ?   18 rulers

9) Sam has six quarters in his bank.
How much money does Sam have in quarters ?   150 cents

10) There were a total of 5 soccer games a month.
The season is played for 4 months. How many soccer games are in the seasons ?
                                        20 games

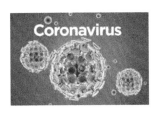

Corona Virus - COVID 19
Pandemic

Student Task: Use the clues and the words in the box to complete this crossword.

Across

1. A virus is considered zoonotic when its origins can be traced to animals.
2. People should stay away from public spaces with large gatherings of people.
3. When an epidemic has spread to multiple continents or countries.
5. The amount of time it takes for an infected person to start showing symptoms,
10. An individual is asymptomatic when they don't show any symptoms

Down

4. A large outbreak of a disease in a short period of time.
6. A restriction of movement and isolation for those exposed to COVID 19.
7. To stay at home in isolation from the general public.
8. The infectious disease caused by the most recently discovered coronavirus
9. A large family of viruses that cause a range of illnesses ranging from the common cold to more severe diseases,

PANDEMIC   COVID19
ZOONOTIC   EPIDEMIC
SOCIAL DISTANCING
ASYMPTOMATIC
QUARANTINE
INCUBATION
CORONAVIRUS   SELF
ISOLATION

Getting Your Temporary Driver's License

No matter what state you live in, there are __legal__ requirements you must meet before you can take the driving test and get your license. Most of the time, these requirements are:

FINISHING A DRIVER EDU COURSE
A LEARNER'S PERMIT IS APPLIED FOR AND RECEIVED
GETTING A CERTAIN NUMBER OF HOURS OF MONITORED PRACTICE

Even though the exact requirements vary from state to state, there will be a __standard__ to meet before taking the driving test. At least six months before you turn 16, find out your state's rules and get everything in order. Do not be without a license on your 18th birthday.

Now comes the hard part, which is passing the test. Even though each state has its own rules, most require that you get a specific score on both a written and a driving test. After about six hours of driver's education, you can usually take the written test. During the written part of the DMV test, you will be asked questions about road signs, traffic laws, and safe driving rules. Find the test __handbook__ for your state to get practice questions and information about the traffic laws in your state.

After you've finished driver's ed, you can take the part of the test where you drive. Depending on where you live, you may have to do this part with a __certified__ driving instructor or a state trooper at the Department of Motor Vehicles (DMV). The examiner will give you a set of driving instructions to see how well you can follow them.

On the day of the exam, you will need to bring proper identification, proof of your social security number, proof of legal residency and school enrollment (when required), a legal __guardian__, and payment for any fees that may be incurred. Believe me when I say nothing could be more frustrating than showing up at the Department of Motor Vehicles, waiting in line for an hour, and finally reaching the attendant, only to find out that you forgot a vital form on the kitchen counter. Before leaving for the test, check and double-check that you have everything you need.

You've done it! You're done with school, you've passed all your tests, and it's finally your 16th birthday. It's time to get your license! Depending on the state, it may be known as the __Department__ of Motor Vehicles (DMV), the Motor Vehicle Division (MVD), the Department of Public Safety (DPS), the Motor Vehicle Agency (MVA), the Department of Revenue (DOR), or the Secretary of State (SOS). Do your research ahead of time, so you know exactly where to go on the day of.

A driving test on-site is required if you haven't already passed either the written or driving portions of the exam. Bring the necessary __paperwork__ and payment, and ensure you look your best. Don't forget that this picture will be on your driver's license for at least a year.

Most states won't give you a full license immediately if you are under 18. Instead, they give you a license that is only good for about 6 months. This is a __trial__ period to see if you are ready to drive without a parent or guardian with you. Be sure to follow all rules and guidelines.

It would be horrible to finally get a license and then have it taken away because you didn't follow all the rules. For example, some states restrict how many hours you can drive per day and how many passengers you can __transport__, while others limit the distance you can travel outside your home county.

Limiting the number of passengers you take on your first few trips, regardless of whether your license is temporary in nature or not, is wise advice irrespective of your license status. Every extra person in the car adds another thing to think about while driving. Driving with friends can be great fun, but if you're not entirely __comfortable__ behind the wheel, this fun can quickly turn into danger.

Of course, it's critical to abide by all state and federal laws and regulations. If you follow the rules of safe driving and use common sense, your first drive after getting your license can be a great time.

Littering

The annual cost of cleaning up litter in the nation's _streets_ , parks, and coastal areas is estimated to be in the millions of dollars. The cleanup of trash has a direct expense, but it also has a _negative_ impact on the surrounding environment, the value of property, and other economic activity. Food packaging, bottles, cans, plastic bags, and paper are the most common sources of litter. Did you know cigarette _butts_ remain the most littered item in the U.S. and across the globe? One of the many strategies that states can use to reduce the amount of litter in their communities is to enact and strictly adhere to laws that carry criminal penalties for the behavior. The penalties for littering vary significantly from state to state, depending on the _amount_ , nature, and location of the litter. The seriousness of the offense is determined by the weight or volume of litter in 10 states, for example. For instance, several states penalize people for disposing of large goods like furniture or major appliances in public places. Legislation addressing trash on public roadways, along the beaches, and in _recreational_ areas has been passed in several states due to these concerns.

In situations that are considered to be relatively small, the courts will typically impose a fine. They may also compel the defendant to perform _community_ service, such as picking up garbage. In Massachusetts, for instance, the minimum _fine_ is $25, whereas, in the state of Maryland, the maximum penalty is $30,000. When a crime is more serious, the offender may be sentenced to up to six years in _jail_ , depending on the state. In addition, the laws in the states of Maryland, Massachusetts, and Louisiana all include provisions that allow the _suspension_ of a driver's license for those who violate the laws. In almost every state, a person's sentence worsens with each subsequent conviction.

It doesn't matter if someone throws trash out on purpose or accidentally; either way, they're contributing to pollution by doing so. Our city's parks, sidewalks, roads, and private property and parks are all impacted by litter. Research has shown that litter leads to the accumulation of even more garbage. A clean _neighborhood_ , on the other hand, lowers the incidence of littering and enhances both the local living standards and the quality of life.

STATE BIKE LAWS

1. State laws and local ordinances often include measures requiring cyclists to wear _____.

    a. headlights

    b. helmets

2. A bicycle violation will not affect your automobile insurance.

    a. True

    b. False

3. Bicyclists are expected to use the appropriate _____ while turning, changing lanes, or stopping, even though some bicycles come equipped with turn signals.

    a. motion sensors

    b. hand signals

4. Rules pertaining to the use of bicycles are enforced at the _____ levels, just like other traffic laws.

    a. state and local

    b. state and countrywide

5. Bicyclists are prohibited from proceeding through a _____ or _____ without first coming to a complete stop, just like vehicles are.

    a. stop sign, stoplight

    b. yield sign, yellow light

6. _____ on back and _____ lights on the front are required in nearly every state, as well as white and red reflectors on the front and back.

    a. Red lights, white

    b. White lights, flashing

UNDERSTANDING RIDESHARE

The way in which people travel is undergoing significant change. Ride-sharing and ride-hailing services, such as Uber, provide an alternative to the taxi business.

When ridesharing startup Uber first debuted its services, the world of private transportation shifted radically. They offered a luxury black car service as an alternative to the usual taxi ride.

In the past, ridesharing was a lot like carpooling , where the person riding along often paid for half of the trip. Both the driver and passenger were traveling in the same direction, and the rider would contribute to the trip's cost.

Ridesharing today is for-profit, and the driver has no destination in mind rather than providing transportation services like a taxi. A third-party app or website charges a fee to connect riders and drivers.

It's common to see the term "rideshare" replaced with "ride-hail." However, this can be deceptive, as "hailing" usually refers to the act of flagging down a cab from a distance.

Hail requests can't be accepted by drivers for ridesharing services like Lyft, Uber, and TappCar because the companies don't support the feature. The legislation also prohibits drivers from receiving hails. Otherwise, the service would be categorized as a taxi service.

Instead, users must use their smartphone to "haul" a driver through their preferred ridesharing app.

Rideshare companies use a smartphone app to connect drivers with passengers in the local region. The driver opens the app and changes their status to "online" to show they are ready to take a ride.

Customer pick-up and drop-off requests are sent to the driver, who responds by accepting or declining the ride.

After accepting the trip and picking up the passenger, the driver proceeds to the passenger's destination.

The passenger will exit the vehicle once the driver reaches the final location.

Because payments for fares are processed within the app, no money exchange occurs between the driver and the passenger.

Additionally, the app enables passengers and drivers to provide ratings for one another. Both the driver and rider benefit from this grading system, which ensures a high level of service and respect for both parties.

Organ Donations

1. You can quickly register to donate organs through the _____ in your state.
   - a. Department of Organ Donations
   - b. Department of Motor Vehicles

2. Donated organs can be _____ into another _____.
   - a. transplanted, person
   - b. translational, facility

3. To remove the DONOR label from your driver's license or ID card, visit any ____office.
   - a. DVM
   - b. DMV

4. There are many different types of _____ that can be donated, including skin, bone, corneas, heart valves, and ____.
   - a. organism, plasma
   - b. tissues, veins

5. Those under the age of ____ may be able to donate their organs if they have the ____ of their parents.
   - a. 18, approval
   - b. 17, agreement

6. If an organ or tissue ____ be transplanted, it may be used for medical research and ____, unless you make other arrangements.
   - a. can, placement
   - b. cannot, teaching

Commonly misspelled words that sound alike but are spelled differently

Carefully circle the correct spelling combinations of words.

	A	B	C	D
1.	Sun/Sn	Son/Son	**Sun/Son**	Son/Sn
2.	Hare/Hiar	Harre/Hair	**Hare/Hair**	Harre/Hiar
3.	Cache/Cassh	**Cache/Cash**	Cache/Casch	Cacha/Cash
4.	Cytte/Sight	**Cite/Sight**	Cyte/Sight	Citte/Sight
5.	Worrn/Warn	Wurn/Warn	Wurrn/Warn	**Worn/Warn**
6.	Minerr/Minor	Miner/Minur	**Miner/Minor**	Minerr/Minur
7.	Wratch/Retch	**Wretch/Retch**	Wrretch/Retch	Wrratch/Retch
8.	Floor/Flower	Flloor/Flower	**Flour/Flower**	Fllour/Flower
9.	Whille/Wile	**While/Wile**	Whylle/Wile	Whyle/Wile
10.	Calous/Callus	Caloos/Callus	**Callous/Callus**	Calloos/Callus
11.	Build/Biled	**Build/Billed**	Boild/Billed	Boild/Biled
12.	Marrten/Martin	**Marten/Martin**	Marten/Martyn	Marrten/Martyn
13.	Humerrus/Humorous	**Humerus/Humorous**	Humerrus/Humoroos	Humerus/Humoroos
14.	Housse/Hoes	**Hose/Hoes**	House/Hoes	Hosse/Hoes
15.	Mei Be/Maybe	Mai Be/Maybe	**May Be/Maybe**	Mey Be/Maybe
16.	Matal/Metle/Meddle	**Metal/Mettle/Meddle**	Matal/Mettle/Meddle	Metal/Metle/Meddle
17.	**Halve/Have**	Hallva/Have	Hallve/Have	Halva/Have
18.	**Wee/We**	Wea/We	We/We	Wa/We
19.	**Taper/Tapir**	Taperr/Tapyr	Taperr/Tapir	Taper/Tapyr
20.	Timberr/Timbre	Tymber/Timbre	Tymberr/Timbre	**Timber/Timbre**
21.	Minse/Mintts	Mince/Mintts	Minse/Mints	**Mince/Mints**
22.	Eies/Ayes	Eyesc/Ayes	**Eyes/Ayes**	Eyess/Ayes
23.	Guesced/Guest	**Guessed/Guest**	Guesed/Guest	Gueced/Guest
24.	**Yore/Your/You'Re**	Yore/Yoor/You'Re	Yorre/Your/You'Re	Yorre/Yoor/You'Re
25.	Oarr/Or/Ora	Oarr/Or/Ore	**Oar/Or/Ore**	Oar/Or/Ora

#			
26.	Bate/Biat	**Bate/Bait**	Batte/Biat	Batte/Bait
27.	**Tax/Tacks**	Tax/Taks	Tax/Tacksc	Tax/Tackss
28.	Bald/Ballad/Bawled	Bald/Baled/Bawled	**Bald/Balled/Bawled**	Bald/Balad/Bawled
29.	Ewe/Yuo/Yew	Ewe/Yoo/Yew	**Ewe/You/Yew**	Ewe/Yoo/Yw
30.	Eei/I/Aye	Eie/I/Ae	**Eye/I/Aye**	Eie/I/Aye
31.	**Hoes/Hose**	Hoess/Hose	Hoess/House	Hoes/House
32.	Tou/Two/To	Tu/Two/To	To/Two/To	**Too/Two/To**
33.	**Ceres/Series**	Cerres/Series	Ceres/Sereis	Cerres/Sereis
34.	**Hansom/Handsome**	Hansum/Handsome	Hanscom/Handsome	Hanssom/Handsome
35.	Residance/Residents	**Residence/Residents**	Ressidence/Residents	Ressidance/Residents
36.	Surrf/Serf	**Surf/Serf**	Surrph/Serf	Surph/Serf
37.	Siall/Sale	Saill/Sale	**Sail/Sale**	Sial/Sale
38.	Therre's/Thiers	There's/Thiers	**There's/Theirs**	Therre's/Theirs
39.	Roed/Rode	Roed/Rude	**Rued/Rude**	Roed/Rue
40.	Aid/Aie	Ayd/Aide	Ayd/Aie	**Aid/Aide**
41.	Taem/Teem	Taem/Tem	Team/Tem	**Team/Teem**
42.	Ilusion/Allusion	Ilution/Allusion	Illution/Allusion	**Illusion/Allusion**
43.	Hi/Hih	Hy/High	**Hi/High**	Hy/Hih
44.	**Barred/Bard**	Bared/Bard	Barad/Bard	Barrad/Bard
45.	Mewll/Mule	**Mewl/Mule**	Mewll/Mole	Mewl/Mole
46.	Rowss/Rose	**Rows/Rose**	Rowss/Rouse	Rows/Rouse
47.	Chep/Cheap	Cheep/Chaep	**Cheep/Cheap**	Chep/Chaep
48.	Bah/Ba	Beh/Ba	**Bah/Baa**	Beh/Baa
49.	**Gofer/Gopher**	Gopher/Gopher	Gophfer/Gopher	Goffer/Gopher
50.	Don/Doe	Dun/Doe	**Dun/Done**	Don/Done
51.	Ryte/Write/Right	Ritte/Write/Right	Rytte/Write/Right	**Rite/Write/Right**
52.	**Mite/Might**	Mitte/Might	Myte/Might	Mytte/Might
53.	**Latter/Ladder**	Later/Ladder	Latar/Ladder	Lattar/Ladder
54.	Gorred/Goord	**Gored/Gourd**	Gored/Goord	Gorred/Gourd
55.	Ball/Belle	**Bell/Belle**	Bal/Belle	Bel/Belle
56.	Ruscell/Rustle	**Russell/Rustle**	Rusell/Rustle	Rucell/Rustle
57.	Tuat/Taught	Tautt/Taught	Tuatt/Taught	**Taut/Taught**

#	Col 1	Col 2	Col 3	Col 4
58.	**Cozen/Cousin**	Cozen/Coosin	Cozen/Coossin	Cozen/Coussin
59.	**Morn/Mourn**	Morrn/Moorn	Morrn/Mourn	Morn/Moorn
60.	Stare/Stiar	**Stare/Stair**	Sttare/Stiar	Sttare/Stair
61.	Wrrap/Rap	Wrrep/Rap	**Wrap/Rap**	Wrep/Rap
62.	Centts/Ssents	Centts/Scents	**Cents/Scents**	Cents/Ssents
63.	Basste/Based	Baste/Baced	**Baste/Based**	Bascte/Based
64.	Foorr/Fore/For	Foor/Fore/For	Fourr/Fore/For	**Four/Fore/For**
65.	Knikers/Nickers	Knickerrs/Nickers	Knikerrs/Nickers	**Knickers/Nickers**
66.	Marre/Mayor	**Mare/Mayor**	Mare/Meyor	Marre/Meyor
67.	Surrje/Serge	Surje/Serge	Surrge/Serge	**Surge/Serge**
68.	**Steal/Steel**	Steal/Stel	Stael/Steel	Stael/Stel
69.	Haerrt/Hart	**Heart/Hart**	Hearrt/Hart	Haert/Hart
70.	**Holed/Hold**	Huled/Hold	Holled/Hold	Hulled/Hold
71.	Way/Wiegh/Whey	Wai/Wiegh/Whey	Wai/Weigh/Whey	**Way/Weigh/Whey**
72.	Diieng/Dying	Dyieng/Dying	Dieing/Dying	**Dyeing/Dying**
73.	Holay/Holy/Wholly	Holay/Holy/Wholy	Holey/Holy/Wholy	**Holey/Holy/Wholly**
74.	Sworrd/Soared	Swurrd/Soared	Swurd/Soared	**Sword/Soared**
75.	Cane/Cyan	Cane/Cian	Cane/Cayn	**Cane/Cain**
76.	Arreil/Aerial	**Ariel/Aerial**	Arriel/Aerial	Areil/Aerial
77.	**Brut/Brute**	Brrot/Brute	Brot/Brute	Brrut/Brute
78.	Frrays/Phrase	**Frays/Phrase**	Frreys/Phrase	Freys/Phrase
79.	**Throne/Thrown**	Thrrune/Thrown	Thrune/Thrown	Thrrone/Thrown
80.	Ha'd/Hed	**He'd/Heed**	He'd/Hed	He'd/Head
81.	Waerr/Where/Ware	**Wear/Where/Ware**	Wearr/Where/Ware	Waer/Where/Ware
82.	Brraed/Bred	**Bread/Bred**	Braed/Bred	Brread/Bred
83.	We've/Waeve	**We've/Weave**	Wa've/Weave	Wa've/Waeve
84.	Hew/Hoe/Huh	**Hew/Hue/Hugh**	Hew/Hoe/Hugh	Hew/Hoe/Hogh
85.	Nikerrs/Knickers	Nickerrs/Knickers	Nikers/Knickers	**Nickers/Knickers**
86.	Call/Sell	**Cell/Sell**	Cal/Sell	Cel/Sell
87.	Isle/I'll/Aisle	**Isle/I'll/Aisle**	Isle/I'll/Aysle	Isle/I'l/Aysle
88.	Brruice/Brews	**Bruise/Brews**	Brruise/Brews	Bruice/Brews
89.	**Except/Accept**	Exsept/Accept	Exsept/Acept	Except/Acept

Grammar: Singular and Plural

1. **Which word is NOT a plural noun?**
   a. books
   b. [hat]
   c. toys

2. **Which word is a singular noun?**
   a. bikes
   b. cars
   c. [pencil]

3. **Which word can be both singular and plural?**
   a. [deer]
   b. bears
   c. mice

4. **Tommy _____ badminton at the court.**
   a. playing
   b. [plays]
   c. play's

5. **They _____ to eat at fast food restaurants once in a while.**
   a. likes
   b. [like]
   c. likies

6. **Everybody _____ Janet Jackson.**
   a. know
   b. known
   c. [knows]

7. **He ___ very fast. You have to listen carefully.**
   a. spoken
   b. speak
   c. [speaks]

8. **Which one is the singular form of women?**
   a. womans
   b. [woman]
   c. women

9. **The plural form of tooth is**
   a. tooths
   b. toothes
   c. [teeth]

10. **The singular form of mice is _____.**
    a. [mouse]
    b. mices
    c. mouses

11. **The plural form of glass is _____.**
    a. glassies
    b. [glasses]
    c. glassy

12. **The plural form of dress is _____.**
    a. dressing
    b. [dresses]
    c. dressy

13. **Plural means many.**
    a. [True]
    b. False

14. **Singular means 1.**
    a. [True]
    b. False

15. **Is this word singular or plural? monsters**
    a. [plural]
    b. singular

16. **Find the plural noun in the sentence. They gave her a nice vase full of flowers.**
    a. they
    b. [flowers]
    c. vase

17. Find the plural noun in the sentence. Her baby brother grabbed the crayons out of the box and drew on the wall.

    a. crayons

    b. box

    c. brothers

18. Find the plural noun in the sentence. My friend, Lois, picked enough red strawberries for the whole class.

    a. strawberries

    b. friends

    c. classes

19. What is the correct plural form of the noun wish?

    a. wishes

    b. wishs

    c. wishy

20. What is the correct plural form of the noun flurry?

    a. flurrys

    b. flurryies

    c. flurries

21. What is the correct plural form of the noun box?

    a. boxs

    b. boxses

    c. boxes

22. What is the correct plural form of the noun bee?

    a. beess

    b. beeses

    c. bees

23. What is the correct plural form of the noun candy?

    a. candys

    b. candyies

    c. candies

24. Find the singular noun in the sentence. The boys and girls drew pictures on the sidewalk.

    a. boys

    b. drew

    c. sidewalk

Grammar: Homophones vs Homographs vs. Homonyms

1. 'there,' 'their,' or 'they're' are examples of _____.
   - a. Homophones
   - b. Homographs

2. ____ are words that have the same spelling or pronunciation but different meanings.
   - a. Homonyms
   - b. Hemograms

3. Choose the correct homophone for this sentence: Please don't drop and _____that bottle of hand sanitizer!
   - a. brake
   - b. break

4. Homographs are two or more words that have the same spelling but different ____.
   - a. ending sounds
   - b. meanings

5. Current (A flow of water / Up to date) is both homograph and homophone.
   - a. True
   - b. False

6. To, two and too are _____.
   - a. Homagraphs
   - b. Homonyms

7. The candle filled the _____ with a delicious scent.
   - a. heir
   - b. air

8. Kim drove _____ the tunnel.
   - a. threw
   - b. through

9. John wants to go to _____ house for dinner, but they don't like her, so _____ going to say no.
   - a. their, they're
   - b. there, they're

10. We won a $95,000 _____!
    - a. cheque
    - b. check

11. For example, a pencil is not really made with _____.
    - a. led
    - b. lead

12. Choose the correct homophone for this sentence: Timmy was standing _____ in line.
    - a. fourth
    - b. forth

13. Homophones are two words that sound the same but have a different meanings.
    - a. True
    - b. False

14. The word ring in the following two sentences is considered what? She wore a ruby ring. | We heard the doorbell ring.
    - a. hologram
    - b. homograph

15. A Homograph is a word that has more than one meaning and doesn't have to sound the same.

    a. [True]

    b. False

16. Homophones occur when there are multiple ways to spell the same sound.

    a. [True]

    b. False

17. Select the correct homophone: I have very little (patience/patients) when students do not follow directions.

    a. patients

    b. [patience]

18. The correct homophone (s) are used in the sentence: Personally, I hate the smell of read meet.

    a. True

    b. [False]

19. The correct homophone(s) is used in the sentence: We saw a herd of cattle in the farmer's field.

    a. [True]

    b. False

20. What is NOT an example of a homograph?

    a. [or, oar]

    b. live, live

Reading a Timeline

Answer Key

Answers

1. 2
2. B
3. 1803
4. 1805
5. 4
6. 1804
7. 1806
8. Yes
9. Use Line
10. Use Line

Lewis and Clark's Expedition

Use the timeline to answer the questions.

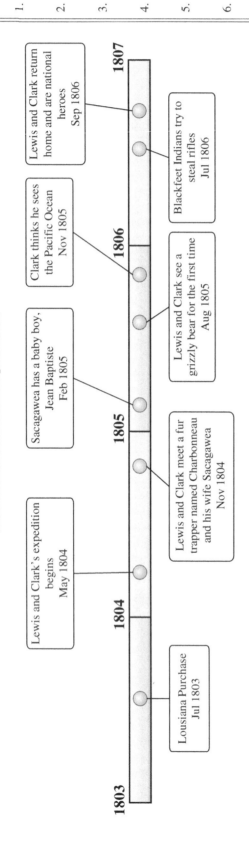

1803

Lousiana Purchase
Jul 1803

1804

Lewis and Clark's expedition
begins
May 1804

Lewis and Clark meet a fur
trapper named Charbonneau
and his wife Sacagawea
Nov 1804

1805

Sacagawea has a baby boy,
Jean Baptiste
Feb 1805

Lewis and Clark see a
grizzly bear for the first time
Aug 1805

Clark thinks he sees
the Pacific Ocean
Nov 1805

1806

Blackfeet Indians try to
steal rifles
Jul 1806

Lewis and Clark return
home and are national
heroes
Sep 1806

1807

1) How many years did Lewis and Clark's expedition take? ___2___

2) Which happened earlier? A. Indians try to steal rifles or B. Lewis and Clark see a grizzly bear ___B___

3) What year was the Louisiana Purchase? ___1803___

4) What year did Sacagawea have her child? ___1805___

5) What is the span (number of years shown) of this timeline? ___4___

6) What year did Lewis and Clark meet Charbonneau? ___1804___

7) What year did Lewis and Clark return home? ___1806___

8) In September of 1804 Lewis and Clark saw a prairie dog. Could you put this event on the timeline above? (Yes / No)

9) What event happened in Nov 1805? ___Clark thinks he sees the Pacific Ocean___

10) What is this timeline about? ___Lewis and Clark's Expedition___

10th Grade Simple Math Refresher

1. Perform the following operation: 12 + 1 + 8 =
   a. 21
   b. 20
   c. 18

2. Solve 1,056 divided by 22.
   a. 92
   b. 48
   c. 36

3. Division is the math operation that tells you to
   _____ and is represented by the symbols
   _____.
   a. separate or combine two numbers together; - and /
   b. separate something into parts; ÷ and /
   c. combine three numbers together; - and /

4. Brad saved $605 for his yearly vacations. He has 11 days of vacation and wants to spend the same amount of money each day, how much will he spend each day?
   a. $95
   b. $55
   c. $104

5. Convert 3/7 to a percent.
   a. 38.1%
   b. 5.9%
   c. 42.9%

6. Change 0.142 to a fraction.
   a. 1/7
   b. 2/4
   c. 1/8

7. Change 2/5 to a decimal.
   a. 0.4
   b. 0.9
   c. 0.5

8. Write 4 8/9 as an improper fraction.
   a. 32/5
   b. 40/8
   c. 44/9

9. A(n) _____ is an improper fraction written with a whole number and a proper fraction.
   a. decimal
   b. proper fraction
   c. mixed number

10. Write 50% as a fraction.
    a. 1/2
    b. 0/5
    c. 5/0

11. Change 79.5% to a decimal.
    a. 0.795
    b. .79.5%
    c. 79.05%

12. Which of the following number has the highest numerical value?
    a. 2.8
    b. 0.28
    c. 4.5%

13. Order the following numbers from smallest to greatest: 0.25, 4.54, 0.015, 1.24

    a. 1.24, 4.54, 0.015, 0.25

    b. 0.015, 0.25, 1.24, 4.54

    c. 4.54, 0.015, 0.25, 1.24

14. What is the 28% of 80?

    a. 28.0

    b. 84%

    c. 22.4

15. Convert 6/7 to a percent.

    a. 7.6%

    b. 6.7%

    c. 86%

16. What is the denominator of 7/9?

    a. 7.9

    b. 7

    c. 9

17. Write 18.7% as a decimal.

    a. 0.187

    b. 1.87

    c. 18.7%

18. Convert 0.00047 to scientific notation.

    a. 4.0×10^{-7}

    b. 4.7×4^{-0}

    c. 4.7×10^{-4}

19. Multiply 4.25×10^{-5} by 4.

    a. 1.7×10^{-4}

    b. 2.7×10^{-4}

    c. 4.5×10^{1}

20. Janes Market sells a pack of 500 napkins for $2.50 and Taylor Grocery sells a pack that has 750 of the same napkins for $3.75. Which pack is the best deal?

    a. Janes Market

    b. Both packs have the same price per napkin

    c. Taylor Grocery

21. Maya earned $4,575 in 3 months. If earned the same amount each month, how much did she earn each month?

    a. $2,575

    b. $925

    c. $1,525

22. The independent variable of an exponential function is the _____.

    a. exponent

    b. logarithm

    c. fraction

23. Solve for X in the following equation $8 + 3^{X} = 35$

    a. X = 3

    b. X = 8

    c. X = 35

24. Grams. liters and centimeters are all examples of _____ units.

    a. pounds

    b. kilogram

    c. metric

25. One kilogram is equivalent to _____ grams.

    a. 100

    b. 10

    c. 1,000

10th Grade Geography Multiple Choice Quiz: Mountain Range

Select the best answer for each question.

1. The _____ run for 1,500 miles along the east coast of the US from northern Alabama to Maine.
   a. Sierra Nevada
   b. Rocky Mountains
   c. Appalachian Mountains

2. Which is of the following is famous for its tall peaks and stretches 1,491 miles through much of central Asia?
   a. Himalayas
   b. Andres
   c. Urals

3. The _____ are the world's longest mountain range, stretching approximately 4,300 miles.
   a. Alps
   b. Rockies
   c. Andes

4. Fault-block mountains were formed along a fault in the Earth's crust. Which of the following is a fault-block mountain?
   a. Appalachian
   b. Sierra Nevada
   c. Rockies

5. What is the process by which the world's tallest mountain ranges are formed?
   a. seafloor spreading
   b. continental drift
   c. plate tectonics

6. The theory of continental drift was proposed by which German meteorologist?
   a. Charles Thomson Rees Wilson
   b. Alfred Wegener
   c. John Dalton

7. Which of the following mountain ranges is the highest and most extensive in Europe?
   a. The Appalachian
   b. The Alps
   c. The Andes

8. What is the highest point of the Rockies that is 14,440 feet above sea level?
   a. Mount Elbert
   b. Mount Chamberlin
   c. Mount Whitney

9. The _____ is a mountain range in northeast New York.
   a. Alaska Range
   b. Adirondacks
   c. Brooks Range

10. Which famous city was built atop a mountain of the Andes Mountain range?
    a. Machu Picchu
    b. Tikal
    c. Tenochtitlan

11. What is the highest mountain range in North America?
    a. Brooks Range
    b. Cascade Range
    c. Alaska Range

12. The _____ is the largest mountain range between the Appalachians and the Rockies.
    a. Ozarks
    b. Urals
    c. Adirondacks

10th Grade Geography Multiple Choice Quiz: Islands

Select the best answer for each question.

1. An island is a body of land smaller than a continent that is surrounded _____ by water.
    a. entirely
    b. on three sides
    c. on two sides

2. A group of related islands, such as the Philippines, is called _____ .
    a. a continent
    b. an island
    c. an archipelago

3. _____ form when volcanoes erupt on the ocean floor.
    a. Artificial Island
    b. Continental islands
    c. Oceanic islands

4. Which of the following islands are classified as oceanic islands?
    a. Padre Island and Cape Hatteras
    b. Greenland and Madagascar
    c. Iceland and Hawaiian

5. Which of the following is the world's largest non-continental island?
    a. Madagascar
    b. Greenland
    c. Great Britain

6. Located off the southeast coast of Africa, _____ is the world's fourth largest island.
    a. Seychelles
    b. Madagascar
    c. Mauritius

7. _____ are sections of the continental shelf that have become isolated due to sea-level rise.
    a. Oceanic islands
    b. Continental islands
    c. Barrier islands

8. Home to the famous volcano Mount Fuji, ____ is Japan's largest island.
    a. Hokkaido
    b. Honshu
    c. Kyushu

9. What is the largest island in the Mediterranean Sea?
    a. Sardinia
    b. Sicily
    c. Cyprus

10. Napoleon Bonaparte, Emperor of France was born on which island in France?
    a. Port-Cros
    b. Levant Island
    c. Corcica

11. _____ is the world's ninth largest island, the largest island in the British Isles, and the world's third most populous island.
    a. Great Britain
    b. Isle of Man
    c. Ireland

12. The largest and southernmost island in the Mariana Islands chain, located in the North Pacific Ocean is _____.
    a. Guam
    b. Saipan
    c. Tinian

10th Grade Geography Multiple Choice Quiz: Glaciers

Select the best answer for each question.

1. A glacier is a huge mass of _____ that moves slowly over _____.
   - a. snow and clouds
   - b. hail and water
   - c. ice and land

2. Glaciers that cover more than 50,000 square kilometers are called?
   - a. Alpine
   - b. Ice caps
   - c. Ice sheets

3. _____ form on mountainsides and move downward through valleys.
   - a. Alpine glaciers
   - b. Ice caps
   - c. Ice sheets

4. A complex of _____ glaciers burying much of a mountain range is called an _____.
   - a. valley and ice sheet
   - b. hill and ice cap
   - c. mountain and ice field

5. Glaciers also exist high in _____ such as the _____ and the _____.
   - a. mountain ranges, Himalayas and Andes
   - b. Plateaus, Arctic and Antarctica
   - c. Hills, Australia and South Africa

6. Melting _____ contribute to rising sea levels.
   - a. ice caps
   - b. ice field
   - c. ice sheets

7. Glaciers carry great amounts of _____, _____, and _____.
   - a. snow, water and rock
   - b. ice, rock and clay
   - c. soil, rock and clay

8. A _____ is one that ends in a body of water like a lake or an ocean.
   - a. hanging glaciers
   - b. cirque glaciers
   - c. calving glacier

9. A _____ glacier is one that is formed in an area where the temperature is always below the freezing point.
   - a. temperate
   - b. polar
   - c. piedmont

10. Most glaciers are located near the _____ or _____.
    - a. Greenland or Iceland
    - b. Arctic or Antarctic
    - c. North or South Poles

11. _____ refers to all processes that contribute mass to a glacier.
    - a. Transformation
    - b. Ablation
    - c. Accumulation

12. _____ is a simple consequence of the weight and creep properties of ice.
    - a. Glacier flow
    - b. Ablation
    - c. Accumulation

10th Grade Geography Multiple Choice Quiz: Deserts

Select the best answer for each question.

1. **Which is the only continent with no large deserts?**
   a. Europe
   b. North America
   c. Australia

2. **Which desert in Asia stretches across parts of China and Mongolia?**
   a. Great Victoria desert
   b. Sahara desert
   c. Gobi desert

3. **What percentage of the world's land surface is a desert?**
   a. 15
   b. 25
   c. 20

4. **The _____ is the world's largest hot desert.**
   a. Sahara
   b. Sonoran
   c. Kalahari

5. **Which of the following is one of the most oil-rich places in the world?**
   a. Mohave desert
   b. Arabian desert
   c. Kalahari desert

6. **An oasis is a place in the desert with _____.**
   a. a collection of desert edible plants
   b. a supply of fresh water
   c. a horde of desert animals

7. **A subtropical desert is -**
   a. a desert that exists near the leeward slopes of some mountain ranges
   b. sometimes called inland deserts
   c. caused by the circulation patterns of air masses

8. **The _____ is a large desert located in Mexico and parts of the Southwestern United States.**
   a. Great Victoria desert
   b. Sonoran desert
   c. Gobi desert

9. **The amount of _____ in a desert often greatly exceeds the annual rainfall.**
   a. condensation
   b. precipitation
   c. evaporation

10. **_____ deserts exist near the leeward slopes of some mountain ranges.**
    a. rain shadow
    b. costal
    c. interior

11. **A home to Death Valley, the hottest and lowest spot in the US is the _____.**
    a. Sonoran desert
    b. Mohave desert
    c. Kalahari desert

12. **The Atacama Desert, on the Pacific shores of Chile, is a _____, where some areas of it are often covered by fog.**
    a. subtropical desert
    b. coastal desert
    c. interior desert

10th Grade The Metric System

Tip: After you've answered the easy ones, go back and work on the harder ones.

gram	metric	liter	Meter	Gram
centimeter	liter	weight	Celsius	Liter
meter	10	milliliters	kilogram	Celsius

Scientists all over the world use the _metric_ system. There's a very good reason for this-it's so everyone is doing the measuring the same way, all over the world. Most other countries already use the metric system for measuring everything.

Another good reason to use metric is that you don't have so much to remember-no 12 inches in a foot or 5,280 feet in a mile. It's all decimal! The larger or smaller units go up or down by _10_, 100, or 1,000.

Meter is for length. A _meter_ is a little longer than a yard. For long distances, there is the kilometer (a thousand meters). For small things, there is the _centimeter_ (100 centimeters in a meter).

Liter is for volume. A _liter_ is a little larger than a quart. There are a thousand _milliliters_ in a _liter_.

Gram is for _weight_. A _gram_ is a little more than the weight of a paper clip. For heavier things, there is the _kilogram_ (a thousand grams).

Temperatures are in degrees Celsius (also called centigrade). Water freezes at 0 degrees _Celsius_ and boils at 100 degrees _Celsius_. That's easy!

Contractions Multiple Choice

A *contraction* is a way of making two words into one. Circle the correct answer.

1. aren't
- a. are not
- b. not are
- c. arenot

2. can't
- a. cants
- b. cannot
- c. cant

3. couldn't
- a. couldnt
- b. couldnts
- c. could not

4. didn't
- a. didn'ts
- b. did nots
- c. did not

5. don't
- a.
- b. do not

6. hadn't
- a. had not
- b. had nots
- c. hadn'ts

7. hasn't
- a. has nots
- b. has not
- c. hasnot

8. haven't
- a. have nots
- b. haven'ts
- c. have not

9. I'm
- a. I am
- b. I'ms
- c. I'am

10. I've
- a. I have
- b. I'ves
- c. I'have

11. isn't
- a. isn'ts
- b. is not
- c. is'not

12. let's
- a. lets
- b. let'us
- c. let us

13. mightn't
- a. mightnt
- b. might not
- c. might'not

14. mustn't
- a. mustnt
- b. must'not
- c. must not

10th Grade Art: Henri Matisse

1. Henri Matisse was born in the north of __France__ . Henri's father was a grain merchant who was strict with him. He went to law school in Paris and graduated from there.

2. In 1888, he passed the __bar__ and began working as a law clerk.

3. Henri was diagnosed with __appendicitis__ in 1889.

4. His mother encouraged him to break the __rules__ of art and experiment with new techniques and paint his

__emotions__ .

5. He studied art for a year at the Academie Julian in Paris before leaving to train under the artist Gustave

Moreau, where he could experiment with more __modern__ painting styles.

6. Russell introduced him to __impressionism__ and van Gogh's work.

7. In 1897, Matisse completed his first __masterpiece__ . It was known as The Dinner Table.

8. He continued to paint, __influenced__ by artists such as Vincent van Gogh and Paul Cezanne.

9. Matisse developed a new style in the early 1900s. He began to paint with __bright__ masses of freely applied

colors.

10th Grade Art: Recycled Art

Recycled art is an unusual but very creative art form in which existing materials are reused and recycled to create works of art. This is in contrast to more traditional art forms in which artists use paint, drawing materials, clay, or other mediums associated with artwork creation. Sometimes the materials used in recycled art are essentially garbage, while other materials are created for a purpose other than art and are being given a new lease on life. Recycled art can be made for several reasons. When people have limited materials to work with, it is often created out of necessity. In other cases, as discussed in this lesson, the materials used in the art are deliberately chosen to challenge viewers' perceptions of what is art, what is trash, and what is beautiful and meaningful. Many recycled art artists use their mediums to convey powerful environmental messages.

There are two types of recycled art: upcycled art and downcycled art. These are two complementary approaches that make use of recycled materials in opposing ways. Upcycled art transforms materials that are typically considered trash into beautiful and meaningful art. This practice is considered more common in the recycled art world because it allows artists to make powerful statements about waste. Upcycled art is created by an artist who creates a portrait out of discarded computer parts that would otherwise end up in a landfill.

Downcycled art is the inverse of upcycled art in that artists deconstruct or destroy objects before transforming them into art. Downcycled art is created by an artist who takes an old armchair and rips the stuffing out of it in an installation piece. While downcycled art exists, it is less common because the goal of recycled art is often to elevate materials that are considered worthless by incorporating them into art.

1. Sometimes the materials used in recycled art are essentially _____.

   a. wood

   b. garbage

   c. luxury items

2. _____ art transforms materials that are typically considered trash into beautiful and meaningful art.

   a. Abstract

   b. Acrylic paint

   c. Upcycled

3. _____ art is the inverse of upcycled art in that artists deconstruct or destroy objects before transforming them into art.

   a. Enamel

   b. Fine art

   c. Downcycled

4. There are two types of recycled art: _____ art and _____ art.

   a. decorative and airbrush

   b. upcycled and downcycled

   c. abstract and recycled

10th Grade Music Vocabulary Crossword

Music has most likely existed for as long as humans have, which could be over a hundred thousand years! The earliest music is thought to have involved singing and clapping, and then early humans began drumming with sticks or other natural objects. Flutes carved from bones, such as bear and woolly mammoth bones, were among the first known musical instruments. Some of these bone instruments date back to 45,000 years!

Scholars agree that there are no 100% reliable methods for determining the exact chronology of musical instruments across cultures. Comparing and organizing instruments based on their complexity is deceptive, because technological advances in musical instruments have sometimes reduced complexity. Early slit drums, for example, required felling and hollowing out large trees; later slit drums were made by opening bamboo stalks, a much simpler task.

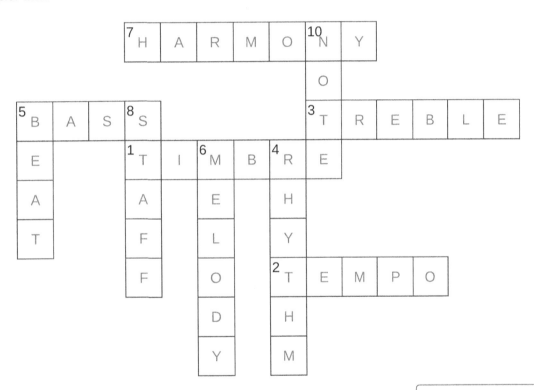

Across

1. the distinctive property of a complex sound
2. the speed at which a composition is to be played
3. having or denoting a high range
5. the lowest part of the musical range
7. compatibility in opinion and action

Down

4. an interval during which a recurring sequence occurs
5. hit repeatedly
6. a succession of notes forming a distinctive sequence
8. a strong rod or stick with a specialized utilitarian purpose
10. a brief written record

BASS   BEAT   STAFF
TIMBRE   HARMONY
TREBLE   MELODY   NOTE
RHYTHM   TEMPO

10th Grade Music: Wolfgang Amadeus Mozart

Wolfgang Amadeus Mozart (January 27, 1756 – December 5, 1791; pronounced MOHT-sart) was an Austrian composer, instrumentalist, and music teacher. Johannes Chrysostomus Wolfgangus Theophillus Mozart was his full baptismal name. He was the youngest child of Leopold and Anna Maria Mozart and was born in Salzburg, Austria. The young Mozart displayed exceptional musical talent from an early age. He toured Europe with his parents and older sister "Nannerl," performing for royalty and the aristocratic elite for several years.

Mozart attempted but failed to establish himself as a composer in Paris as a young man. He returned to Salzburg and briefly worked in the Archbishop of Salzburg's court. He was restless, aware of his brilliance, and thought Salzburg was too small for him. He moved to Vienna, where he had some success. He married Constance Weber and had two sons with her.

Mozart composed over 600 musical works, all of which are of the highest quality. The operas, The Marriage of Figaro, Don Giovanni, Cos fan tutte, and The Magic Flute; the symphonies in E-flat major, G minor, and C major ("Jupiter"); concertos for piano, violin, and various wind instruments; and numerous chamber pieces, and the Requiem are among his works. Along with Bach and Beethoven, Mozart is regarded as one of the greatest composers of all time.

There are several stories about Mozart's final illness and death, and it's difficult to know what happened. He was working on The Magic Flute, one of his best works and still a popular opera today. It is written in German rather than Italian, as are the majority of his other operas. It's similar to an English pantomime in some ways. At the same time, he was working on this, he was approached by a stranger and asked to compose a requiem. He was instructed to write this in private. Then he was commissioned to write the Italian opera La Clemenza di Tito, which premiered in Prague in September 1791. The Magic Flute received its first performance at the end of September. The Requiem was then a labor of love for Mozart. He must have realized that he was already gravely ill and that the Requiem (a mass for the dead) was for himself in some ways. He died in Vienna before completing it. Constanze commissioned another composer, Franz Xaver Süssmayr, to complete the work. Mozart was laid to rest in the St. Marx Cemetery.

1. When Mozart returned to Salzburg, he worked in the_____.
   a. Archbishop of Salzburg's court
   b. Salzburg's Music Store
   c. Archbishop High School

2. Mozart was an Austrian _____.
   a. composer, English teacher, singer
   b. science teacher, piano player and composer
   c. composer, instrumentalist, and music teacher

3. Mozart married _____ and had two sons with her.
   a. Constance Weber
   b. Courtney Webber
   c. Countesses Wilson

4. Mozart was laid to rest in the _____.
   a. Mozart family cemetery
   b. Dr. Mary Cemetery
   c. St. Marx Cemetery

10th Grade Spelling Words
Word Scramble

Look carefully at the jumbled words and unscramble the spelling words below.

1. eenegtl   g e n t e e l

2. luieedbg   b e g u i l e d

3. tramanel   m a t e r n a l

4. ucmuevialt   c u m u l a t i v e

5. dandeut   d a u n t e d

6. lnarabmo   a b n o r m a l

7. geossua   g a s e o u s

8. rirantpiopoap   a p p r o p r i a t i o n

9. iamlemd   d i l e m m a

10. lmaedu   m a u l e d

11. iinnutoti   i n t u i t i o n

12. tiuneaecn   e n u n c i a t e

13. ioeaulgd   d i a l o g u e

14. orecirtd   c r e d i t o r

15. iietdcfne   d e f i c i e n t

16. lntceleie   c l i e n t e l e

17. mtoidte   o m i t t e d

18. inoocslvun   c o n v u l s i o n

19. ietlxpo   e x p l o i t

20. roancgi   o r g a n i c

10th Grade Spelling Words Quiz

Circle the best definition meaning for each spelling word provided below.

1. emboss

   a. to design with a sunken or recessed pattern

   b. to decorate with a raised pattern or design

   c. to print a material with flat pattern or design

2. perseverance

   a. the act or power of continuing to do something in spite of difficulties

   b. the act of giving up on something because it is difficult

   c. the act of being uninterested, unenthusiastic, or unconcerned

3. chagrin

   a. a feeling of being safe or protected

   b. a feeling of being annoyed by failure or disappointment

   c. a feeling of being sleepy and lethargic

4. mediocre

   a. not very often

   b. not very effective

   c. not very good

5. frugal

   a. careful, unwavering attention or persistent application

   b. careful in spending or using supplies

   c. careful in spending time and effort

6. benefactor

   a. someone who helps another especially by giving money

   b. someone who helps another find a job

   c. someone who helps another buy a house

7. personnel

   a. a group of kids who are members of a sports club

   b. a group of people employed in a business or an organization

   c. a group of elderly citizens that are members of senior social programs

8. journal

   a. a book in which we collect photographs

   b. a book in which you write down your personal experiences and thoughts

   c. a book in which map are compiled and collected

9. amphitheater

   a. a room built to enable an audience to hear and watch performances

   b. an arena with seats rising in curved rows around an open space

   c. a large room for public meetings or performances

10. horticulture

   a. the science and art of cultivating silkworms to produce silk

   b. the science and art of growing fruits, vegetables, flowers, or ornamental plants

   c. the science and art of cultivating plants and livestock

10th Grade Geometry Reading Comprehension

90-degree	segment	Acute	angles	Obtuse
directions	straight	halves	height	formulas

The study of shapes and space is known as geometry. It provides answers to size, area, and volume questions. The earliest known geometry works date back to 2000 BC and are from Egypt. There were formulas for lengths, areas, and volumes, as well as one for pyramids. Thales of Miletus calculated the height of pyramids in the 7th century BC, and the Greek mathematician Pythagoras proved the well-known Pythagorean Theorem.

Euclid, another Greek mathematician, introduced Euclidean geometry around 300 BC by demonstrating how to prove theorems using basic definitions and truths. We still use Euclidean geometry to prove theorems today.

Geometric terms include points, lines, and angles . A point is a non-dimensional object with no length or width. A dot is commonly used to represent it. A line is an object that extends in both directions without end. It is usually depicted with arrowheads to indicate that it continues indefinitely. A line segment is a section of a line that has two ends. A ray is one-half of a line with a single endpoint. Two rays with the same endpoint form an angle. The angle is called a straight angle if the rays are the two halves of a single line. A straight angle is analogous to a book open flat on a desk. A right angle is defined as an angle that is opened half that far.

Angles are expressed in degrees. A right angle is defined as a 90-degree angle. Acute angles are those that are less than a right angle. Obtuse angles are those that are larger than a right angle but smaller than a straight angle.

10 Grade Math Algebraic Equation

Algebraic equations are made up of two algebraic expressions that are equal on either side of an equal sign. Constants, variables, and exponents are included, and they are also considered polynomial equations when the exponents are positive whole numbers.

1. An algebraic equation is the same thing as _____ being set equal to one another.

   a. three expressions

   b. 1 algebraic 2 expressions

   c. two algebraic expressions

2. The word equation is related to the word 'equal' meaning that there is___.

   a. an equal sign between the two expressions

   b. an equal sign between the x and y.

   c. an equal sign after y and x.

3. Polynomials are algebraic expressions that are created by ___,

   a. dividing by a variable

   b. combining negative exponents

   c. combining numbers and variables

4. A linear equation is one that usually only has two variables ____.

   a. 'x' and 'y'

   b. 'y' and 'z'

   c. 'x' and 'l'

5. Linear equations will only have ___line when graphed.

   a. two

   b. one

   c. three

6. A quadratic equation is an _____ equation of the second degree.

   a. coefficient

   b. polynomial

   c. quadratic equations

7. Linear equations sometimes can have ___ variables.

   a. zero

   b. only one

   c. one, two or three

8. When solving algebraic equations, the goal is to find out what number the ___ is representing.

   a. variable

   b. expression inside first

   c. figures

9. What type of equation is $-2x + 7 = 4$?

   a. proportional to

   b. linear equation

   c. integers

10. What type of equation is $7x^2 + 5x + 3 = 0$?

   a. cubic equation

   b. positive number

   c. quadratic equation

10th Grade Spelling Words
Word Search

Circle the 12 words listed below. Words appear straight across, back- word straight across, up and down.

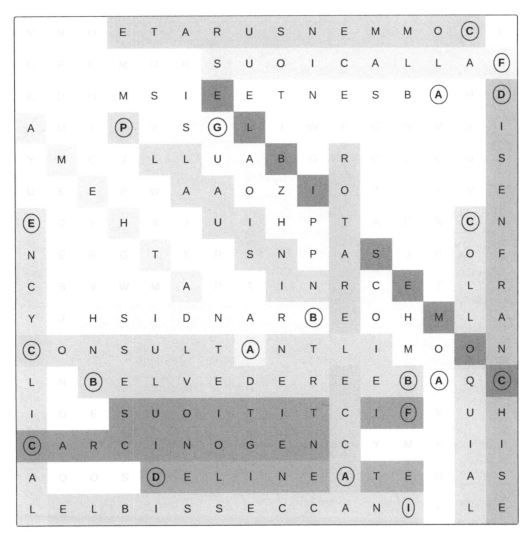

			E	T	A	R	U	S	N	E	M	M	O	Ⓒ	
				S	U	O	I	C	A	L	L	A	Ⓕ
		M	S	I	E	E	T	N	E	S	B	Ⓐ	Ⓓ
A		Ⓟ	S	Ⓖ	L				R				I
M		L	L	U	A	B		R				S
E		A	A	O	Z	I	O				E
Ⓔ	H		U	I	H	P	T			Ⓒ	N
N	T		S	N	P	A	S		O	F
C		A		I	N	R	C	E		L	R
Y	H	S	I	D	N	A	R	Ⓑ	E	O	H	M	L	A
Ⓒ	O	N	S	U	L	T	Ⓐ	N	T	L	I	M	O	O	N
L	Ⓑ	E	L	V	E	D	E	R	E	E	Ⓑ	Ⓐ	Q	Ⓒ
I		S	U	O	I	T	I	T	C	I	Ⓕ	U	H
Ⓒ	A	R	C	I	N	O	G	E	N	C		I	I
A		Ⓓ	E	L	I	N	E	A	T	E		A	S
L	E	L	B	I	S	S	E	C	C	A	N	Ⓘ	L	E

consultant →   inaccessible ←   fictitious ←   brandish ←   plausible ↘   absenteeism ←

accelerator ↑   amorphous ↖   anathema ↖   belvedere →   biennial ↖   carcinogen →   colloquial ↓

comestible ↖   commensurate ←   delineate →   disenfranchise ↓   encyclical ↓   fallacious ←

gazpacho ↘

20 words in Wordsearch: 4 vertical, 10 horizontal, 6 diagonal. (11 reversed.)

10th Grade Spelling Test

Encircle the word with the correct spelling.

	A	B	C	D
1.	imperrturbible	imperrturbable	**imperturbable**	imperturbible
2.	largese	largesce	largece	**largesse**
3.	narcisus	**narcissus**	narciscus	narcisos
4.	neofyte	neophytte	neofytte	**neophyte**
5.	obstetricain	**obstetrician**	obsstetrician	obsstetricain
6.	elloquent	**eloquent**	eloqoent	elloqoent
7.	**cryptic**	criptic	crryptic	crriptic
8.	**hypocrite**	hypucrite	hypocrrite	hypucrrite
9.	**assertive**	acertive	ascertive	asertive
10.	**parables**	paribles	parribles	parrables
11.	**assess**	asess	asesc	ascess
12.	**indisposed**	indissposed	indispoused	indisspoused
13.	calloos	caloos	**callous**	calous
14.	ilustrious	ilustroius	**illustrious**	illustroius
15.	crredibiliti	**credibility**	crredibility	credibiliti
16.	**allure**	allore	alore	aeure
17.	pascive	**passive**	pasive	pasyve
18.	conscolidate	**consolidate**	conssolidate	cunsolidate
19.	percepsion	**perception**	perrception	perrcepsion
20.	obgecttivity	**objectivity**	objecttivity	obgectivity

10th Grade Biology: ANIMAL KINGDOM

Animals are the most numerous and diverse of the five kingdoms of living things. Over two million animal species have been identified so far. All animals share certain characteristics. Animals, unlike plants, obtain their energy from food. They are all made up of many cells, and many animals move quickly. Most reproduce sexually and have sense organs that allow them to respond rapidly to their environment.

Jellyfish, for example, has a relatively simple structure. They lack a skeleton, have few muscles, and move in an uncoordinated manner? They float along with the ocean currents. Jellyfish are classified as invertebrates because, like 98% of all animals, they lack a backbone.

Animals with backbones, such as these zebras, are known as vertebrates. Vertebrates include mammals, birds, fish, amphibians, and reptiles. Zebras are classified as mammals. Mammalian animals, which include humans, are the most complex in the animal kingdom.

1. What are 5 examples of a vertebrate?

   fishes, amphibians, reptiles, birds, and mammals.

2. What are 5 examples of invertebrates?

   insects, snail, squids, earthworms and leeches

3. What exactly is a mammal?

   A mammal is an animal that breathes air, has a backbone, and at some point in its life grows hair. Furthermore, all female mammals have milk-producing glands. Mammals are among the most intelligent creatures on the planet. Mammals are a diverse group of animals that include everything from cats to humans to whales.

4. Amphibians are a class of what cold-blooded vertebrates?

   rogs, toads, salamanders, newts, and caecilians

5. Reptiles use a variety of methods to defend themselves such as...

   avoidance, camouflage, hissing and biting

6. What are the 4 types of arthropods?

   insects, myriapods, arachnids, crustaceans

7. Oviparous animals lay eggs where?

   outside their body

8. An herbivore is an organism that mostly feeds on what?

   plants

9. A carnivore is an organism that mostly eats?

   meat, or the flesh of animals

10. An omnivore is an organism that eats?

    plants and animals

ARTS Vocabulary Terms 1

Choose the best answer to each question.

1	G	The arrangement of the parts of a work of art.	⇢	Composition
2	F	Coarse cloth or heavy fabric that must be stretched and primed to use for painting, particularly for oil paintings.	⇢	Canvas
3	C	The use of found objects or three-dimensional objects to create a work of art.	⇢	Assemblage
4	D	Colors next to each other on the color wheel.	⇢	Analogous colors
5	I	An arrangement of shapes adhered to a background.	⇢	Collage
6	K	The organization of colors on a wheel. Used to help understand color schemes.	⇢	Color wheel
7	A	The "glue" the holds pigment together and makes it stick to a surface.	⇢	Binder
8	L	Originally the study of beautiful things; currently refers to the study or understanding of anything that is visually pleasing or "works" within the boundaries of the principles of art.	⇢	Aesthetics
9	H	A print made from a collage of assorted pasted materials such as papers, cardboards, string etc.	⇢	Collagraph
10	J	The art principle which refers to the arrangement of elements in an art work. Can be either formal symmetrical, informal asymmetrical or radial.	⇢	Balance
11	B	Italian word for "light-shade". The use and balance of light and shade in a painting, and in particular the use of strong .contrast.	⇢	Chiaroscuro
12	E	Clay objects that have been fired one time. (unglazed).	⇢	Bisque

ARTS Vocabulary Terms 2

Choose the best answer to each question.

1	D	Computer art	→→	Art made with the use of a computer program.
2	B	Diptych	→→	Painting, usually an altarpiece, made up of hinged panels.
3	H	Earth colors	→→	Pigments made using earth (dirt) that contain metal oxides mixed with a binder such as glue
4	K	Eye-level	→→	The artists' view of where the perceived line or perspective came from.
5	A	Environmental art	→→	Art made on a grand scale, involving the creation of a man-made environment such as architecture, sculpture, light or landscape.
6	I	Facade	→→	The front or face of a building.
7	C	Figurative	→→	Artwork based on the human form.
8	L	Foreshortening	→→	A rule in perspective to create the illusion of coming forward or receding into space
9	E	Gilding	→→	Applying gold leaf to a painting or other surface.
10	G	Greenware	→→	Dried clay forms that have not been fired.
11	J	Gum Arabic	→→	A binder used in watercolors made from the gum of an acacia tree.
12	F	Horizon line	→→	The horizontal line that distinguishes the sky from the earth, or the ground from the wall. The eye-level of the artists view. Also, where the vanishing point lies in a perspective drawing.

ARTS Vocabulary Terms 3

Choose the best answer to each question.

1	A, E	India ink	→	A waterproof ink made from lampblack.
2	A, E	Impressionism	→	A movement in the 19th century which bridged the "realist" tradition with the modern movements of the 20th century. The focus was on light and atmosphere.
3	J	Kiln	→	A large "oven" used for firing clay work.
4	H	Linear perspective	→	Creating the illusion of depth on a picture plane with the use of lines and a vanishing point.
5	D	Marquette	→	French word for "small model". Used particularly by sculptors as a "sketch" of their work.
6	L	Medium	→	The process or material used in a work of art.
7	F	Monochrome	→	Light and dark tones of a singular color.
8	B	Mural	→	A painting either on a wall or on a surface to be attached to a wall.
9	K	Newsprint	→	Newspaper stock used for sketching, preliminary drawings and printing.
10	G	Oil pastel	→	Oil based crayons.
11	I	Palette	→	The surface used to dispense and mix paint on.
12	C	Pattern	→	Design, motif or symbol repeated over and over.

My First Resume

When you're a high school student, writing a résumé can be __intimidating__ . The good news is that you probably have more work experience than you realize, even if this is your first résumé. Experiences such as childcare, yard work, and volunteerism all __contribute__ to developing key work skills that companies seek. Simply because you have not held a position similar to the one you are seeking does not indicate you lack the requisite abilities to succeed.

Be sure to include any previous employment, especially if it was for pay. Other than that, you can consist of informal work such as pet sitting, cutting grass, snow shoveling, and any other tasks you've done for money. Although you may not have received a __regular__ income for your informal employment, your talents and reliability as an employee can still be shown via it.

Given that the majority of teenagers have not held many jobs, it is critical to draw on all elements of your life that prove you possess the attitude, willingness to work hard, competencies, and personality necessary for job success.

Please list any __leadership__ positions you held (for example, a president of an organization or as team captain), as well as any honors or awards you have received. Include a list of your duties and accomplishments under each heading.

Employers are more concerned with your work __habits__ and attitude than anything else. Nobody expects you to be an expert in your field. When recounting an experience, you might use language to the effect that you have perfect or near-perfect attendance and are on time for school and other commitments.

Employers are looking for employees who have a history of positively impacting the company. Ask yourself whether there are any accomplishments that you can include from your time in school, your clubs, or your employment. Use verbs like "upgraded," "started," and "expanded" to describe what you've done if you want to illustrate what you've accomplished. To demonstrate to __potential__ employers that you are both bright and ambitious, include any demanding advanced academic assignments on your resume.

Keep it short: Keep it simple (But Include All Necessary Information). A single page is all you need. Contact information and previous work experience are both required in some way on every resume. On the other hand, you can exclude things like a career objective or summary.

Create a narrative. Match your talents and expertise to the job's requirements. For example, in the case of a cashier position, if you've never had a position with that precise title before, emphasize your customer service abilities, aptitude for mathematical calculations, work ethic, and ability to operate as part of a team. Examine the job description and make sure your __qualifications__ meet the requirements.

It is also appropriate to add information about your academic achievements, such as participation in organizations and the necessary curriculum you finished while producing a college __freshman__ resume or a resume for a college application. Suppose you're applying for work as a front desk receptionist at a hotel. You could want to include the talents you gained while studying hospitality at a school.

Finally, be sure to double- or even triple-check your resume for typos and __grammatical__ errors. You may be tempted to send in your resume as soon as you finish it, but take a few minutes to review it.

As a last resort, ask for a second opinion on your resume from friends, family, or school teachers. Have them go it through to see if there's anything you missed or if you can make any __improvements__ .

Financial: Taxes

Every citizen pays taxes to the government to _fund_ critical services.

Have you ever been curious about how schools and parks are constructed? Or who is responsible for funding and maintaining roads? In a nutshell, you are! That is if you are of tax-paying age. The government uses taxes to raise funds for _public_ services such as schools and roads.

Taxation has existed for _centuries_, dating back to the earliest human civilizations. Animals or goods were used as tax payments in ancient Mesopotamia because the concept of paper money had not yet been developed. Over time, different types of money were made, and taxes were still being collected, but differently.

Consider the following scenario: you've just landed a fantastic job working at a video game store. You are aware that you earn $10 an hour and work ten hours per week after school. Because you're a math whiz, you're aware that 10 x 10 equals 100. Therefore, your initial _compensation_ should be $100, correct? Sadly, you won't get $100 because the federal and state governments take a percentage of your earnings as tax.

So, you've got a great job, and you'd like to buy a car or a house when you're older. What do you imagine will happen? Automobiles and homes, too, are subject to _taxation_. This is referred to as property tax, and it is frequently paid to local governments, such as the county in which you _reside_. Once you own a home, you are responsible for paying property taxes on it each year until you sell it.

Sales taxes are another method by which states and municipalities collect tax revenue. This means that when you purchase an item in a store or online, an additional charge in the form of a tax is _added_. Different categories of goods are taxed differently, and the proceeds benefit the state and _local_ governments.

While there may be numerous taxes, consider for a moment all of the public goods that taxes support. What about your educational institution? Taxes cover the cost of _textbooks_, desks, and even the building itself. What about your favorite teacher? They are compensated monthly with tax dollars. Taxes also fund the _construction_ and maintenance of roads and bridges, the employment of police officers to protect neighborhoods, and the operation of some parks and museums.

Geography: Time Zones

Have you ever tried to call or send a message to someone who was on the other side of the country or the world? It can be tough to reach a faraway location from you because the time of day may be different from your own. The purpose of time zones and why we have them will be discussed in this session.

Kim, Mike's classmate who recently relocated across the country, is texting him. After a short time, Kim sends Mike a text message saying that it is time for her to go to sleep for the night. The sun is beaming brightly outside , and Mike is confused about why Kim would choose this time of day to go to sleep. 'Can you tell me what time it is, please?' Mike asked. 'It's 9:00 p.m. now!' Kim replies.

What exactly is going on here? Was Mike able to travel back in time in some way?

What is happening to Mike and Kim is nothing more than a natural occurrence that occurs on our planet daily. Since Kim relocated across the country, she is now in a different time zone than she was previously.

A time zone is a geographical location on the planet with a fixed time that all citizens can observe by setting their clocks to that time. As you go from east to west (or west to east) on the globe's surface, you will encounter different time zones. The greater the distance traveled, the greater the number of time zones crossed.

Time zones are not something that arises in nature by chance. Humans created the concept of time zones and determined which regions of the world are located in which time zones.

Because of time zones, everyone experiences the same pattern of dawn in the early morning and sunset in the late afternoon. We require time zones because the earth is shaped like a ball and therefore requires them. As the sun beams down on the planet, not every location receives the same amount of sunshine. The sun shines on one side of the earth and brightens it during the day, while the other side is dark during the night (nighttime). If time-zones didn't exist , many people worldwide would experience quite strange sunshine patterns during the day if there were no time zones.

Science: Albert Einstein

Albert Einstein was born in Germany on March 14, 1879. Because he was Jewish, he fled to the United States to avoid Hitler and the Second World War.

His father gave him a simple pocket compass when he was about five years old, and it quickly became his favorite toy!

He developed an interest in mathematics and science at the age of seven.

When Einstein was about ten years old, a much older friend gave him a large stack of science, mathematics, and philosophy books .

He'd published his first scientific paper by the age of sixteen. That is absolutely incredible!

Numerous reports have shown that Einstein failed math in school, but his family has stated that this is not the case. They claimed he was always at the top of his class in math and could solve some challenging problems.

As an adult, he frequently missed appointments, and because his mind was all over the place, his lectures were a little difficult to understand.

He didn't wear socks and had uncombed hair! Even at posh dinners, he'd arrive unkempt, with crumpled clothes and, of course, no socks!

An experiment in 1919 proved the theory correct. He became famous almost overnight , and he suddenly received invitations to travel worldwide, as well as honors from all over the world!

In 1921, he was awarded the Nobel Prize for Physics. He'd come a long way from the boy who was told he'd never amount to anything!

Today, his other discoveries enabled us to have things like garage door openers, televisions, and DVD players. Time magazine named him "Person of the Century" in 1999.

One of his favorite activities was to take a boat out on a lake and take his notebook with him to think and write everything down. Perhaps this is what inspired him to create his inventions!

Einstein's first marriage produced two sons. His daughter, Lierserl, is believed to have died when she was young. He married twice, and she died before him.

Government History: How Laws Are Made

1. If the Senate approves the bill, it will be sent to the _____.
   a. President
   b. House Representee

2. The _____ may decide to make changes to the bill before it is passed.
   a. governor
   b. committee

3. The bill must then be _____ by a member of Congress.
   a. signed
   b. sponsored

4. The President has the option of refusing to sign the bill. This is known as a ___.
   a. voted
   b. veto

5. The Senate and House can choose to override the President's veto by _____ again.
   a. creating a new bill
   b. voting

6. The bill is assigned to a committee after it is _____.
   a. introduced
   b. vetoed

7. Bills are created and passed by _____.
   a. The House
   b. Congress

8. A bill must be signed into law by the President within ___-days.
   a. 10
   b. 5

9. The President's _____ is the final step in a bill becoming law.
   a. signature
   b. saying yes

10. If the committee agrees to pass the bill, it will be sent to the House or Senate's main ___ for approval.
    a. chamber
    b. state

Extra Credit: What are some of the weirdest laws in the world? List at least 5. (Independent student's answers)

[Student worksheet has a 19 line writing exercise here.]

History: United States Armed Forces

1. The United States military is divided into ___ branches.
   a. six
   b. five

2. _____ is managed by the United States Department of Homeland Security.
   a. The National Guard
   b. The Coast Guard

3. The _____ of the United States is the Commander in Chief of the United States Armed Forces.
   a. Governor
   b. President

4. The United States maintains a military to safeguard its _____ and interests.
   a. borders
   b. cities

5. DoD is in charge of controlling each _____ of the military.
   a. branch
   b. army

6. The Marines are prepared to fight on both land and ____.
   a. battlefield
   b. sea

7. The United States Space Force is in charge of operating and defending military ____ and ground stations.
   a. soldiers
   b. satellites

8. The mission of the _____ is to defend the country from outside forces.
   a. United States DoD Forces
   b. United States Air Force

9. There are _____ units in all 50 states.
   a. Army National Guard
   b. Armed Nations Guard

10. The United States Navy conducts its missions at sea to secure and protect the world's _____.
    a. oceans
    b. borders

11. The primary concern of the United States Coast Guard is to protect_____.
    a. domestic waterways
    b. domesticated cities

12. The United States military is: the Amy Force, Army, Coast Guard, Mario Corps, Old Navy, and Space Force.
    a. True
    b. False

Extra Credit: Has America ever been invaded? (Independent student research answer)

[Student worksheet has a 19 line writing exercise here.]

Science: Water Cycle

1. NMSALIITBOU	s u b l i m a t i o n	
2. IARTASRPONTIN	t r a n s p i r a t i o n	
3. OMLLECUE	m o l e c u l e	
4. NEIRAVOTAOP	e v a p o r a t i o n	
5. ALEIGCR	g l a c i e r	
6. TONOINSNCEDA	c o n d e n s a t i o n	
7. DARRWOGENTU	g r o u n d w a t e r	
8. TUNLOPLAT	p o l l u t a n t	
9. EPITITARINCPO	p r e c i p i t a t i o n	
10. ITNIOILRNFAT	i n f i l t r a t i o n	
11. ODRLPET	d r o p l e t	
12. NIEDTSOPIO	d e p o s i t i o n	
13. WTAEERH	w e a t h e r	
14. EONNTIGR	n i t r o g e n	
15. RWANTREAI	r a i n w a t e r	
16. REBGICE	i c e b e r g	
17. TNOAIADRI	r a d i a t i o n	
18. EOXNGY	o x y g e n	
19. SGOMRNIA	o r g a n i s m	
20. YNEDRHOG	h y d r o g e n	
21. EARTLWTME	m e l t w a t e r	
22. COTNCLEOLI	c o l l e c t i o n	
23. PAROV	v a p o r	
24. NEVOEMTM	m o v e m e n t	
25. ORENINTNVEM	e n v i r o n m e n t	
26. OCSANE	o c e a n s	

Prevent Food Poisoning

Did you know that approximately 1 in every 6 Americans will contract food poisoning this year? Food poisoning not only _hospitalizes_ 128,000 Americans each year, but it can also result in long-term health problems.

In general, a foodborne illness is defined as an infection of the _digestive_ system caused by consuming food or beverages contaminated with harmful bacteria, parasites, or viruses. Disease-causing microorganisms are waiting for the right moment to get into your food. There are more than 200 of them. Salmonella, E. coli, and Listeria are three of the most common. Vomiting, diarrhea, _abdominal_ pain, fever, and chills are all symptoms of foodborne illnesses. They aren't always the same, but they can all happen. Most foodborne illnesses are short-lived, meaning they come on quickly and last for only a few days.

At any point before consumption, your food can become _contaminated_ with dangerous microorganisms. The best way to avoid getting a foodborne illness is to store, cook and clean food properly. Here are a few ideas for how to keep foodborne illnesses at bay.

Refrigerate or freeze perishable raw and cooked foods promptly. Make sure your refrigerator is set to the correct _temperature_ to ensure proper storage. It's best to thaw frozen food in the refrigerator or microwave and then cook it right away.

Seafood, eggs, poultry, and meat should be cooked all the way through. Ensure that the juices from meat and poultry are clear, not _pink_. A meat thermometer can be used to check the internal temperature of foods. Boiling is a good idea for things like soups and stews. Cooked food should always be completely reheated.

Before eating, cutting, or cooking, wash fruits and vegetables under running water. If you want to clean fruits and vegetables with hard skin, you can use a produce _brush_. Hands should be washed in warm, soapy water for at least 20 seconds. It would help if you washed your hands before and after handling raw meats and poultry and after using the bathroom, changing diapers, or interacting with animals to prevent the _spread_ of bacteria. Before and after use, wash utensils and surfaces with hot, soapy water.

The majority of people recover completely from mild cases of foodborne illness. For mild foodborne illnesses, rehydrating and replenishing _electrolytes_ like sodium, potassium, and chloride are the most common treatment. Anti-diarrhea medications are available over the counter. On the other hand, these medications should not be used if you have _bloody_ diarrhea, as they may prolong your infection. If your symptoms persist for more than three days, you should seek medical attention.

Grammar: Adjectives Matching

Adjectives are words that describe people, places, and things, or nouns. Adjectives are words that describe sounds, shapes, sizes, times, numbers/quantity, textures/touch, and weather. You can remember this by saying to yourself, "an adjective adds something."

If you need to describe a friend or an adult, you can use words that describe their appearance, size, or age. When possible, try to use positive words that describe a person.

#				
1	O	disappointed	⇢	sad because something is worse than expected
2	K	anxious	⇢	worried
3	C	delighted	⇢	very pleased
4	G	terrified	⇢	very frightened
5	I	ashamed	⇢	feeling bad because you did sg wrong
6	H	envious	⇢	wanting something another person has
7	N	proud	⇢	feeling pleased and satisfied
8	F	shocked	⇢	very surprised and upset
9	A	brave	⇢	nothing frightens him/her
10	L	hard-working	⇢	has 2 or more jobs
11	B	organized	⇢	everything is in order around him
12	D	punctual	⇢	always arrives in time
13	J	honest	⇢	uprightness and fairness
14	E	outgoing	⇢	loves being with people
15	M	loyal	⇢	always supports his friends
16	P	reliable	⇢	one can always count on him

Math: Arithmetic Refresher

Select the best answer for each question.

1. Use division to calculate 6/3. The answer is _____.
   - a. 2
   - b. 4
   - c. 3.5

2. Fill in the blank 2 + √5 _____ 7 - √10
   - a. >
   - b. ≤
   - c. ≥

3. Use division to calculate 50/10. The answer is _____.
   - a. 5.5
   - b. 8
   - c. 5

4. Which family of numbers begins with the numbers 0, 1, 2, 3, …?
   - a. Integers
   - b. Whole numbers
   - c. Rational numbers

5. Use division to calculate 7/4. The answer is _____.
   - a. 2 R4
   - b. 1.5
   - c. 1 R3

6. Which of the answer choices is an INCORRECT statement?
   - a. 0 > -1
   - b. -2 < -4
   - c. 32 < -25x

7. Simplify: 7 * 5 - 2 + 11
   - a. 44
   - b. 23
   - c. 21

8. -18 + (-11) = ?
   - a. 28
   - b. 32
   - c. -29

9. 16 - (-7) = ?
   - a. 20
   - b. 23
   - c. 19

10. -12 - (-9) = ?
   - a. -3
   - b.

11. Simplify: 37 - [5 + {28 - (19 - 7)}]
   - a. 16
   - b. 36
   - c. 46

12. The numbers 1, 2, 3, 4, 5, 6, 7, 8, ..., i.e. natural numbers, are called_____.
   - a. Positive integers
   - b. Rational integers
   - c. Simplify numbers

13. _____is the number you are dividing by.
   - a. divisor
   - b. equation
   - c. dividend

14. _____ is the leftover amount when dividend doesn't divide equally.
   - a. remainder
   - b. quotient
   - c. dividend

Math: Decimals Place Value

Our basic number system is decimals. The decimal system is built around the number ten. It is sometimes referred to as a base-10 number system. Other systems use different base numbers, such as binary numbers, which use base-2.

The place value is one of the first concepts to grasp when learning about decimals. The position of a digit in a number is represented by its place value. It determines the value of the number.

When the numbers 800, 80, and 8 are compared, the digit "8" has a different value depending on its position within the number.

8 - ones place
80 - tens place
800 - hundreds place

The value of the number is determined by the 8's place value. The value of the number increases by ten times as the location moves to the left.

Select the best answer for each question.

1. Which of the following is a decimal number?
   a. 1.852
   b. 1.123
   c. 15

2. For the number 125.928, what is in the tenths place?
   a. 9
   b. 2
   c. 5

3. For the number 359, which number is in the tens place?
   a. 3
   b. 5
   c. 9

4. Write the number 789.1 as an addition problem.
   a. 70 + 800 + 90 + 1
   b. 700 + 80 + 9 + 1 / 10
   c. 700 + 80 + 9+10

5. When we say 7 is in the hundreds place in the number 700, this is the same as 7x102.n.
   a. True
   b. False

6. For the number 2.14, what digit is in the hundredths place?
   a. 4
   b. 1
   c. 2

7. When you start to do arithmetic with decimals, it will be important to_____ properly.
   a. line up the numbers
   b. line up all like numbers
   c. line up numbers ending in 0

8. Depending upon the position of a digit in a number, it has a value called its_____.
   a. tenth place
   b. decimals place
   c. place value

9. The place value of the digit 6 in the number 1673 is 600 as 6 is in the hundreds place.
   a. True
   b. False

10. What is the place value of the digits 2 and 4 in the number 326.471?
    a. 2 is in the tens place. 4 is in the tenths place.
    b. 2 is in the tenths place. 4 is in the tens place.
    c. 2 is in the ones place. 4 is in the tenths place.

Math: Roman Numerals

The Ancient Romans used Roman numerals as their numbering system. We still use them every now and then. They can be found in the Super Bowl's numbering system, after king's names (King Henry IV), in outlines, and elsewhere. Roman numerals are base 10 or decimal numbers, just like the ones we use today. However, they are not entirely positional, and there is no number zero.

Roman numerals use letters rather than numbers. You must know the following seven letters:

I = 1

V = 5

X = 10

L = 50

C = 100

D = 500

M = 1000

Select the best answer for each question.

1. III = ___
   a. 33
   b. 30
   c. 3

2. XVI=___
   a. 60
   b. 61
   c. 16

3. IV = 5 - 1 =____
   a. 40
   b. 4
   c. 14

4. What number does the Roman numeral LXXIV represent?
   a. 79
   b. 74
   c. 70

5. Which of the following is the Roman numeral for the number 5?
   a. IV
   b. VI
   c. V

6. How many of the same letters can you put in a row in Roman numerals?
   a. 4 or more
   b. 3
   c. 2

7. Which of the following is the Roman numeral for the number 10?
   a. X
   b. IX
   c. XXI

8. What is the Roman numeral for 33?
   a. XXXIII
   b. XIII
   c. XVIII

9. Which of the following is the Roman numeral for the number 50?
   a. X
   b. L
   c. I

10. Which of the following is the Roman numeral for the number 100?
   a. C
   b. IVV
   c. LII

Social Skill Interests: Things To Do

A **hobby** is something that a person actively pursues relaxation and enjoyment. On the other hand, a person may have an **interest** in something because they are curious or concerned. Hobbies usually do not provide monetary compensation. However, a person's interests can vary and may lead to earning money or making a living from them. Hobbies are typically pursued in one's spare time or when one is not required to work. Interests can be followed in one's spare time or while working, as in the case of using one's passion as a source of income. A hobby can be a recreational activity that is done regularly in one's spare time. It primarily consists of participating in sports, collecting items and objects, engaging in creative and artistic pursuits, etc. The desire to learn or understand something is referred to as interest. If a person has a strong interest in a subject, he or she may pursue it as a hobby. However, an interest is not always a hobby. Hobbies such as stamp and flower collecting may not be a source of income for a person, but the items collected can sometimes be sold. Hobbies frequently lead to discoveries and inventions. Interests could be a source of income or something done for free. If a person is interested in cooking or enjoys creating dishes, he can do so at home or make it a career by becoming a chef.

_____

Put the words in the correct category.

pottery	card making	candle making	reading	weaving	knitting
gym	jewellery	chess	surfing	computer games	collecting
woodwork	Soccer	art	swimming	cooking	skateboarding
embroidery	skiing	gardening	writing	chatting	sewing
netball	stamp collecting	football	music	rugby	basketball

Sport (10)	Handcrafts (10)	Interests (10)
Soccer	knitting	reading
rugby	sewing	cooking
football	card making	music
netball	woodwork	stamp collecting
basketball	weaving	gardening
surfing	jewellery	chess
skateboarding	pottery	computer games
skiing	candle making	writing
swimming	embroidery	collecting
gym	art	chatting

Health: Check Your Symptoms

1. I've got a pain in my head.
   - a. Stiff neck
   - b. headache

2. I was out in the sun too long.
   - a. Sunburn
   - b. Fever

3. I've got a small itchy lump or bump.
   - a. Rash
   - b. Insect bite

4. I might be having a heart attack.
   - a. Cramps
   - b. Chest pain

5. I've lost my voice.
   - a. Laryngitis
   - b. Sore throat

6. I need to blow my nose a lot.
   - a. Runny nose
   - b. Blood Nose

7. I have an allergy. I have a
   - a. Rash
   - b. Insect bite

8. My shoe rubbed my heel. I have a
   - a. Rash
   - b. Blister

9. The doctor gave me antibiotics. I have a/an
   - a. Infection
   - b. Cold

10. I think I want to vomit. I am
    - a. Nauseous
    - b. Bloated

11. My arm is not broken. It is
    - a. Scratched
    - b. Sprained

12. My arm touched the hot stove. It is
    - a. Burned
    - b. Bleeding

13. I have an upset stomach. I might
    - a. Cough
    - b. Vomit

14. The doctor put plaster on my arm. It is
    - a. Sprained
    - b. Broken

15. If you cut your finger it will
    - a. Burn
    - b. Bleed

16. I hit my hip on a desk. It will
    - a. Burn
    - b. Bruise

17. When you have hay-fever you will
    - a. Sneeze
    - b. Wheeze

18. A sharp knife will
    - a. Scratch
    - b. Cut

Grammar: 8 Parts of Speech
Matching

- NOUN. used to identify any of a class of people, places, or things
- PRONOUN. a word (such as I, he, she, you, it, we, or they) that is used instead of a noun or noun phrase
- VERB. a word used to describe an action, state, or occurrence
- ADJECTIVE. modify or describe a noun or a pronoun
- ADVERB. word that modifies (describes) a verb (she sings loudly), adverbs often end in -ly
- PREPOSITION. word or phrase that connects a noun or pronoun to a verb or adjective in a sentence
- CONJUNCTION. word used to join words, phrases, sentences, and clauses
- INTERJECTION. word or phrase that expresses something in a sudden or exclamatory way, especially an emotion

1	C	Identify the noun.	⇢	Lion
2	I	Identify the verb.	⇢	barked
3	F	What is an adjective?	⇢	a word that describes nouns and pronouns
4	B	Three sets of nouns	⇢	mother, truck, banana
5	E	Three sets of adverbs	⇢	always, beautifully, often
6	G, H	above, across, against	⇢	preposition
7	D	but, and, because, although	⇢	conjunctions
8	J	Wow! Ouch! Hurrah!	⇢	Interjection
9	A	Mary and Joe are friends.	⇢	verb
10	G, H	Jane ran <u>around</u> the corner yesterday.	⇢	preposition

[Student worksheet has a 4 line writing exercise here.]

Grammar:
Subjunctive Mood

Wishes, proposals, ideas, imagined circumstances, and assertions that are not true are all expressed in the subjunctive mood. The subjunctive is frequently used to indicate an action that a person hopes or wishes to be able to undertake now or in the future. In general, a verb in the subjunctive mood denotes a scenario or state that is a possibility, hope, or want. It expresses a conditional, speculative, or hypothetical sense of a verb.

When verbs of advice or suggestion are used, the subjunctive mood is utilized. After verbs of recommendation or advice, the subjunctive appears in a phrase beginning with the word -that.

Here are a few verbs that are commonly used in the subjunctive mood to recommend or advise.

- advise, ask, demand, prefer

1. Writers use the subjunctive mood to express ____ or ____conditions.
   a. imaginary or hoped-for
   b.

2. Which is NOT a common marker of the subjunctive mood?
   a.
   b. memories

3. Which is NOT an example of a hope-for verb?
   a. demand
   b. need

4. Subjunctive mood is used to show a situation is not _____.
   a. fictional or fabricated
   b. entirely factual or certain

5. Which of the below statements is written in the subjunctive mood?
   a. I wish I were a millionaire.
   b. What would you do with a million dollars?

6. The indicative mood is used to state facts and opinions, as in:
   a. My mom's fried chicken is my favorite food in the world.
   b. Smells, taste, chew

7. The imperative mood is used to give commands, orders, and instructions, as in:
   a. Eat your salad.
   b. I love salad!

8. The interrogative mood is used to ask a question, as in:
   a. Have you eaten all of your pizza yet?
   b. I ordered 2 slices of pizza.

9. The conditional mood uses the conjunction "if" or "when" to express a condition and its result, as in:
   a. Blue is my favorite color, so I paint with it often.
   b. If I eat too much lasagna, I'll have a stomach ache later.

10. The subjunctive mood is used to express wishes, proposals, suggestions, or imagined situations, as in:
    a. Yesterday was Monday, and I ate pizza.
    b. I prefer that my mom make pasta rather than tuna.

Proofreading Shakespeare:
Romeo and Juliet

There are **24** mistakes in this passage. 5 capitals missing. 3 unnecessary capitals. 4 unnecessary apostrophes. 3 punctuation marks missing or incorrect. 2 incorrect homophones. 7 incorrectly spelled words.

In 1597, William Shakespeare published "Romeo and ~~Juliet"~~ Juliet," which would go on to become one of the world's most famous love stories. The plot of Shakespeare's ~~pley~~ play takes place in Verona, where the two main ~~characters~~ characters, ~~romeo~~ Romeo and Juliet, meet and fall in ~~love~~ love. Both are descended from two feuding families, the Capulets, and the Montagues. As a result, ~~thay~~ they choose to keep their ~~luve~~ love hidden and are married by Friar Laurence. Romeo gets into a fight with ~~Juliet"s~~ Juliet's cousin Tybalt, whom he ~~Kills~~ kills in a ~~Brawl~~ brawl despite his best efforts. Romeo is expelled from Verona and escapes to Mantua.

When ~~juliet's~~ Juliet's parents press her to marry, she ~~Seeks~~ seeks the assistance of Friar Laurence once more, who provides her with a sleeping potion designed to simulate her death. In a letter that never reaches Romeo, he explains his plan. Disgusted by the alleged death of his beloved Juliet, ~~Rumeo~~ Romeo returns to Verona and commits suicide at Juliet's open coffin. Juliet awakens from her slumber, sees what has happened, and decides to end her ~~liphe.~~ life. The two feuding families now recognize their complicity and reconcile at their children's graves.

The medieval old town of Verona is ideal for putting oneself in the shoes of Romeo and ~~juliet.~~ Juliet. Every year, many loving couples and tourists come to walk in the footsteps of ~~romeo~~ Romeo and Juliet. A photograph of Juliet's famous balcony, a visit to Romeo's home, or ~~sum~~ some ~~queit~~ quiet time spent at Julia's grave. No matter ~~were~~ where you look in the city, you ~~wall~~ will find loving ~~couple's~~ couples who stick declarations of love and initials on small slips of paper to the walls or immortalize ~~themselve's~~ themselves on the walls or stones of ~~house's~~ houses - often illegally.

Although Shakespeare's drama never corresponded to reality, ~~verona~~ Verona has a unique charm, especially for lovers, who imagine they can feel the true story behind the literary work, almost as if Romeo and Juliet had really existed.

Proofreading Interpersonal Skills: Peer Pressure

Tony is mingling with a large group of what he considers to be the school's cool kids. Suddenly, someone in the group begins mocking Tony's friend Rob, who walks with a limp due to a physical ~~dasability.~~ **disability.**

They begin to imitate ~~rob's~~ **Rob's** limping and ~~Call~~ **call** him 'lame cripple' and other derogatory terms. Although Tony disapproves of their behavior, he does not want to risk being excluded from the group, and thus joins them in mocking Rob.

Peer pressure is the influence exerted on us by ~~member's~~ **members** of our social group. It can manifest in a variety of ways and can lead to us engaging in behaviors we would not normally ~~consider~~ **consider,** such as Tony joining in and mocking his friend Rob.

However, peer pressure is not always detrimental. Positive peer pressure can motivate us to make better ~~chioces,~~ **choices,** such as studying harder, staying in school, or seeking a better job. ~~Whan~~ **When** others influence us to make poor ~~Choices,~~ **choices,** such as smoking, using illicit drugs, or bullying, we succumb to negative peer pressure. We all desire to belong to a group and fit in, so ~~Developing~~ **developing** strategies for resisting peer pressure when necessary can be beneficial.

Tony and his friends are engaging in bullying by ~~moking~~ **mocking** Rob. Bullying is defined as persistent, ~~unwanted.~~ **unwanted,** aggressive behavior directed toward another person. It is ~~moust~~ **most** prevalent in school-aged children but can also ~~aphfect~~ **affect** adults. Bullying can take on a variety of forms, including the following:

~~· Verbil~~
· **Verbal** bullying is when someone is called names, threatened, or taunted verbally.
· Bullying is physical in nature - ~~hitting~~ **hitting,** spitting, tripping, or ~~poshing~~ **pushing** someone.
· Social ~~Bullying~~ **bullying** is intentionally excluding ~~Someone~~ **someone** from ~~activities~~ **activities,** spreading rumors, or embarrassing ~~sumeone.~~ **someone.**
· Cyberbullying is the act of verbally or socially bullying someone via the internet, such as through social media sites.

Peer pressure exerts a significant influence on an individual's decision to engage in bullying ~~behavoir.~~ **behavior.** In Tony's case, even though Rob is a friend and ~~tony~~ **Tony** would never consider mocking his disability, his desire to belong to a group outweighs his willingness to defend his ~~friend~~ **friend.**

Peer pressure is a strong force that is exerted on us by our social group members. Peer pressure is classified into two types: negative peer pressure, which results in poor decision-making, and positive peer pressure, which influences us to make the correct choices. Adolescents are particularly susceptible to peer pressure because of their desire to fit ~~in~~ **in.**

Peer pressure can motivate someone to engage in bullying behaviors such as mocking someone, threatening to harm them, taunting them online, or excluding them from an activity. Each year, bullying ~~affect's~~ **affects** an astounding 3.2 million school-aged children. ~~Severil~~ **Several** strategies for avoiding peer pressure bullying include the following:

- ~~consider~~ **Consider** your actions by surrounding yourself with good company.
- Acquiring the ability to say no to someone you trust.

Speak up - bullying is never acceptable and is taken ~~extramely~~ **extremely** ~~seroiusly~~ **seriously** in schools and the workplace. If someone is attempting to convince you to bully another person, speaking with a trusted adult such as a teacher, coach, counselor, or coworker can frequently help put ~~thing's~~ **things** into perspective and highlight the issue.

Credit Scores

1. Credit scores typically range from 300 to _____.
   a. 850
   b. 800

2. Experian, _____, and _____ are three credit reporting agencies that generate credit scores.
   a. Fico, and TransCredit
   b. TransUnion, and Equifax

3. The majority of lenders use the Fair _____ Corporation's score model.
   a. Isaac
   b. Credit

4. A credit score is a number that is used to figure out how well someone manages their money.
   a. True
   b. False

5. An individual's payment history is a _____ of the payments made to lenders.
   a. contract agreement
   b. record

6. The VantageScore® model was developed by VantageScore Solutions LLC, a company formed by the _____ in the United States.
   a. three major credit bureaus
   b. federal reserve

7. The amount a person _____ to a lender reveals how much of their credit they've used.
   a. owes
   b. loaned

8. How long you been using and maintaining a credit card account is referred to as _____.
   a. credit score factor
   b. credit history length

9. _____ refers to a credit profile with a variety of credit sources.
   a. Credit maintaining
   b. Credit mix

10. A credit card account that has been open for several years will almost certainly have a positive effect on a credit score because it adds to the _____.
    a. credit history
    b. TransUnion score

Introvert vs. Extrovert

Introvert is a person who prefers calm environments, limits social engagement, or embraces a greater than average preference for solitude.

SYNONYMS:
brooder
loner
solitary

Extrovert is an outgoing, gregarious person who thrives in dynamic environments and seeks to maximize social engagement.

SYNONYMS:
character
exhibitionist
show-off
showboat

Fill in the blank with the correct word. [introvert, introverts, extrovert, extroverts]

1. Sue is the **extrovert** in the family; opinionated, talkative and passionate about politics.

2. He was described as an **introvert** , a reserved man who spoke little.

3. **Extroverts** are often described as the life of the party.

4. An **introvert** is often thought of as a quiet, reserved, and thoughtful individual.

5. **Extroverts** enjoy being around other people and tend to focus on the outside world.

6. Typically **introverts** tend to enjoy more time to themselves.

7. Jane is an **introvert** whose only hobby is reading.

8. I am still not as "outgoing" as an **extrovert** is.

9. I had been a very **extrovert** person, living life to the full.

10. I am an **introvert** , I am a loner.

11. Because Pat is an **extrovert** who enjoys chatting with others, she is the ideal talk show host.

12. She is basically an **introvert** , uncomfortable with loud women and confrontations.

Dealing With Acne

Acne is a skin disorder that results in bumps. Whiteheads, blackheads, pimples, and pus-filled bumps are all sorts of blemishes. What's the source of these annoying bumps? Pores and hair follicles make up most of your skin's top layer. Sebum (pronounced "see-bum"), the natural oil that moisturizes hair and skin, is produced in the pores by oil glands.

Generally, the glands produce adequate sebum, and the pores are good. However, oil, dead skin cells, and bacteria can block a pore if they accumulate in it to an unhealthy level. Acne may result as a result of this.

Puberty-induced hormonal changes are to blame for acne in children. If your parent suffered from acne as a teen, you will likely as well because your pores may produce more sebum when under stress; stress may worsen acne. Acne is usually gone by the time a person reaches their twenties.

Here are a few tips for preventing breakouts if you suffer from acne:

- It would help if you washed your face with warm water and a light soap or cleanser in the morning before school and before bed.
- Avoid scrubbing your face. Acne can be exacerbated by irritating the skin, so scrubbing is not recommended.
- Makeup should be washed off at the end of the day if you wear it.
- Ensure to wash your face after a workout if you've been sweating heavily.
- Acne-fighting lotions and creams are readily available over-the-counter. Talk to your parents or doctor about the options available to you.

Make sure you follow the guidelines on any acne medication you use. If you're unsure whether you're allergic to the cream or lotion, use a small amount at first. If you don't notice results the next day, don't give up. Acne medication can take weeks or months to take effect. If you use more than recommended, your skin may become extremely dry and red.

Acne-suffering children can seek treatment from their doctor. Doctors can prescribe stronger medications than what you can get over the counter.

The following are some other factors to consider:

- Avoid touching your face if you can.
- Pimples should not be picked, squeezed, or popped.
- Long hair should be kept away from the face, and it should be washed regularly to reduce oil production.

It is possible to get pimples on the hairline by wearing headgear like baseball caps. Stay away from them if you suspect they're contributing to your acne problems.

Despite their best efforts, many children will get acne at some point in their lives. The situation isn't out of the ordinary.

If you suffer from acne, you now have several options for treating it. Remind yourself of this: You are not alone. Take a look around at your buddies and you'll notice that the majority of children and adolescents are dealing with acne, too!

1. Puberty _____ changes are to blame for acne in children.
   a. harmonic
   b. hormonal

2. Pores and hair _____ make up most of your skin's top layer.
   a. follicles
   b. folate

3. Avoid _____ your face.
   a. using cleanser
   b. scrubbing

4. _____ is the oil that moisturizes hair and skin, is produced in the pores by oil glands.
   a. Acne
   b. Sebum

Smart Ways to Deal With a Bully

One of the most serious issues in our society today is bullying. It's not uncommon for young people to experience a range of negative emotions due to this. Bullies may use physical force (such as punches, kicks, or shoves) or verbal abuse (such as calling someone a name, making fun of them, or scaring them) to harm others.

Some examples of bullying include calling someone names, stealing from them and mocking them, or ostracizing them from a group.

Some bullies want to be the center of attention. As a strategy to be popular or get what they want, they may believe bullying is acceptable. Bullies are usually motivated by a desire to elevate their own status. As a result of picking on someone else, they can feel more power and authority.

Bullies frequently target someone they believe they can control . Kids who are easily agitated or have difficulty standing up for themselves are likely targets. Getting a strong reaction from someone can give bullies the illusion that they have the power they desire. There are times when bullies pick on someone who is more intelligent than them or who looks different from them somehow.

Preventing a Bully's Attack
Do not give in to the bully. Avoid the bully as much as possible. Of course, you aren't allowed to disappear or skip class. However, if you can escape the bully by taking a different path, do so.

Bravely stand your ground . Scared people aren't usually the most courageous people. Bullies can be stopped by just showing courage in the face of them. Just how do you present yourself as a fearless person? To send a message that says, "Don't mess with me," stand tall. It is much easier to be brave when you are confident in yourself.

Don't Pay Attention to What the Bully Says or Does. If you can, do your best not to listen to the bully's threats . Act as though you aren't aware of their presence and immediately go away to a safe place. It's what bullies want: a big reaction to their teasing and being mean. If you don't respond to a bully's actions by pretending you don't notice or care, you may be able to stop them.

Defend your rights. Pretend you're confident and brave. In a loud voice, tell the bully, "No! Stop it!" Then take a step back or even take off running if necessary. No matter what a bully says, say "no" and walk away if it doesn't feel right. If you do what a bully tells you to do, the bully is more likely to keep bullying you; kids who don't stand up for themselves are more likely to be targeted by bullies.

Don't retaliate by being a bully yourself. Don't fight back against someone who's bullying you or your pals by punching, kicking, or shoving them. Fighting back only makes the bully happier, and it's also risky since someone can be injured. You're also going to be in a lot of trouble. It's essential to stick with your friends, keep safe, and seek adult assistance.

Inform a responsible adult of the situation. Telling an adult if you're being bullied is crucial. Find someone you can confide in and tell them what's going on with you. It is up to everyone in the school, from teachers to principals to parents to lunchroom assistants, to stop the bullies. As soon as a teacher discovers the bullying, the bully usually stops because they are worried that their parents will punish them for their behavior. Bullying is terrible, and everyone who is bullied or witnesses bullying should speak up.

Your Identity and Reputation Online

Your online identity grows every time you use a social network, send a text, or make a post on a website, for example. Your online _persona_ may be very different from your real-world persona – the way your friends, parents, and teachers see you.

One of the best things about having an online life is trying on different personas. If you want to change how you act and show up to people, you can. You can also learn more about things that you like. Steps to help you maintain control on the internet can be taken just like in real life.

Here are some things to think about to protect your online identity and reputation:

Nothing is temporary online. The worldwide web is full of opportunities to connect and share with other people. It's also a place with no " _take-backs_ " or "temporary" situations. It's easy for other people to copy, save, and forward your information even if you delete it.

Add a "private" option for your profiles. Anyone can copy or screen-grab things that you don't want the world to see using social _networking_ sites. Use caution when using the site's default settings. Each site has its own rules, so read them to ensure you're doing everything you can to keep your information safe.

Keep your passwords safe and change them often. Someone can ruin your _reputation_ by pretending to be you online. The best thing to do is pick passwords that no one can guess. The only people who should know about them are your parents or someone else who you can trust. Your best friend, boyfriend, or girlfriend should not know your passwords.

Don't put up pictures or comments that are _inappropriate_ or sexually provocative. In the future, things that are funny or cool to you now might not be so cool to someone else, like a teacher or admissions officer. If you don't want your grandmother, coach, or best friend's parents to see it, don't post it. Even on a private page, it could be hacked or copied and sent to someone else.

Don't give in to unwanted advances. There are a lot of inappropriate messages and requests for money that teenagers get when they're on the web. These things can be scary, weird, or even _embarrassing_ , but they can also be exciting and fun. Do not keep quiet about being bullied online. Tell an adult you trust right away if a stranger or someone you know is bullying you. It's never a good idea to answer. If you respond, you might say something that makes things even worse.

You can go to www.cybertipline.org to report bad behavior or other problems.

Avoid "flaming" by taking a break now and then. Do you want to send an angry text or comment to someone? Relax for a few minutes and realize that the _remarks_ will be there even if you have cooled off or change your mind about them.

People may feel free to write hurtful, _derogatory_ , or abusive remarks on the internet if they can remain anonymous. We can be painful to others if we share things or make angry comments when we aren't facing someone. If they find out, it could change how they see us. If you wouldn't say it, show it, or do it in person, don't do it online.

Make sure you don't break copyright laws. Don't upload, share, or distribute copyrighted photographs, sounds, or files. Be aware of copyright restrictions. Sharing them is great, but doing so illegally runs the risk of legal _repercussions_ down the road.

It's time for a self-evaluation. Take a look at your "digital footprint," which people can find out about you. When you search for your screen name or email address, see what comes up. That's one way to get a sense of what other people think of you online.

In the same way that your _real-life_ identity is formed, your online identity and reputation are also formed. It's different when you're on the internet because you don't always have the chance to explain how you feel or what you mean. Thinking about what you're going to say and being responsible can help you avoid leaving an online trail that you'll later be sorry about.

This, That, These, and Those

This, that, these and those are demonstratives. We use this, that, these, and those to point to people and things. This and that are singular. These and those are plural.

1. _____ orange I'm eating is delicious.
   a. This
   b. These
   c. Those
   d. That

2. It is better than _____ apples from last week.
   a. that
   b. those
   c. these
   d. this

3. Let's exchange _____ bread for these crackers.
   a. those
   b. this
   c. these
   d. that

4. Let's try some of _____ freeze-dried steak.
   a. this
   b. this here
   c. them
   d. those there

5. Is _____ water boiling yet?
   a. these here
   b. that
   c. that there
   d. this here

6. _____ granola bars are tasty too.
   a. These
   b. This here
   c. Them
   d. These here

7. _____ mountains don't look that far away.
   a. This
   b. Those
   c. These
   d. That

8. I like _____ pictures better than those.
   a. this
   b. that
   c. those
   d. these

9. _____ car at the far end of the lot is mine.
   a. That
   b. This
   c. These
   d. Those

10. I like the feel of _____ fabric.
   a. those
   b. this here
   c. that there
   d. this

11. In _____ early days, space travel was a dream.
   a. that
   b. them
   c. those
   d. this

12. _____ days, we believe humans will go to Mars.
   a. These
   b. This
   c. Those
   d. That

HEALTH: Non-Communicable Disease Word Scramble

A non-communicable disease (NCD) is a noninfectious health condition lasting for a long period of time. This is also known as a chronic disease. NCD is a disease that is not transmissible directly from one person to another.

Traumatic Brain Injury	Liver Disease	Kidney Disease	Eczema	Ulcerative Colitis	Bipolar Disorder
Down Syndrome	Muscular Dystrophy	Seizure Disorder	Crohn's Disease	Epilepsy	Autism
Arthritis	Bell's Palsy	Psoriasis	Cerebral Palsy	Chronic Kidney Disease	

1. rtrshitai   A r t h r i t i s

2. atiums   A u t i s m

3. s'blel lyasp   B e l l ' s   P a l s y

4. orabipl rddoreis   B i p o l a r   D i s o r d e r

5. raeclrbe laysp   C e r e b r a l   P a l s y

6. ocrnihc nekyid ieedssa   C h r o n i c   K i d n e y   D i s e a s e

7. h'ocnsr sdieesa   C r o h n ' s   D i s e a s e

8. wodn ymedrson   D o w n   S y n d r o m e

9. emzeac   E c z e m a

10. eielypsp   E p i l e p s y

11. dikyen deiseas   K i d n e y   D i s e a s e

12. ivrle asiesde   L i v e r   D i s e a s e

13. smuracul hposytdyr   M u s c u l a r   D y s t r o p h y

14. rpssisioa   P s o r i a s i s

15. euirsze dderirso   S e i z u r e   D i s o r d e r

16. micratuat inrba yrjinu   T r a u m a t i c   B r a i n   I n j u r y

17. arvectluei osicitl   U l c e r a t i v e   C o l i t i s

Test Your Mathematics Knowledge

1. To add fractions_____

    a. the denominators must be the same

    b. the denominators can be same or different

    c. the denominators must be different

2. To add decimals, the decimal points must be?

    a. column and carry the first digit(s)

    b. lined up in any order before you add the columns

    c. lined up vertically before you add the columns

3. When adding like terms_____

    a. the like terms must be same and they must be to the different power.

    b. the exponent must be different and they must be to the same power.

    c. the variable(s) must be the same and they must be to the same power.

4. The concept of math regrouping involves_____

    a. regrouping means that 5x + 2 becomes 50 + 12

    b. the numbers you are adding come out to five digit numbers and 0

    c. rearranging, or renaming, groups in place value

5. _____ indicates how many times a number, or algebraic expression, should be multiplied by itself.

    a. Denominators

    b. Division-quotient

    c. Exponent

6. _____is the numerical value of a number without its plus or minus sign.

    a. Absolute value

    b. Average

    c. Supplementary

7. Any number that is less than zero is called_____

    a. Least common multiple

    b. Equation

    c. Negative number

8. 23 = 2 x 2 x 2 = 8, 8 is the

    a. third power of 2

    b. first power of 2

    c. second power of 2

9. -7, 0, 3, and 7.12223 are

    a. all real numbers

    b. all like fractions

    c. all like terms

10. How do you calculate 2 + 3 x 7?

    a. 2 + 3 x 7 = 2 + 21 = 23

    b. 2 + 7 x 7 = 2 + 21 = 35

    c. 2 + 7 x 3 = 2 + 21 = 23

11. How do you calculate (2 + 3) x (7 - 3)?

    a. (2 + 2) x (7 - 3) = 5 x 4 = 32

    b. (2 + 3) x (7 - 3) = 5 x 4 = 20

    c. (2 + 7) x (2 - 3) = 5 x 4 = 14

12. The Commutative Law of Addition says_____

    a. positive - positive = (add) positive

    b. that it doesn't matter what order you add up numbers, you will always get the same answer

    c. parts of a calculation outside brackets always come first

13. The Zero Properties Law of multiplication says_____

    a. that any number multiplied by 0 equals 0

    b. mathematical operation where four or more numbers are combined to make a sum

    c. Negative - Positive = Subtract

14. Multiplication is when you_____

    a. numbers that are added together in multiplication problems

    b. take one number and add it together a number of times

    c. factor that is shared by two or more numbers

15. When multiplying by 0, the answer is always_____

    a. 0

    b. -0

    c. 1

16. When multiplying by 1, the answer is always the _____

    a. same as the number multiplied by 0

    b. same as the number multiplied by -1

    c. same as the number multiplied by 1

17. You can multiply numbers in_____

    a. any order and multiply by 2 and the answer will be the same

    b. any order you want and the answer will be the same

    c. any order from greater to less than and the answer will be the same

18. Division is____

    a. set of numbers that are multiplied together to get an answer

    b. breaking a number up into an equal number of parts

    c. division is scaling one number by another

19. If you take 20 things and put them into four equal sized groups

    a. there will be 6 things in each group

    b. there will be 5 things in each group

    c. there will be 10 things in each group

20. The dividend is_____

    a. the number you are multiplied by

    b. the number you are dividing up

    c. the number you are grouping together

21. The divisor is _____

    a. are all multiples of 3

    b. the number you are dividing by

    c. common factor of two numbers

22. The quotient is _____

    a. the answer

    b. answer to a multiplication operation

    c. any number in the problem

23. When dividing something by 1_____

    a. the answer is the original number

    b. the answer produces a given number when multiplied by itself

    c. the answer is the quotient

24. Dividing by 0_____

    a. the answer will always be more than 0

    b. You will always get 1

    c. You cannot divide a number by 0

25. If the answer to a division problem is not a whole number, the number(s) leftover_____

    a. are called the Order Property

    b. are called the denominators

    c. are called the remainder

26. You can figure out the 'mean' by_____

    a. multiply by the sum of two or more numbers

    b. adding up all the numbers in the data and then dividing by the number of numbers

    c. changing the grouping of numbers that are added together

27. The 'median' is the_____

    a. last number of the data set

    b. middle number of the data set

    c. first number of the data set

28. The 'mode' is the number_____

    a. that appears equal times

    b. that appears the least

    c. that appears the most

29. Range is the_____

    a. difference between the less than equal to number and the highest number.

    b. difference between the highest number and the highest number.

    c. difference between the lowest number and the highest number

30. Please Excuse My Dear Aunt Sally: What it means in the Order of Operations is____

    a. Parentheses, Exponents, Multiplication and Division, and Addition and Subtraction

    b. Parentheses, Equal, Multiplication and Decimal, and Addition and Subtraction

    c. Parentheses, Ellipse, Multiplication and Data, and Addition and Subtraction

31. A ratio is_____

    a. a way to show a relationship or compare two numbers of the same kind

    b. short way of saying that you want to multiply something by itself

    c. he sum of the relationship a times x, a times y, and a times z

32. Variables are things_____

    a. that can change or have different values

    b. when something has an exponent

    c. the simplest form using fractions

33. Always perform the same operation to_____of the equation.

    a. when the sum is less than the operation

    b. both sides

    c. one side only

34. The slope intercept form uses the following equation:

    a. $y = mx + b$

    b. $y = x + ab$

    c. $x = mx + c$

35. The point-slope form uses the following equation:

    a. $y - y1 = m(y - x2)$

    b. $y - y1 = m(x - x1)$

    c. $x - y2 = m(x - x1)$

36. Numbers in an algebraic expression that are not variables are called____

    a. Square

    b. Coefficient

    c. Proportional

37. A coordinate system is _____

    a. a type of cubed square

    b. a coordinate reduced to another proportion plane

    c. a two-dimensional number line

38. Horizontal axis is called_____

    a. h-axis

    b. x-axis

    c. y-axis

39. Vertical axis is called____

    a. v-axis

    b. y-axis

    c. x-axis

40. Equations and inequalities are both mathematical sentences____

    a. has y and x variables as points on a graph

    b. reduced ratios to their simplest form using fractions

    c. formed by relating two expressions to each other

ANSWERS
Adding Fractions

1) $\dfrac{5}{7} + \dfrac{4}{7} = \dfrac{5}{7} + \dfrac{4}{7} = \dfrac{9}{7} = 1\dfrac{2}{7}$

2) $\dfrac{2}{8} + \dfrac{5}{8} = \dfrac{2}{8} + \dfrac{5}{8} = \dfrac{7}{8}$

3) $\dfrac{6}{7} + \dfrac{4}{7} = \dfrac{6}{7} + \dfrac{4}{7} = \dfrac{10}{7} = 1\dfrac{3}{7}$

4) $\dfrac{5}{4} + \dfrac{3}{4} = \dfrac{5}{4} + \dfrac{3}{4} = \dfrac{8}{4} = \dfrac{2}{1} = 2\dfrac{0}{1}$

5) $\dfrac{1}{8} + \dfrac{3}{8} = \dfrac{1}{8} + \dfrac{3}{8} = \dfrac{4}{8} = \dfrac{1}{2}$

6) $\dfrac{2}{6} + \dfrac{5}{6} = \dfrac{2}{6} + \dfrac{5}{6} = \dfrac{7}{6} = 1\dfrac{1}{6}$

7) $\dfrac{2}{6} + \dfrac{2}{6} = \dfrac{2}{6} + \dfrac{2}{6} = \dfrac{4}{6} = \dfrac{2}{3}$

8) $\dfrac{5}{4} + \dfrac{3}{4} = \dfrac{5}{4} + \dfrac{3}{4} = \dfrac{8}{4} = \dfrac{2}{1} = 2\dfrac{0}{1}$

9) $\dfrac{8}{8} + \dfrac{6}{8} = \dfrac{8}{8} + \dfrac{6}{8} = \dfrac{14}{8} = \dfrac{7}{4} = 1\dfrac{3}{4}$

10) $\dfrac{3}{7} + \dfrac{5}{7} = \dfrac{3}{7} + \dfrac{5}{7} = \dfrac{8}{7} = 1\dfrac{1}{7}$

11) $\dfrac{7}{9} + \dfrac{1}{9} = \dfrac{7}{9} + \dfrac{1}{9} = \dfrac{8}{9}$

12) $\dfrac{3}{9} + \dfrac{6}{9} = \dfrac{3}{9} + \dfrac{6}{9} = \dfrac{9}{9} = 1$

13) $\dfrac{2}{7} + \dfrac{4}{7} = \dfrac{2}{7} + \dfrac{4}{7} = \dfrac{6}{7}$

14) $\dfrac{3}{6} + \dfrac{2}{6} = \dfrac{3}{6} + \dfrac{2}{6} = \dfrac{5}{6}$

15) $\dfrac{3}{6} + \dfrac{5}{6} = \dfrac{3}{6} + \dfrac{5}{6} = \dfrac{8}{6} = \dfrac{4}{3} = 1\dfrac{1}{3}$

Greatest Common Factor ANSWERS

1)   15 , 3   3

2)   24 , 12   12

3)   10 , 4   2

4)   40 , 4   4

5)   8 , 40   8

6)   10 , 4   2

7)   12 , 20   4

8)   5 , 20   5

9)   8 , 2   2

10)   24 , 40   8

11)   6 , 8   2

12)   10 , 3   1

13)   8 , 6   2

14)   24 , 10   2

15)   24 , 12   12

16)   40 , 24   8

17)   8 , 10   2

18)   10 , 20   10

19)   2 , 3   1

20)   6 , 12   6

Prime Factors ANSWERS

1) 38   2 , 19
2) 49   7
3) 35   5 , 7
4) 25   5
5) 15   3 , 5
6) 44   2 , 11
7) 32   2
8) 48   2 , 3
9) 22   2 , 11
10) 21   3 , 7
11) 30   2 , 3 , 5
12) 20   2 , 5
13) 39   3 , 13
14) 14   2 , 7
15) 12   2 , 3
16) 26   2 , 13
17) 46   2 , 23
18) 40   2 , 5
19) 24   2 , 3
20) 10   2 , 5

ANSWERS

Find the Prime Factors of the Numbers

1)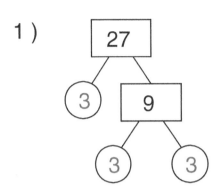

2)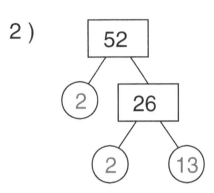

3)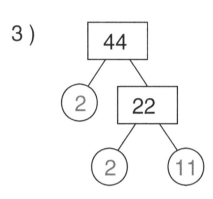

Factors
3 x 3 x 3 = 27

Factors
2 x 2 x 13 = 52

Factors
2 x 2 x 11 = 44

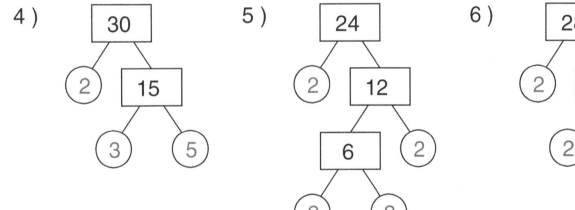

4)

5)

6)

Factors
2 x 3 x 5 = 30

Factors
2 x 2 x 2 x 3 = 24

Factors
2 x 2 x 7 = 28

TIME ANSWERS

What time is on the clock?   6:00

What time was it 1 hour ago?   5:00

What time was it 3 hours and 40 minutes ago?   2:20

What time will it be in 4 hours and 20 minutes?   10:20

What time is on the clock?   7:40

What time was it 2 hours ago?   5:40

What time will it be in 3 hours ?   10:40

What time will it be in 4 hours and 20 minutes?   12:00

What time is on the clock?   10:20

What time was it 1 hour ago?   9:20

What time was it 3 hours and 20 minutes ago?   7:00

What time will it be in 2 hours ?   12:20

What time is on the clock?   10:00

What time will it be in 3 hours and 20 minutes?   1:20

What time was it 2 hours ago?   8:00

What time was it 1 hour ago?   9:00

ANSWER SHEET
Visually Adding Simple Fractions

1) $\frac{1}{11}$ + $\frac{7}{11}$ = $\frac{8}{11}$

2) $\frac{1}{10}$ + $\frac{7}{10}$ = $\frac{8}{10}$

3) $\frac{1}{5}$ + $\frac{3}{5}$ = $\frac{4}{5}$

4) $\frac{2}{11}$ + $\frac{6}{11}$ = $\frac{8}{11}$

5) $\frac{3}{7}$ + $\frac{3}{7}$ = $\frac{6}{7}$

Matching Pictographs to Charts

Answer Key

Determine which pictograph best represents the information in the chart.

1)

Month	Cats Sold
June	56
July	32
August	24
September	40
October	80

2)

Month	Cats Sold
June	24
July	56
August	8
September	32
October	40

3)

Month	Cats Sold
June	16
July	8
August	56
September	48
October	24

4)

Month	Cats Sold
June	48
July	40
August	24
September	32
October	64

5)

Month	Cats Sold
June	24
July	80
August	48
September	56
October	32

6)

Month	Cats Sold
June	32
July	48
August	80
September	16
October	8

1. F
2. B
3. C
4. A
5. D
6. E

A.

Month	Cats Sold
June	🐈🐈🐈🐈🐈
July	🐈🐈🐈🐈🐈
August	🐈🐈🐈
September	🐈🐈🐈🐈
October	🐈🐈🐈🐈🐈🐈🐈🐈🐈🐈

Each 🐈 = 8 cat

B.

Month	Cats Sold
June	🐈🐈🐈
July	🐈🐈🐈🐈🐈🐈🐈
August	🐈
September	🐈🐈🐈🐈
October	🐈🐈🐈🐈🐈

Each 🐈 = 8 cat

C.

Month	Cats Sold
June	🐈🐈
July	🐈
August	🐈🐈🐈🐈🐈🐈🐈
September	🐈🐈🐈🐈🐈🐈
October	🐈🐈🐈

Each 🐈 = 8 cat

D.

Month	Cats Sold
June	🐈🐈🐈
July	🐈🐈🐈🐈🐈🐈🐈🐈🐈🐈
August	🐈🐈🐈🐈🐈🐈
September	🐈🐈🐈🐈🐈🐈🐈
October	🐈🐈🐈🐈

Each 🐈 = 8 cat

E.

Month	Cats Sold
June	🐈🐈🐈🐈
July	🐈🐈🐈🐈🐈🐈
August	🐈🐈🐈🐈🐈🐈🐈🐈🐈🐈
September	🐈🐈
October	🐈

Each 🐈 = 8 cat

F.

Month	Cats Sold
June	🐈🐈🐈🐈🐈🐈
July	🐈🐈🐈🐈
August	🐈🐈🐈
September	🐈🐈🐈🐈🐈
October	🐈🐈🐈🐈🐈🐈🐈🐈🐈🐈

Each 🐈 = 8 cat

Examining Number Value by Place Value

Solve each problem.

1) What is the value of the 6 in the number 154,637?

2) What is the value of the 1 in the number 417,298?

3) What is the value of the 9 in the number 97?

4) What is the value of the 3 in the number 9,673,824?

5) What is the value of the 4 in the number 14,697?

6) What is the value of the 4 in the number 42?

7) What is the value of the 1 in the number 29,158?

8) What is the value of the 1 in the number 268,514?

9) What is the value of the 7 in the number 3,576?

10) What is the value of the 5 in the number 3,956,728?

11) What is the value of the 1 in the number 4,781,392?

12) What is the value of the 4 in the number 734,168?

13) What is the value of the 6 in the number 68,435?

14) What is the value of the 2 in the number 51,627?

15) What is the value of the 2 in the number 235?

16) What is the value of the 3 in the number 31,475?

17) What is the value of the 5 in the number 9,536?

18) What is the value of the 7 in the number 37,681?

19) What is the value of the 6 in the number 3,264,871?

20) What is the value of the 1 in the number 76,183?

Finding Ten More & Ten Less   Name:

Fill in the blanks for each problem.

What is 10 more than 59?   69

What is 10 less than 13?   3

What is 10 more than 2?   12

What is 10 less than 15?   5

What is 10 more than 87?   97

What is 10 less than 17?   7

What is 10 more than 25?   35

What is 10 less than 19?   9

What is 10 more than 85?   95

What is 10 less than 21?   11

What is 10 more than 72?   82

What is 10 less than 23?   13

What is 10 more than 79?   89

What is 10 less than 25?   15

What is 10 more than 1?   11

What is 10 less than 27?   17

What is 10 more than 39?   49

What is 10 less than 29?   19

What is 10 more than 27?   37

What is 10 less than 31?   21

What is 10 more than 86?   96

What is 10 less than 33?   23

What is 10 more than 7?   17

What is 10 less than 35?   25

What is 10 more than 69?   79

What is 10 less than 37?   27

What is 10 more than 60?   70

What is 10 less than 39?   29

What is 10 more than 31?   41

What is 10 less than 41?   31

What is 10 more than 11?   21

What is 10 less than 43?   33

What is 10 more than 12?   22

What is 10 less than 45?   35

What is 10 more than 63?   73

What is 10 less than 47?   37

What is 10 more than 97?   107

What is 10 less than 49?   39

What is 10 more than 41?   51

What is 10 less than 51?   41

What is 10 more than 99?   109

What is 10 less than 53?   43

What is 10 more than 92?   102

What is 10 less than 55?   45

What is 10 more than 67?   77

What is 10 less than 57?   47

What is 10 more than 51?   61

What is 10 less than 59?   49

What is 10 more than 16?   26

What is 10 less than 61?   51

Math Terms Crossword

Solve the puzzle below with the correct math vocabulary word.

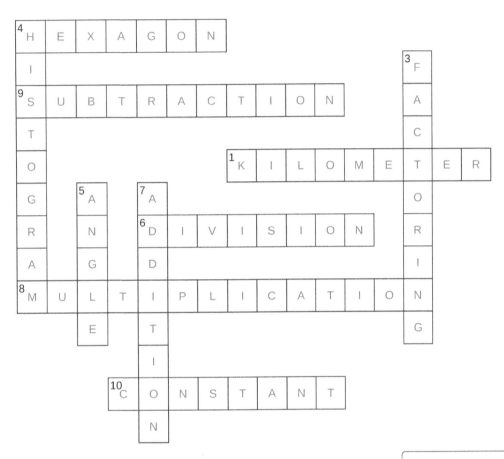

Across

1. A unit of measure equal to 1000 meters.
4. A six-sided and six-angled polygon.
6. Quotient, Goes Into, How Many Times
8. Multiply, Product, By, Times, Lots Of
9. Minus, Less, Difference, Decrease, Take Away, Deduct
10. A value that does not change.

Down

3. The process of breaking numbers down into all of their factors.
4. A graph that uses bars that equal ranges of values.
5. Two rays sharing the same endpoint (called the angle vertex).
7. Sum, Plus, Increase, Total

MULTIPLICATION
HEXAGON   KILOMETER
CONSTANT   ANGLE
FACTORING   DIVISION
SUBTRACTION
HISTOGRAM   ADDITION

Math Terms Matching

Match each math term to the correct meaning.

1	A	Rectangle	→	A parallelogram with four right angles.
2	G	Negative Number	→	A number less than zero.
3	C	Triangle	→	A three-sided polygon.
4	D	X	→	The Roman numeral for 10.
5	P	X-Axis	→	The horizontal axis in a coordinate plane.
6	B	Weight	→	The measure of how heavy something is.
7	M	Like Fractions	→	Fractions with the same denominator.
8	K	Like Terms	→	____ with the same variable and same exponents/powers.
9	F	Mode	→	The ____ is a list of numbers are the values that occur most frequently.
10	H	Midpoint	→	A point that is exactly halfway between two locations.
11	E	Line	→	A straight infinite path joining an infinite number of points in both directions.
12	I	Numerator	→	The top number in a fraction.
13	Q	Octagon	→	A polygon with eight sides.
14	N	Logic	→	Sound reasoning and the formal laws of reasoning.
15	O	Outcome	→	Used in probability to refer to the result of an event.
16	J	Polynomial	→	The sum of two or more monomials.
17	L	Quotient	→	The solution to a division problem.
18	R	Proper Fraction	→	A fraction whose denominator is greater than its numerator.

Mean, Mode, Median

1) 2, 2, 3, 4, 4, 9, 4
2, 2, 3, 4, 4, 4, 9

Mean 4   Median 4   Mode 4

2) 7, 7, 9, 7, 2, 8, 3, 6, 4, 7
2, 3, 4, 6, 7, 7, 7, 7, 8, 9

Mean 6   Median 7   Mode 7

3) 8, 4, 2, 7, 5, 6, 2, 3, 4, 9
2, 2, 3, 4, 4, 5, 6, 7, 8, 9

Mean 5   Median 4.5   Mode 2, 4

4) 7, 7, 3, 2, 6
2, 3, 6, 7, 7

Mean 5   Median 6   Mode 7

5) 5, 6, 6, 7, 6, 5, 6, 7, 6
5, 5, 6, 6, 6, 6, 6, 7, 7

Mean 6   Median 6   Mode 6

6) 9, 7, 4, 4, 4, 2
2, 4, 4, 4, 7, 9

Mean 5   Median 4   Mode 4

7) 8, 8, 4, 3, 4, 7, 9, 4, 7
3, 4, 4, 4, 7, 7, 8, 8, 9

Mean 6   Median 7   Mode 4

8) 2, 4, 6, 2, 5, 2, 9, 2
2, 2, 2, 2, 4, 5, 6, 9

Mean 4   Median 3   Mode 2

9) 6, 5, 8, 2, 9
2, 5, 6, 8, 9

Mean 6   Median 6   Mode None

10) 6, 3, 3, 5, 8, 1, 9
1, 3, 3, 5, 6, 8, 9

Mean 5   Median 5   Mode 3

Solve each problem.

1) What is the value of the 6 in the number 154,637?

2) What is the value of the 1 in the number 417,298?

3) What is the value of the 9 in the number 97?

4) What is the value of the 3 in the number 9,673,824?

5) What is the value of the 4 in the number 14,697?

6) What is the value of the 4 in the number 42?

7) What is the value of the 1 in the number 29,158?

8) What is the value of the 1 in the number 268,514?

9) What is the value of the 7 in the number 3,576?

10) What is the value of the 5 in the number 3,956,728?

11) What is the value of the 1 in the number 4,781,392?

12) What is the value of the 4 in the number 734,168?

13) What is the value of the 6 in the number 68,435?

14) What is the value of the 2 in the number 51,627?

15) What is the value of the 2 in the number 235?

16) What is the value of the 3 in the number 31,475?

17) What is the value of the 5 in the number 9,536?

18) What is the value of the 7 in the number 37,681?

19) What is the value of the 6 in the number 3,264,871?

20) What is the value of the 1 in the number 76,183?

#	Answer
1.	600
2.	10,000
3.	90
4.	3,000
5.	4,000
6.	40
7.	100
8.	10
9.	70
10.	50,000
11.	1,000
12.	4,000
13.	60,000
14.	20
15.	200
16.	30,000
17.	500
18.	7,000
19.	60,000
20.	100

Write the Names for the Decimal Numbers.

1)   **3.48**   Three and Forty Eight Hundredths _____

2)   **8.20**   Eight and Two Tenths _____

3)   **2.19**   Two and Nineteen Hundredths _____

4)   **2.38**   Two and Thirty Eight Hundredths _____

5)   **9.47**   Nine and Forty Seven Hundredths _____

6)   **3.51**   Three and Fifty One Hundredths _____

7)   **2.25**   Two and Twenty Five Hundredths _____

8)   **9.47**   Nine and Forty Seven Hundredths _____

9)   **6.76**   Six and Seventy Six Hundredths _____

10)   **3.28**   Three and Twenty Eight Hundredths _____

Find the Mystery Numbers

1) **The mystery number has ...**

A 2 in the Thousands place.
A 8 in the Tens place.
A 2 in the Hundreds place.
A 3 in the Ones place.
What is the mystery number ?   2,283

2) **The mystery number has ...**

A 1 in the Tens place.
A 6 in the Hundreds place.
A 1 in the Thousands place.
A 7 in the Ones place.
What is the mystery number ?   1,617

3) **The mystery number has ...**

A 7 in the Thousands place.
A 1 in the Hundreds place.
A 3 in the Tens place.
A 2 in the Ones place.
What is the mystery number ?   7,132

4) **The mystery number has ...**

A 5 in the Ones place.
A 1 in the Thousands place.
A 4 in the Hundreds place.
A 7 in the Tens place.
What is the mystery number ?   1,475

5) **The mystery number has ...**

A 1 in the Ones place.
A 8 in the Hundreds place.
A 8 in the Tens place.
A 6 in the Thousands place.
What is the mystery number ?   6,881

Combining Like Terms

1) $8 + 13y - 15y$

   $-2y + 8$

2) $14 - 6y + 3$

   $-6y + 17$

3) $-11 + 2 - 14y - 4y$

   $-18y - 9$

4) $-14(5 - 2f) - 8$

   $28f - 78$

5) $12n + 6n$

   $18n$

6) $13k + k$

   $14k$

7) $16(-14z - 4) - 3$

   $-224z - 67$

8) $-19(16 + 13s)$

   $-247s - 304$

9) $3 + 9r - 7r + 6$

   $2r + 9$

10) $14(-19c + 8)$

    $-266c + 112$

Look It Up! Pop Quiz

Learn some basic vocabulary words that you will come across again and again in the course of your studies in algebra. By knowing the definitions of most algebra words, you will be able to construct and solve algebra problems much more easily.

Find the answer to the questions below by *looking up each word. (The wording can be tricky. Take your time.)*

1. improper fraction
   a. a fraction that the denominator is equal to the numerator
   b. a fraction in which the numerator is greater than the denominator, is always 1 or greater

2. equivalent fraction
   a. a fraction that has a DIFFERENT value as a given fraction
   b. a fraction that has the SAME value as a given fraction

3. simplest form of fraction
   a. an equivalent fraction for which the only common factor of the numerator and denominator is 1
   b. an equivalent fraction for which the only least factor of the denominator is -1

4. mixed number
   a. the sum of a whole number and a proper fraction
   b. the sum of a variable and a fraction

5. reciprocal
   a. a number that can be divided by another number to make 10
   b. a number that can be multiplied by another number to make 1

6. percent
   a. a percentage that compares a number to 0.1
   b. a ratio that compares a number to 100

7. sequence
   a. a set of addition numbers that follow a operation
   b. a set of numbers that follow a pattern

8. arithmetic sequence
   a. a sequence where EACH term is found by adding or subtracting the exact same number to the previous term
   b. a sequence where NO term is found by multiplying the exact same number to the previous term

9. geometric sequence
   a. a sequence where each term is found by multiplying or dividing by the exact same number to the previous term
   b. a sequence where each term is solved by adding or dividing by a different number to the previous term

10. order of operations
    a. the procedure to follow when simplifying a numerical expression
    b. the procedure to follow when adding any fraction by 100

11. variable expression
    a. a mathematical phrase that contains variables, numbers, and operation symbols
    b. a mathematical phrase that contains numbers and operation symbols

12. absolute value
    a. the distance a number is from zero on the number line
    b. the range a number is from one on the number line

13. integers
    a. a set of numbers that includes whole numbers and their opposites
    b. a set of numbers that includes equal numbers and their difference

14. x-axis
    a. the horizontal number line that, together with the y-axis, establishes the coordinate plane
    b. the vertical number line that, together with the y-axis, establishes the coordinate plane

15. y-axis

    a. the vertical number line that, together with the x-axis, establishes the coordinate plane

    b. the horizontal number line that, together with the x-axis, establishes the coordinate plane

16. coordinate plane

    a. plane formed by one number line (the horizontal y-axis and the vertical x-axis) intersecting at their -1 points

    b. plane formed by two number lines (the horizontal x-axis and the vertical y-axis) intersecting at their zero points

17. quadrant

    a. one of two sections on the four plane formed by the intersection of the x-axis

    b. one of four sections on the coordinate plane formed by the intersection of the x-axis and the y-axis

18. ordered pair

    a. a pair of numbers that gives the location of a point in the coordinate plane. Also known as the "coordinates" of a point.

    b. a pair of equal numbers that gives the range of a point in the axis plane. Also known as the "y-axis" of a point.

19. x-coordinate

    a. the number that indicates the position of a point to the left or right of the y-axis

    b. the number that indicates the range of a point to the left ONLY of the y-axis

20. y-coordinate

    a. the number that indicates the position of a point above or below the x-axis

    b. the number that indicates the value of a point only above the x-axis

21. inverse operations

    a. operations that equals to each other

    b. operations that undo each other

22. inequality

    a. a math sentence that uses a letter (x or y) to indicate that the left and right sides of the sentence hold values that are different

    b. a math sentence that uses a symbol ($<, >, \leq, \geq, \neq$) to indicate that the left and right sides of the sentence hold values that are different

23. perimeter

    a. the distance around the outside of a figure

    b. the distance around the inside of a figure

24. circumference

    a. the distance around a circle

    b. the range around a square

25. area

    a. the number of square units inside a 2-dimensional figure

    b. the number of circle units inside a 3-dimensional figure

26. volume

    a. the number of cubic units inside a 3-dimensional figure

    b. the number of cubic squared units inside a 2-dimensional figure

27. radius

    a. a line segment that runs from the middle of the circle to end of the circle

    b. a line segment that runs from the center of the circle to somewhere on the circle

28. chord

    a. a line segment that runs from somewhere on the circle to another place on the circle

    b. a circle distance that runs from somewhere on the far left to another place on the circle

29. diameter

    a. a chord that passes through the center of the circle

    b. a thin line that passes through the end of the circle

30. mean

    a. the sum of the data items added by the number of data items minus 2

    b. the sum of the data items divided by the number of data items

31. median

    a. the first data item found after sorting the data items in descending order

    b. the middle data item found after sorting the data items in ascending order

32. mode

    a. the data item that occurs most often

    b. the data item that occurs less than two times

33. range

    a. the difference between the highest and the lowest data item

    b. the difference between the middle number and the lowest number item

34. outlier

    a. a data item that is much higher or much lower than all the other data items

    b. a data item that is much lower or less than all the other data items

35. ratio

    a. a comparison of two quantities by multiplication

    b. a comparison of two quantities by division

36. rate

    a. a ratio that has equal quantities measured in the same units

    b. a ratio that compares quantities measured in different units

37. proportion

    a. a statement (ratio) showing five or more ratios to be equal

    b. a statement (equation) showing two ratios to be equal

38. outcomes

    a. possible results of action

    b. possible answer when two numbers are the same

39. probability

    a. a ratio that explains the likelihood of the distance and miles between to places

    b. a ratio that explains the likelihood of an event

40. theoretical probability

    a. the probability of the highest favorable number of possible outcomes (based on what is not expected to occur).

    b. the ratio of the number of favorable outcomes to the number of possible outcomes (based on what is expected to occur).

41. experimental probability

    a. the ratio of the number of times by 2 when an event occurs to the number of times times 2 an experiment is done (based on real experimental data).

    b. the ratio of the number of times an event occurs to the number of times an experiment is done (based on real experimental data).

42. distributive property

    a. a way to simplify an expression that contains a equal like term being added by a group of terms.

    b. a way to simplify an expression that contains a single term being multiplied by a group of terms.

43. term

    a. a number, a variable, or probability of an equal number and a variable(s)

    b. a number, a variable, or product of a number and a variable(s)

44. Constant

    a. a term with no variable part (i.e. a number)

    b. a term with no variable + y part (i.e. 4+y)

45. Coefficient

    a. a number that divides a variable

    b. a number that multiplies a variable

Polynomial Understanding Quiz

Need help? Try Google.

1. A polynomial is an expression consisting of_____.
- a. variables and coefficients
- b. variables and constant

2. A polynomial can have____.
- a. constants, variables, exponents
- b. terms, variables, exponents

3. To add polynomials you simply_____.
- a. add any like terms together
- b. divide any like terms together

4. If the variable in a term is multiplied by a number, then this number is called?
- a. polynomial
- b. coefficient

5. The exponent on the variable portion of a term tells you the ____ of that term.
- a. the degree
- b. the term

6. The "poly-" prefix in "polynomial" means many
- a. few
- b. many

7. Monomial
- a. is a one-term polynomial
- b. is a two-term polynomial

8. Linear
- a. is a first-degree polynomial
- b. is a second-degree polynomial

9. Cubic
- a. is a third/fourth-degree polynomial
- b. is a third-degree polynomial

10. Binomial
- a. is a one-term polynomial
- b. is a two-term polynomial

11. Quadratic
- a. is a zero-degree polynomial
- b. is a second-degree polynomial

12. Trinomial
- a. is a three-term polynomial
- b. is a two-term polynomial

13. The degree of a polynomial is the degree of the_____.
- a. term with the smallest degree
- b. term with the largest degree

14. Quintic
- a. is a fifth-degree polynomial
- b. is a fifth/sixth-degree polynomial

15. Quartic
- a. is a fourth-degree polynomial
- b. is a fifth-degree polynomial

16. What is a polynomial with 4 terms?
- a. trinomial
- b. quadrinomial

17. A polynomial is the sum or _____.
- a. difference of monomials
- b. difference of exponent

18. The degree of a monomial is the sum of the?
- a. degree of the variables
- b. exponents of the variables

19. Leading coefficient is the____.
- a. term with the smallest degree
- b. term with the largest degree

20. Standard Form of a polynomial is the list of the monomials in order from?
- a. smaller to largest degree
- b. largest to smaller degree

10th Grade Geometry Reading Comprehension

segment	Obtuse	90-degree	straight	halves
directions	Acute	height	formulas	angles

The study of shapes and space is known as geometry. It provides answers to size, area, and volume questions. The earliest known geometry works date back to 2000 BC and are from Egypt. There were formulas for lengths, areas, and volumes, as well as one for pyramids. Thales of Miletus calculated the height of pyramids in the 7th century BC, and the Greek mathematician Pythagoras proved the well-known Pythagorean Theorem.

Euclid, another Greek mathematician, introduced Euclidean geometry around 300 BC by demonstrating how to prove theorems using basic definitions and truths. We still use Euclidean geometry to prove theorems today.

Geometric terms include points, lines, and angles . A point is a non-dimensional object with no length or width. A dot is commonly used to represent it. A line is an object that extends in both directions without end. It is usually depicted with arrowheads to indicate that it continues indefinitely. A line segment is a section of a line that has two ends. A ray is one-half of a line with a single endpoint. Two rays with the same endpoint form an angle. The angle is called a straight angle if the rays are the two halves of a single line. A straight angle is analogous to a book open flat on a desk. A right angle is defined as an angle that is opened half that far.

Angles are expressed in degrees. A right angle is defined as a 90-degree angle. Acute angles are those that are less than a right angle. Obtuse angles are those that are larger than a right angle but smaller than a straight angle.

10 Grade Biology: Reading Comprehension Viruses

When we catch a cold or get the flu, we are dealing with the effects of a viral infection. Viruses, despite sharing some characteristics with living organisms, are neither cellular nor alive. The presence of cells, the ability to reproduce, the ability to use energy, and the ability to respond to the environment are all important characteristics of living organisms. A virus cannot perform any of these functions on its own.

A virus, on the other hand, is a collection of genetic material encased in a protective coat, which is typically made of proteins. Viruses are obligate parasites because they must replicate on the host. To replicate itself, a virus must first attach to and penetrate a host cell, after which it will go through the various stages of viral infection. These stages are essentially the virus lifecycle. A virus can enter the host cell via one of several methods by interacting with the surface of the host cell. The virus can then replicate itself by utilizing the host's energy and metabolism.

Bacteriophages, viruses that infect bacteria, either use the lysogenic cycle, in which the host cell's offspring carry the virus, or the lytic cycle, in which the host cell dies immediately after viral replication. Once viral shedding has occurred, the virus can infect additional hosts. Viral infections can be productive in the sense that they cause active infection in the host, or they can be nonproductive in the sense that they remain dormant within the host. These two types of infection can result in chronic infections, in which the host goes through cycles of illness and remission, as well as latent infections, in which the virus remains dormant for a period of time before causing illness in the host.

1. A virus is encased in a protective coat, which is typically made of _____.
   a. proteins
   b. molecules
   c. cells

2. To replicate itself, a virus must first attach to and penetrate a ___ cell.
   a. healthy
   b. living atom
   c. host

3. Viruses are neither cellular nor __.
   a. alive
   b. moving
   c. a threat

4. The virus can replicate itself by utilizing the host's ___ and ___.
   a. cells and DNA
   b. molecules and cell
   c. energy and metabolism

5. A virus can remain _____ for a period of time before causing illness in a host.
   a. metabolized
   b. dormant
   c. infected

Match Politics Terms

Learn how to *look up* words in a *Spanish-English dictionary or online. Write the corresponding letter(s).*

1	M	Campaign	⇢	la campaña
2	K	Candidate	⇢	el candidato
3	S	Coalition	⇢	la coalición
4	H	Coup	⇢	el golpe de Estado
5	F	Democracy	⇢	la democracia
6	Q	Demonstration	⇢	la manifestación
7	N	Demonstrator	⇢	el/la manifestante
8	I	Deputy, Representative	⇢	el diputado
9	Z	Dictatorship	⇢	la dictadura
10	A	Diplomacy	⇢	la diplomacia
11	P	Elections	⇢	las elecciones
12	G	Electoral	⇢	electoral
13	AE	Foreign Policy	⇢	la política exterior
14	C	Freedom Of Speech	⇢	la libertad de expresión
15	U	Government	⇢	el gobierno
16	AA	Internal Affairs	⇢	la política interior
17	Y	Majority	⇢	la mayoría
18	L	Minister	⇢	el ministro

19	W	Ministry	⇢	el ministerio
20	O	Minority	⇢	la minoría
21	AD	Movement	⇢	el movimiento
22	E	Opposition	⇢	la oposición
23	AB	Parliament	⇢	el parlamento
24	V	Party	⇢	el partido
25	B	Politician	⇢	el político
26	J	President	⇢	el presidente
27	T	Prime Minister	⇢	el primer ministro
28	AC	Referendum	⇢	el plebiscito/referendo
29	D	Spokesperson	⇢	el/la portavoz
30	X	State	⇢	el estado
31	R	Vote	⇢	el voto

Pick 7 politics Spanish words from above and work on arranging them in order alphabetically:

[Student worksheet has a 7 line writing exercise here.]

The History of the Calendar

Tuesday	Saturday	November	February	Monday	March
Friday	weekend	May	Wednesday	Sunday	January
weekday	October	June	September	December	August
April	Thursday	July			

1. rauanjy — January

2. uraeybfr — February

3. macrh — March

4. iralp — April

5. yma — May

6. nuej — June

7. luyj — July

8. suagut — August

9. ebpmeetrs — September

10. btcreoo — October

11. vmbeneor — November

12. eedcrmbe — December

13. dmnyoa — Monday

14. saetudy — Tuesday

15. deeawysnd — Wednesday

16. shtayudr — Thursday

17. rdayfi — Friday

18. yuartdas — Saturday

19. ydsaun — Sunday

20. eenekwd — weekend

21. kaewedy — weekday

Acronym

A common way to make an acronym is to use the first letter of each word in a phrase to make a word that can be spoken. This is a great way to make a longer, more complicated phrase easier to say and shorter.

Carefully choose the acronym for each word or phrase.

1. Also Known As
   a. AKA
   b. KAA

2. Central Standard Time
   a. CST
   b. TCS

3. Doing Business As
   a. DBA
   b. ASDOING

4. Do Not Disturb
   a. NOTDN
   b. DND

5. Electronic Data Systems
   a. SDE
   b. EDS

6. End of Day
   a. EOD
   b. ENDDAY

7. Eastern Standard Time
   a. EST
   b. TSE

8. Estimated Time of Arrival
   a. ET
   b. ETA

9. Human Resources
   a. HRS
   b. HR

10. Masters of Business Administration
   a. MOBA
   b. MBA

11. MST - Mountain Standard Time
   a. MST
   b. MSTS

12. Overtime
   a. OTIME
   b. OT

13. Point Of Service
   a. POS
   b. POOS

14. Pacific Standard Time
   a. PST
   b. PSTE

15. Anti-lock Braking System
   a. LOCKBS
   b. ABS

16. Attention Deficit Disorder
   a. ADD
   b. ATTDD

17. Attention Deficit Hyperactivity Disorder

    a. ADHP

    b. ADHD

18. Acquired Immune Deficiency Syndrome

    a. ACQIMDEF

    b. AIDS

19. Centers for Disease Control and Prevention

    a. CDC

    b. CDCP

20. Dead On Arrival

    a. DONA

    b. DOA

21. Date Of Birth

    a. DOB

    b. DOFB

22. Do It Yourself

    a. DIY

    b. DIYO

23. Frequently Asked Questions

    a. FAQA

    b. FAQ

24. Graphics Interchange Format

    a. GIF

    b. GIFF

25. Human Immunodeficiency Virus

    a. HIV

    b. HIMMV

26. Medical Doctor

    a. MD

    b. MED

27. Over The Counter

    a. OTC

    b. OTHEC

28. Pay Per View

    a. PPV

    b. PAYPPV

29. Sound Navigation And Ranging

    a. SONAR

    b. SONAVR

30. Sports Utility Vehicle

    a. SPOUV

    b. SUV

ADDITIONAL ASSIGNMENTS PLANNER

○ MONDAY

GOALS THIS WEEK

○ TUESDAY

○ WEDNESDAY

WHAT TO STUDY

○ THURSDAY

○ FRIDAY

EXTRA CREDIT WEEKEND WORK
○ SATURDAY / SUNDAY

ADDITIONAL ASSIGNMENTS PLANNER

○ MONDAY

GOALS THIS WEEK

○ TUESDAY

○ WEDNESDAY

WHAT TO STUDY

○ THURSDAY

○ FRIDAY

EXTRA CREDIT WEEKEND WORK
○ SATURDAY / SUNDAY

ADDITIONAL ASSIGNMENTS PLANNER

○ MONDAY

GOALS THIS WEEK

○ TUESDAY

○ WEDNESDAY

WHAT TO STUDY

○ THURSDAY

○ FRIDAY

EXTRA CREDIT WEEKEND WORK
○ SATURDAY / SUNDAY

GRADES TRACKER

Week	Monday	Tuesday	Wednesday	Thursday	Friday
1					
2					
3					
4					
5					
6					
7					
8					
9					
10					
11					
12					
13					
14					
15					
16					
17					
18					

Notes

GRADES TRACKER

Week	Monday	Tuesday	Wednesday	Thursday	Friday
1					
2					
3					
4					
5					
6					
7					
8					
9					
10					
11					
12					
13					
14					
15					
16					
17					
18					

Notes

GRADES TRACKER

Week	Monday	Tuesday	Wednesday	Thursday	Friday
1					
2					
3					
4					
5					
6					
7					
8					
9					
10					
11					
12					
13					
14					
15					
16					
17					
18					

Notes

End of the Year Evaluation

Name: _____

Grade/Level: _____ Date: _____

Subjects Studied: _____

_____

_____

Goals Accomplished: _____

_____

_____

_____

Most Improved Areas:_____

_____

_____

_____

Areas of Improvement:_____

_____

_____

Main Curriculum Evaluation	Satisfied		A= Above Standards	Final Grades
_____	Yes	No	S= Meets Standards	_____
			N= Needs Improvement	
			98-100 A+	
_____	Yes	No	93-97 A	_____
			90-92 A	
_____	Yes	No	88-89 B+	_____
			83-87 B	
_____	Yes	No	80-82 B	_____
			78-79 C+	
_____	Yes	No	73-77 C	_____
			70-72 C	
_____	Yes	No	68-69 D+	_____
			62-67 D	
_____	Yes	No	60-62 D	_____
			59 & Below F	

Most Enjoyed:_____

_____

Least Enjoyed:_____

_____